THE ECOLOGY OF AGGRESSION

Arnold P. Goldstein

Syracuse University
Syracuse, New York

PLENUM PRESS • NEW YORK AND LONDON

Library of Congress Cataloging-in-Publication Data

Goldstein, Arnold P.
    The ecology of aggression / Arnold P. Goldstein.
        p.   cm. -- (The Plenum series in social/clinical psychology)
    Includes bibliographical references and index.
    ISBN 0-306-44741-X
    1. Aggressiveness (Psychology) 2. Environmental psychology.
3. Personality and situation.   I. Title.   II. Series.
BF575.A3G644   1994
155.2'32--dc20   94-26532
                                                               CIP

ISBN 0-306-44741-X

©1994 Plenum Press, New York
A Division of Plenum Publishing Corporation
233 Spring Street, New York, N.Y. 10013

Printed in the United States of America

With love and deep appreciation
to my wife, Susan,
a most special partner

PREFACE

Most efforts to better understand, and reduce, human aggressive behavior focus upon the perpetrator. Whether specialist or general public; psychologist, sociologist, or criminologist; theoretician, researcher, or practitioner; or concerned with prediction, prevention, rehabilitation, or public policy—the person or persons actually committing the aggressive act are almost always the primary target of attention. Who he or she is, the person's relevant background experiences, history of similar behaviors, mood and rationality at the time the act occurred, and related intraindividual matters are the typical questions addressed. The abuser's parenting; the delinquent's early temperament; the offender's personality traits; hormonal levels; television viewing habits; and other in-the-person markers are posited, examined, and held responsible. For most of those concerned, aggression is in the perpetrator, by the perpetrator, and from the perpetrator. This book presents an alternative view.

Our perspective is responsive to one of the most significant developments in the study of human behavior in recent decades—the ascendance of interactionism. Broadly defined, interactionism is a philosophical stance toward understanding and predicting human behavior which holds that such efforts will be optimized when they reflect both intraindividual (e.g., trait) qualities and relevant characteristics of the individual's environment. These latter ecological features may be other people (e.g., victims, fellow group members) or qualities of the immediate or larger physical location in which the perpetration occurs.

In recent years, this interactionist perspective has been brought to bear upon a wide range of behaviors, and aggression is certainly among them. This body of aggression-relevant knowledge is the central focus of the present book. Aggression, we hold, is invariably a person–environment event. After describing more fully the historical evolvement of interactionism, we present and evaluate the substantive relevance of this perspective to aggression at different levels of the physical and social ecologies in which such behavior typically occurs. Thus, the physical ecological contribution to an interactionist determination of aggressive behavior is examined at the micro level (i.e., home, street, bar, etc.), the meso level (i.e., neighborhood), and the macro level (i.e., regional), as are parallel social ecological components—micro (the victim), meso (the group), and macro (the mob).

However, it is not only the causes of aggression that may be profitably viewed from an interactionist perspective. So, too, its prevention and remediation. In chapters devoted to environmental design as a strategy for diminishing criminal opportunity, and to interpersonal contact as a conflict-reduction strategy, we seek to demonstrate, respectively, the potency of physical and social ecological settings as aggression-moderating and minimizing venues. The book concludes with a look ahead, seeking to suggest yet further avenues via which a person–environment interactionist stance may prove valuable to the theoretician, researcher, or practitioner concerned about more adequately understanding and more successfully reducing human aggression.

Four valued colleagues, each of whose own significant works has helped shape and sharpen my thinking about aggression and its reduction, read earlier drafts of this book. Their generous efforts and perceptive critique have substantially improved it and are warmly appreciated. Thus, to Don Ford, Fred Kanfer, Len Krasner, and Mark Sherman, a special thank you.

CONTENTS

III. SOCIAL ECOLOGY

PART I

INTRODUCTION

CHAPTER 1

THE PERSON–ENVIRONMENT DUET

Every act of aggression is a person–environment event. The singular goal of this book is to provide supportive substance for this assertion. For many decades, the study of aggression was the study of aggressors; the study of crime was the study of criminals. In this early era of near exclusive focus on perpetrators, first constitutional, then psychoanalytic, and then personality theories of aggressive and criminal behavior held sway. In its own way, each perspective was dispositional in its central tenet: antisocial behavior grew from something *in* the perpetrator. For the constitutional theorist Lombroso (1911), it was a combination of moral deficiency (lazy, shameless, cruel, impulsive) and physical primitiveness, as evidenced by cranial asymmetries, large ears, sloping shoulders, short legs, and numerous other facial and bodily characteristics. Though such "criminaloid" propositions never gained appreciable scientific stature, a later incarnation of constitutional causation theorizing by Sheldon (1949), of body type correlates of both temperament and overt behavior, did gain a measure of credibility. Mesomorphy—the muscular, broad-chested, large-boned, low-waisted body type—was shown by several independent investigators to be disproportionately characteristic of delinquent, as compared to nondelinquent youth (Cortes & Gatti, 1972; Epps & Parnell, 1952; Gibbens, 1963; Glueck & Glueck, 1950). Not unimportantly, however, the same physique appears to be more frequently characteristic of salesmen, politicians, and other extroverted, domineering, high-activity subgroups.

3

For Freud (1961), and later in their own ways for the ethologists Lorenz (1963), Ardrey (1966), and Morris (1967), aggression was an internal, instinctive energy. For Freud it was a destructive energy, the self-directed death instinct turned outward. For the others, aggression grew from an innate fighting instinct, an instinct spontaneously generated within the person in a continuous manner. It builds up, they held, and, as time passes, the weaker is the stimulus needed to "release" it. Eventually, its accumulation is inexorable; its expression is inevitable. The best one can hope for is some sort of nonantisocial sublimation or channeling of the instinctive energy. Such a theoretical stance, more accurately a blend of anecdote, analogical leaps, unsystematic journalism, and undefined concepts than a formal theory, although seductively appealing and still widely held, has failed to gather any appreciable degree of scientific support, and has functioned primarily as a detour diverting attention from more useful and credible beliefs about aggression and its sources. So, too, for psychoanalytic thinking about criminal behavior. Freud's (1961) view saw criminal behavior growing from a compulsive need for punishment stemming from unconscious, incestuous oedipal wishes. Crimes were committed, in his view, in an effort by the perpetrator to be caught, punished, and thus cleansed of guilt. Other psychoanalytic writers, alternatively, stressed inability to delay gratification (Alexander & Healy, 1935), the role of maternal separation and parental rejection (Bowlby, 1949), crime as substitute behavior for gaining love, nurturance, and attention (Johnson & Szurek, 1952), or as reflecting a superego lacuna (Johnson, 1949, 1959). While such offerings were useful in the general sense of pointing to early-life and familial antecedents of criminal behavior, their specific contents, as Cohen and Land (1987), Nietzel (1979), and we (Goldstein, 1990) have pointed out, are tautological. As Nietzel (1979) puts it, "Aggressive or acquisitive acts are often explained by underlying aggressive or acquisitive impulses. The evidence for these impulses. . .turns out to be the aggressive or acquisitive acts" (p. 78).

Personality trait theory is the third orientation to place the full etiological locus for aggression and crime within its perpetrators. Such thinking typically grew from research comparing, for example, samples of delinquent and nondelinquent youth on a wide array of personality measures. Although these studies showed some such between-sample differences, e.g., on assertiveness, suspiciousness, impulsiveness, anxiety, dependency, and conventionality (Glueck & Glueck, 1950), both Metfessel and Lovell's (1942) and Schuessler and Cressey's (1950) reviews in this domain concluded that such personality traits are distributed in the criminal population in about the same proportion as in the general population. Later studies, more fully controlling for the socioeconomic, intelligence, and institutionalization artifacts operating in many of the earlier studies, began to yield reliable trait differences between criminal and noncriminal samples. These included extroversion, neuroticism, and psychoticism (Eysenck, 1977), psychopathy (McCord & McCord, 1964; Quay, 1965), moral reasoning (Arbuthnot & Gordon, 1987; Laufer & Day, 1983), conceptual level (Hunt, 1972), irresponsible thinking (Yochelson & Samenow, 1976), and rational choicefulness (Hunt, 1972). These several, largely cognitive/personality dispositional findings help remind us, in this book intentionally focussing disproportionately on the environmental component of the person–environment duet, that person variables do indeed account for a significant portion of the behavioral outcome variance of interest.

Constitutional, psychoanalytic, and personality trait theories of crime and aggression, as noted, are each internal theories, that is, the behaviors of interest are located in, and derive from characteristics of or dispositions within the perpetrator. The journey out of the skin, the beginnings of looking at least to a modest degree *outside* of the aggressor/perpetrator to explain at least in some part the individual's behavior began in modern times with the view of aggression as an externally motivated inner-drive state. As Baron (1977) observes:

> The notion of spontaneously generated energy has been largely dismissed by the majority of researchers in this field. The more general suggestion that aggression stems from an aggressive motive or drive (i.e., a heightened state of arousal that can be reduced through overt acts of aggression) has enjoyed a much more favorable reception....Basically, such theories hold that human aggression stems mainly from the arousal of a drive to harm or injure others, which is itself elicited by various environmental conditions. (p. 21)

The view of aggression as an externally stimulated internal drive was centrally concretized by and introduced via the frustration–aggression hypothesis (Dollard, Doob, Miller, Mowrer, & Sears, 1939). This well-known thesis held frustration to be the only antecedent of aggression, and aggression always to stem from frustration. It proved a provocative notion, giving rise in subsequent years to a great deal of productive research on the instigation of aggression, on the arousal process, and even on means toward aggression reduction (e.g., Berkowitz, 1962; Buss, 1961; Feshbach, 1970; Zillman, 1979). In 1973, in the midst of a time in which psychology in general was moving swiftly toward much greater reliance on person-plus-environment thinking to explain many types of behavior, Bandura offered his social learning perspective on aggression. Unlike the mostly internal, modestly external quality of drive theory, social learning theory was a major step toward giving equal due to both internal and external determinants of aggressive behavior. The flavor of this dualism is captured by, for example, Bandura's (1973) comment:

> In a vigorous effort to avoid spurious inner causes it [psychology] neglected determinants of man's behavior arising from his cognitive functioning.... People can represent external influences symbolically and later use such representations to guide their actions; they can solve problems mentally without having to enact the various alternatives; and they can see the probable consequences of different actions and alter their behavior accordingly. (p. 42)

Social learning theory of aggression is, therefore, an *interactionist* theory, in which such external stimulus conditions as the nature of the potential target of aggression and the social context of the perpetrator–target interaction, as well as the anticipated reward consequences of aggressive actions, interplay with the actor's own past direct and vicarious learning history to determine which behaviors are and are not acquired, instigated, and maintained.

At approximately the same time as Bandura's (1973) important contribution appeared, there occurred in psychology and its central concern with understanding and predicting behavior a major acceleration of person–environment thinking. This movement, termed *interactionism*, had been brewing in psychology for decades. Its central tenet is captured well in the following quotations:

> The trait model and the psychodynamic model propose that actual behavior is primarily determined by latent, stable dispositions. Both assume that the sources for the initiation and direction of behavior come primarily from within the organism. The situational model assumes that the sources for the initiation and direction of behavior come primarily from factors external to the organism. The interactional model assumes that the sources for the initiation and direction of behavior come primarily from the continuous interactions between the person and the situations that he or she encounters. The individual's behavior is influenced by meaningful aspects of the situation in which behavior occurs. Subsequently the person's behavior affects these situations and their meaning. The reciprocal influence of person factors on situations and situation factors on behavior operates continuously. (Endler & Magnusson, 1976, p. 960)

> People and psychological processes are embedded in and inseparable from their physical and social contexts. According to this principle, phenomena are viewed as holistic unities rather than combinations of separate elements....There are no separate actors in an event; the actions of one person are understood in relation to the actions of other people, and in relation to spatial, situational, and temporal circumstances in which the actors are embedded. These different aspects of an event are mutually defining and lend meaning to one another, and are so intermeshed that understanding one aspect requires simultaneous inclusion of other aspects in the analysis. (Altman, Brown, Staples, & Werner, 1992, p. 195)

This person-plus-situation interactionism had its early roots in the seminal works of Lewin (1935, 1936) and Murray (1938). In Lewin's well-known formula, $B = f(p,e)$, not only was behavior considered a function of both the person and the environment, but also the environment that was most influential in this regard was considered subjective in nature (i.e., the environment-as-perceived, also termed the *phenomenal field* or the *psychological situation*). Murray (1938) also described human behavior as a result of both needs (the person variable) and environmental press or need-satisfying potential (the situation variable).

Research support of this person-by-situation view of human behavior began to emerge even at this early point in interactionist thinking. In 1928, Hartshorne and May reported their now well-known studies of "deceit," a type of behavior originally assumed to be determined by enduring qualities and consistencies within the person and not substantially influenced by such environmental considerations as where, when, and with whom the behavior occurs. In these studies, later largely replicated by Burton (1963) and Nelson, Grinder, and Mutter (1969), children were placed in a series of situations in which cheating behavior was possible, and their reactions across situations were examined. Results clearly supported an interactionist view. Cheating was a function of both the individual youngster and qualities of particular situations. In later years, such joint person-plus-situation determinism has been shown to be operative for other types of behaviors, including aggression on the one hand (Campbell, 1986; Cordilia, 1986; Forgas, 1986; Gibbs, 1986; Page & Moss, 1976; Raush, 1965, 1972) and an array of prosocial behaviors on the other (Leming, 1978; Zimmerman, 1983).

Others followed Lewin (1935) and Murray (1938). Angyal's (1959) phenomenological theory emphasized the inseparability of organism and environment and the subjectivity of environment in shaping human behavior. Murphy's (1947) "organism-situation field" offered a similar view. The social learning theorists, starting with Rotter (1954) and Mischel (1968), promoted a similarly strong emphasis on situational, as well as person, determinants. In addition to the phenomenologists and social learning theorists, a third view advancing interactionism emerged, variously called *ecological psychology* and *environmental psychology*. Roger Barker and his research group's studies of the "stream of behavior" in a variety of field settings were the pioneering works in this context (Barker & Gump, 1964; Barker & Wright, 1954). These investigations involved both an effort to examine the effects of diverse real-world "behavior settings" on the ability to predict individual behavior and an initial search for answers to the central methodological questions that have made interactionism, since its inception, a difficult position to concretize. Specifically, Barker's work sought to clarify how situational influences are optimally defined, classified, and measured. His investigations and those of Moos examining the influence of institutional environments on behavior (Moos, 1968, 1973; Moos & Houts, 1968) went beyond the important but broad generalizations of the early interactionist theorists and began pointing to specific situational characteristics that seemed potent as behavior change influences. Price and Bouffard (1974) extended this effort further, demonstrating in their study of "behavioral appropriateness and situational constraints" how an array of common situations and settings (e.g., class, date, bus, own room, church, job interview, and sidewalk) constrained, influenced the occurrence of, or were judged to fit or not to fit a similarly lengthy array of common behaviors (e.g., run, talk, kiss, write, eat, sleep, read, and fight) and how, reciprocally, these behaviors were variously judged appropriate or inappropriate to the situations represented.

We have introduced this book and titled this chapter, "The Person–Environment Duet," as our way of indicating that the person and context (social or physical) interactions at the heart of the interactionist position taken here are probabilistic and reciprocal. Probabilism contrasts with both determinism and possibilism. Determinism views the environment as the shaper of human behavior and the individual as the passive responder, inexorably led, with little ability or opportunity to select or alter his or her environment. Possibilism, alternatively, sees the person as acting upon the environment, an environment which provides opportunities to grasp but does little or no selecting or shaping of its own. Probabilism views an environment as neither determining nor merely providing possibilities. Instead, it makes certain choices more likely, enlarges, reinforces, and, in Krupat's (1985) view:

> ...the relationship of person to environment is dynamic, rather than static. There is a give and take, with each part of the system providing reciprocal influences on each other. We shape our environment and in turn are shaped by them in a never-ending cycle of mutual influence. (p. 12)

Both the spirit and substance of this interactionist perspective have continued to grow in modern psychology (e.g., Altman et al., 1992; Little, 1987; Pervin, 1986; Stokols & Altman, 1987) and have come to influence substantially the manner in which aggression and criminal behavior are viewed. Berkowitz (1989), Campbell (1986), Green (1976), and Toch (1986) are but a few of the contemporary aggression researchers asserting the interactional significance of situational, contextual, and environmental variables. It is not only psychology marching in this direction, but also sociology and criminology. In sociology, predominantly person-oriented theories of criminal behavior, such as the control and social bonding views of Hirschi (1969) and Elliott, Ageton, and Canter (1979) and the almost exclusively environmental subcultural (Miller, 1958; Sutherland & Cressey, 1974), labeling (Becker, 1963; Hawkins & Tiedemann, 1975; Lemert, 1967), and radical (Abadinsky, 1979; Meier, 1976) viewpoints, are increasingly yielding to positions much more fully reflecting person–environment interactionism. These include differential association–differential reinforcement theory (Akers, 1985), social development theory (Hawkins & Weiss, 1985), integrated learning theory (Feldman, 1977), criminal opportunity theory (Cohen & Land, 1987), Kornhauser's (1978) social disorganization theory, Hogan and Jones's (1985) socioanalytic theory, Warren's (1983) interpersonal maturity theory, and Aultman and Wilford's (1978) combined model of control, strain, and labeling theories. In criminology, as will be described more fully later, there has been the advent and growth of such interactionist perspectives as situational crime prevention (Clarke, 1992; Jeffery, 1977), crime prevention through environmental design (Angel, 1968; Jacobs, 1961; Wood, 1991), defensible space (Coleman, 1985; Newman, 1972), and environmental criminology (Brantingham & Brantingham, 1991).

We believe that what has been lacking for the fuller development of an interactional approach to aggression and crime is not relevant theoretical perspectives, which, as just noted, abound, but a thorough, critical statement and examination of those characteristics of the physical and social environment which have played or profitably might play a significant role in the person–environment duet leading to aggression. This book's title is *The Ecology of Aggression*. We will seek to share and evaluate what is known, and what needs to be known, about the place and person context of aggression in order to better understand its sources of initiation and its venues for remediation. We seek, in short, to provide substance for an ecological perspective on aggressive and criminal behavior.

Part II seeks to do so for relevant layers of the physical ecologies which are the frequent settings of such antisocial actions. Chapter 2 conducts this exploration and evaluation at the level of the microsite at which aggression and crime may occur: the home, street, bar, car, store, and school. Here, as in all subsequent chapters, it will become clear that the behaviors of interest have been the focus of several professional disciplines, and thus we are catholic in our reportorial and evaluative efforts, drawing generously not only upon psychological findings, but quite heavily also from criminology and sociology. Chapter 3 offers a mesolevel focus on the neighborhood—its taxonomies, its social and physical ecology, its incivilities, its density, its criminogenic opportunity features, and its role as a venue for social support. A substantial portion of the existing literature on the "geography of crime" is at this neighborhood level, and its findings are both numerous and consequential. Historically, however, study of the ecology of crime was initiated at a broader physical level via the regional comparisons popularly put forth in the Europe of the mid-1800s. Chapter

4 begins with these data and carries the regionally comparative and nationally comparative picture of crime and aggression through to modern times.

Part III, "Social Ecology," shifts the perspective from the physical context of antisocial behavior to its person context. The diverse roles of the victim (Chapter 5), the group (Chapter 6), and the mob (Chapter 7) are each examined and collectively give strong support for the view that aggression is always a person–environment interactional event. However innocently or unintentionally, the individual persons or collectives constituting the social environment in which aggressive or criminal actions occur contribute to such an occurrence. The abused child, the rape victim, and the assaulted or murdered individual each help precipitate their own victimization. They do not cause it, nor are they responsible for it, but contribute they do. At the group level, three diverse theoretical approaches—realistic group conflict theory, social identity theory, and information-processing theory—each demonstrate via their propositions and supporting data the (often dramatic) power of group membership as a conflict-generating and conflict-sustaining social ecological force. Although such potency, in groups, can be for better or worse (not only instigating aggression but at times also restraining it), in mobs it is much more typically for worse. Our consideration of mobs and mob violence focuses on convergence theory, contagion theory, emergent norm theory, and deindividuation theory. We find that elements of each perspective, in combination, serve as useful means of comprehending what often is the most volatile social ecological context for aggression, the mob.

We seek to end this book (in Part IV, "Intervention") on a hopeful, constructive note. Wearing ecological glasses to better see the roots of crime and aggression also enables us to better discern means for its prevention and reduction. Chapter 8 describes and catalogs the several dozen environmental-design alternatives which have been implemented in various settings as crime-opportunity-diminishing, crime-reward-reducing, or crime-surveillance-increasing steps and devices. The existing research evaluating the real-world impact of such physical ecological intervention is examined. One may also seek to alter the social environment for aggression and crime prevention or reduction purposes, and a central aspect of such an effort is examined in Chapter 9. Here, the literature on interpersonal contact as a social ecological intervention is examined. At the level of intergroup aggression (whether the group is a tribe, gang, nation, or otherwise), nonaggression often begins with facilitative interpersonal and intergroup contact. How such contact may be initiated and sustained toward the ends of reducing antisocial interactions and promoting prosocial interactions is our chapter focus.

We conclude the book (in Part V) with a reiteration of our central theme, as stated at the outset, that every act of aggression is a person–environment event. We do so by pointing, more briefly than in our earlier chapter discussions, to yet further aggression- and crime-relevant domains in which enhanced subscription to the use of physical and social ecological theory and data has apparent potential for a substantially better understanding of the sources of aggression and crime, and for a better opportunity to prevent or reduce their occurrence.

PART II

PHYSICAL ECOLOGY

CHAPTER 2

MICROLEVEL: THE SITE

Aggression occurs in an immediate, often circumscribed, largely identifiable location, which we term the *site*. Although its distal and proximal antecedents may have begun in a near or distant "elsewhere," and may continue in other locations, a discrete aggressive event can typically be specified and situated as to place. We will examine such aggression sites in the present chapter, both for their relative incidence data, and for their person–place transactional nature as it bears upon the facilitation or inhibition of aggressive behavior.

THE HOME

Home is many things, including, but well beyond, a physical structure. It is, according to Dovey (1985), *order*, the patterning of environmental experience, as well as *orientation*, in space, time, and society. It is *identity*, implying a bonding of place and person "such that the place takes its identity from the dweller and the dweller takes his or her identity from the place" (p. 39). It is also, he adds, *connectedness* with place and, temporally, with past, present, and future. It is a place of *ritual*, of repeatable, cyclical activities and events (Saile, 1985). It is a place of *social rules* and *social relationships* (Werner, Altman, & Oxley, 1985). Lastly, it is a place of both *affordances*, the positive meanings and behaviors which a physical environment may facilitate, and—perhaps more relevant to our present theme—*impedances*. In this latter regard, Silverstein and Krate (1975), in their *Children of the Dark Ghetto*, observe:

> Most of the children we knew lived in old buildings in need of significant repair
> and renovation, often lacking heat or hot water. In the cold Northern winter,

many inner-city apartments were freezing. In the hot summer, they were sweatboxes, and often there was no running water at all. Many of the children lived in crowded apartments....It was not uncommon for children to come to school very tired in the morning...because it was too noisy in their building or on their block. (p. 10)

And Yancy (1976) reports:

Within the buildings themselves, the neglect is more apparent. Entering the building...one is struck with the stale air and the stench of urine, trash, and garbage on the floors. One is also struck by the unfinished construction—the unpainted cinderblocks and cement. These unfinished walls...are decorated with colorful graffiti. The elevator is used as a public restroom, as well as a means of transportation....Residents of Pruitt-Igoe continually expressed concern with being assaulted, beaten, or raped. (p. 173)

Home is also, as we shall see below, one of America's most favorite hitting places.

Home is the place of intimates, an opportunity ground for small slights and major perceived insults, where old grudges can smolder and flare, an arena for unobserved incivilities, a private domain often ruled by a self-anointed familial dictator, a location permitting and at times encouraging disinhibition of restraint, a tavern of sorts for excessive drinking, a safe island for acting up and acting out with little fear of punitive consequences, and a physical structure and space often populated by potential aggressors and (literally) near-at-hand targets. It is perhaps then little wonder that Wolfgang (1958) found that 112 of 136 homicides (82 per cent) in which offender and victim were from the same family took place in the home, a finding essentially replicated by Gelles (1972), Harries (1990), Pittman and Handy (1964), Pokorny (1965), and others.

Romero (1985) found the home to be the most frequent setting for sexual assault at all four of the age levels he studied: children, adolescents, young adults, and older (ages 40–76) adult victims. Members of the latter three groups typically met their assailants outdoors but, via guile or force, were moved indoors, where the assault occurred. Gelles's (1972) site-level analysis of assault goes even further spatially, to examine the exact within-home locations by room for different types of offenders. He reported that the only room in the house where there was no violence for the sample studied was the bathroom, which, he observes, is often a family refuge or demilitarized zone and may have the only lockable inside door in the house. Gelles (1972) found, as had Pokorny (1965) and Wolfgang (1958) with their homicide data, that the bedroom is the deadliest room in the house. A precondition for highly aggressive behavior is high levels of arousal, which is precisely the frequent accompaniment of bedroom-based conjugal arguments about sex, intimacy, and other volatile concerns. In the bedroom, these studies reveal, the perpetrator is most likely to be male, the victim female. In the kitchen, the next most frequent site for in-house assault (and homicide), women are the usual offenders, males the victims. Gelles (1972) comments, with regard to kitchen violence:

> The potential for family arguments and family conflict is quite high here considering that family members are somewhat constrained to remain in the kitchen until dinner is complete, and that conflict-prone topics such as children's behavior during the day and financial matters are frequently discussed over dinner. (p. 97)

After bedroom and kitchen, it appears that the house's living room is the next most likely location for aggressive behavior. Much of this site's violence appears to occur in front of and, in a sense, in response to television viewing, i.e., conflict over one's view of the screen being blocked or which channel to watch, or arguments initiated by differing reactions to program content.

What of burglary? We will examine later the literature which compares diverse neighborhoods, cities, and regions for their respective crime probabilities, but what about *within* a neighborhood? It will be clear that the homes within any given neighborhood do not have equal potential for becoming the target site for a burglary. Instead, matters of opportunity and routine activity will greatly influence target selection. Cromwell, Olson, and Avary (1991) conducted an ethnographic analysis of home burglaries in an urban Texas metropolitan area, in which 30 active burglars were recruited to serve as research subjects. Acceptability for participation required that the individual admit to committing a minimum of two burglaries a month and meet related criteria concerned with court involvement and self-perception or labeling by others as a burglar. Subjects were asked to reconstruct and simulate their past burglaries, participate in an interview series about these events, and engage in a sequence of "ride-alongs," during which they were asked to discuss and evaluate a number of residential sites which they or others had previously burglarized, as well as homes they had rejected as too high-risk. Much of this discussion sought to examine both the salient and the subtle cues used by the burglar subjects in selecting a target, including especially cues associated with occupancy, potential gain, and likely risks.

The authors comment:

> The sites, more often than not, were targets of opportunity rather than purposeful selections. There were three common patterns: (a) the burglar happened by the potential burglary site at an opportune moment when the occupants were clearly absent and the target was perceived as vulnerable (open garage door, windows, etc.); (b) the site was one that had been previously visited by the burglar for a legitimate purpose (as a guest, delivery person, maintenance worker); (c) the site was chosen after "cruising" neighborhoods searching for a criminal opportunity. (p. 41)

Opportunity theory based upon routine activities (Cohen & Felson, 1979) holds that the likelihood of the occurrence of a criminal act is a joint function of (1) the presence of motivated offenders, (2) the availability of suitable targets, and (3) the absence of capable guardians. In Cromwell et al.'s (1991) sample of motivated offender burglars, considerable creativity was often employed by them in seeking to estimate target suitability and guardian absence. The most common opportunity-estimating probe was for one of the burglars to knock on the door or ring the doorbell. If anyone answered, the prober would ask for a nonexistent person, or for directions to a nearby address. Some noted the resident's name from the mailbox, left, looked up and called the resident's phone number, and left the phone ringing to return to the potential site. If the burglar could hear the phone still ringing when he or she arrived back at the house, it was deemed unoccupied and thus safe to break into. Another burglar donned jogging clothes, removed a piece of mail from the potential target's mailbox, and knocked on the door. If no one answered, the burglary ensued. If someone answered, he or she was told the mail had been found on the street and was being returned to him or her. Yet another burglar, dressed more conservatively, sought out homes next to those with "For Sale" signs (diminished guardianship) and, acting as a potential buyer, walked around the yard of the for-sale house while estimating accessibility of the adjacent home. Still other burglars simply watched the target home until seeing the occupants leave for work in the morning and, after a quick probe for remaining occupants, entered the house. In each instance, burglars may also estimate the likelihood of being seen based upon the physical location and characteristics of the potential target houses. Considered here are such characteristics as their location vis-à-vis pedestrian and automobile traffic, fences, shrubs, hedges, paths, and facing windows from other homes.

As noted, opportunity estimates according to routine activity theory require not only a person desiring to commit a crime (motivated offender) and an acceptably low probability of being surveilled (guardian absence), but also target availability and suitability. What cues do burglars use to estimate their potential payoffs? One is the socioeconomic sense of both the neighborhood and the specific location of the potential target houses. In Cromwell et al.'s (1991) sample, also factored in were such target-specific "gain cues" as

> "I look for those satellite TV dishes. If they got one of those, they got expensive electronic stuff inside."
>
> "If you see a jeep in the driveway or an RV or a boat, you can usually find some sporting equipment."
>
> "If they got an old wreck parked outside, they don't have nothing....I look for a new car. Something like an Oldsmobile." (p. 34)

In a follow-up attempt to partially validate the findings of their burglar interview study, which, as noted, are consistent with routine activity theory, the same authors compared 300 previously burglarized homes with 300 homes having no official record of being burglarized. Again consistent with the theory, the two home categories were highly distinguishable on a number of relevant characteristics. For example, the slower the auto traffic in front of the residence, or the closer the residence to (people-gathering and thus opportunity-revealing) schools, churches, stop signs, or stop lights, the greater the likelihood the residence had been burglarized. A second example: homes with no garages or with open carports—both of which more readily reveal if the occupants may be home—had more frequently been burglarized than those with closed garages.

Cromwell et al. (1991) conclude:

> These results tend to suggest that as burglars go about their everyday activities, traveling to and from activity hubs such as school, work, and recreational facilities, they come into contact with residential sites near those facilities. When burglars stop at a traffic light or a stop sign they have a brief opportunity to view the sites nearby and may choose a potential target during those moments. It is possible that this...accounts for the disproportionate selection of corner houses as burglar targets. (p. 46)

What are the physical borders of "home"? Are they the exterior walls, the surrounding shrubs, a fence, the property line? Taylor and Brower (1985) assert:

> Home does not end at the front door, but extends beyond. [It includes] that region beyond those exterior spaces adjoining the home: porches, steps, front yards, back yards, driveways, sidewalks, and alleys. (p. 212)

These are, the author suggest, the near-home areas in which the private and the public, the owned and the shared, the personal and the open interpenetrate. They are areas, depending on their distance from "home," which may be characterized by varying degrees of both control and threat. In the authors' words, "As we move from more central to less central spaces, desired control progressively decreases, and perceived threat progressively increases" (p. 198). Such near-home control decrement and threat increment may lead to an attempt to restore or expand control and reduce threat (i.e., *reassertion*), to establish strong defensive barriers by means of increased surveillance devices or physical means such as fencing or gates (i.e., *bulwarking*), or to reduce or even abandon territorial claims to the area of concern (i.e., *retreat*). In all three instances, reassertion, bulwarking, or retreat, the individual is increasingly concerned with, focused upon, and responsive to activity in the next microlevel site we wish to examine: the street.

THE STREET

The street is many places, a site for much of the best and much of the worst in human interaction. It may be a positive microsite, a place of safety, surveillance, and socialization. Or it may be a site for acts of aggression, a location for rape, assault, or homicide.

In her book, *The Death and Life of Great American Cities*, Jacobs (1961) talks positively of street life in a way that can only be responded to now, over 30 years later, with nostalgia for an era largely gone by in many American neighborhoods:

> The trust of a city street is formed over time from many, many little public sidewalk contacts. It grows of people stopping by at the bar for a beer, getting advice from the grocer and giving advice to the newsstand man, comparing opinions with other customers at the bakery and nodding hello to the two boys drinking pop on the stoop, eyeing the girls while waiting to be called for dinner, admonishing the children, hearing about a job from the hardware man and borrowing a dollar from the druggist....Most of it is ostensibly utterly trivial but the sum is not trivial at all. The sum of such casual, public contact at a local level...is a feeling for the public identity of people, a web of public respect and trust, and a resource in time of personal or neighborhood need. The absence of this trust is a disaster to a city street. (p. 56)

The social patterning thus described by Jacobs (1961), and before her by Suttles (1958) and Whyte (1943), occurring on narrow, ball-playing, inner-city, tenement traversing streets with adults watching at their windows or on their stoops, may describe a "physical slum," but not necessarily a "social slum." Instead, such streets have been, and on occasion still are, vital, healthy arenas of safety, surveillance, security, belonging, growth, and socialization.

There is, as our daily newspapers remind us, a much darker side of life and events on America's streets. Because they are a frequent venue for murder (Wolfgang, 1967a), assault (Brown, Flanagan, & McLeod, 1984), and rape (Stoks, 1982), they can be very dangerous places indeed. Wolfgang's (1967a) analysis of Philadelphia murder statistics revealed that for men, but not women, the street was the single most frequent location for homicide. Brown et al. (1984) report that 53 per cent of assaults occur in street or other outside locations, usually near the victim's home. In many low-income neighborhoods in particular, the street is often a site for hanging around, demonstrating machismo, commanding respect, claiming territorial rights, rapping, signifying, drinking, and in other ways building and maintaining a positive self-image (Blau & Blau, 1982). All of these street transactions hold potential for escalation to overt aggression. Street violence is high, but it must be noted in evaluating its incidence that, as Campbell (1986b) points out, it is also the most public (and thus the most countable) site of aggressive behaviors. Violence in the home is likely to be underreported for reasons associated with threat of more of the same, embarrassment, or mistrust of the police. Barroom violence may reflect poorly on the bar's image and affect future patronage, and therefore it is also likely to be underreported. Such recalcitrance is less possible following a street murder, assault, or rape. These reporting artifacts notwithstanding, the thrust of the available data concurs that for these three major forms of overt aggression, the home (first) and the street (a close second) are the primary sites, a finding demonstrated in Atlanta, Boston, and San Francisco (Curtis, 1974); Houston (Bullock, 1955; Pokorny, 1960); St. Louis (Pittman & Handy, 1964); Seattle (Stoks, 1982); Philadelphia (Amir, 1971; Wolfgang, 1967a); Chicago (Block, 1977; Voss & Hepburn, 1968); and the state of California (Allen, 1980).

Such home and street incidence findings accord with popular observation. What is less obvious, and much less frequently investigated, is the microspatial location of such violent crimes *within* the home and the street. As Stoks (1982), who fills a substantial portion of this investigative void, notes:

> Knowledge of where violent crimes occur in urban public space is limited to rather unspecific, imprecise classification. Without knowing precisely where crime sites are located (for example, exactly where in the alley, exactly where on the street) it is extremely difficult to gather information concerning the physical environmental characteristics of crime sites and opportunities for criminal behavior they provide. (p. 29)

Some, largely anecdotal and impressionistic, violent crime microlevel-site information does exist. Angel (1968) mentions vacant lots and spaces between buildings. Brill (1977) points to poorly lit areas, areas with difficult access, and areas of what he terms "unassigned space." Harries (1976) suggests sites which are concealed, have low pedestrian traffic, or have a poor opportunity for surveillance. Jeffery (1977) indicates isolated institutional regions (e.g., a university) and areas with substantial foliage. Westinghouse (1978) suggests that dark areas, densely shrubbed locations, parking lots, and, more generally, untraveled areas will be likely sites for crimes of violence. Newman (1972), concretizing his notions of defensible space, points to stairwells, elevators, lobbies, and "blind areas" as problem locations. Stoks (1982), treating many of these observations as hypotheses to be tested, conducted a major microanalytic investigation of 590 rape sites in the city of Seattle, for the year 1981.

Stoks's (1982) objective was to identify where and when these rapes occurred, as well as the site characteristics influencing the outcome of the rape attempt. Consistent with the findings of several other investigators (Amir, 1971; Hindelang & Davis, 1977; McDermott, 1979b), Stoks found that rapes in Seattle occur most frequently on weekends, in the evening, peaking in the summer months. Although a rape's location is frequently a moving crime scene (meet at one location and move to another where the rape occurs), primary sites of occurrence for those rapes which took place outdoors (23 per cent of the total took place in the offender's home) were in a vehicle (38 per cent), on or next to a sidewalk (19 per cent), or in an alley (9 per cent), a wooded area (7 per cent), a park (6 per cent), a parking lot (5 per cent), or a school (4 per cent).

In a still more fine-grained site analysis, Stoks sought to identify the rape-facilitating and rape-inhibiting microfeatures of these several incident locations. His findings included:

Vegetation. Sixty per cent of the sites had trees, shrubs, long grass, or other forms of vegetation defining and often obscuring the location where the rape occurred. At 80 per cent of these sites, the vegetation was over four feet tall and, in over half the locations, judged to be so dense at the time of the rape that it would have been very difficult to observe the crime as it took place from where potential witnesses might have been.

Other barriers. Over three quarters of the rape sites had substantial nonvegetation barriers to escape or surveillance: walls, fences, ground slopes, and the like. The greater the number and/or height of such barriers, the greater the likelihood the attempted rape would be successful.

Lighting. Completed rapes were most likely to occur in Stoks's data set when the rape scene had no lighting. In over 70 per cent of the cases, the quality of the lighting was such that the ability of a witness to identify a suspected perpetrator at 25 yards was estimated to be unlikely.

Predictability of victim movement and location. Stoks (1982) comments with regard to this site feature:

> I assumed from the outset that predatory rapists (like predatory animals) need to know where to find their victims, and to be able to some extent anticipate what their movements will be. For over half the cases, I estimated that the configuration of the rape site and its immediate vicinity was such that the offender could most likely (35.1%) and definitely (15.8%) predict where the victims would move in that area. For example, if a victim began to descend a flight of steps, an offender might consider it most likely that she will arrive at the landing midway, and at the bottom if there are no opportunities for leaving along the way. (p. 177)

Analysis revealed that in fact in successful rapes there frequently were high levels of movement and location predictability, i.e., sidewalk paths (68.4 per cent), steep terrain (26.5 per cent), alleys (12.2 per cent), bus stops (10.5 per cent), and stair landings (7.7 per cent).

Potential witnesses. In general, as the estimated number of people within 100 yards of the rape site decreases, the number of successfully completed rapes increases. In a third of the Seattle rapes, based on time of day, day of week, and site location, Stoks estimated there to be fewer than five potential witnesses within 100 yards of the rape site. In two thirds of the instances, however, more than five such possible witnesses were estimated to be present, suggesting that the location at which outdoor rapes occur need not be isolated areas.

In combination, these several site characteristics jointly appear to enhance perpetrator predictability and control, and to diminish both the victim's potential for escape and the offender's likelihood of surveillance and apprehension. In a cross-validational attempt to discern the predictive accuracy of this cluster of successful rape site characteristics, Stoks arranged to have identified five urban areas, each approximately 250 square yards in size, somewhere in each of which a successful rape had occurred. Only the police knew the precise location of each of the five rapes. In four of the five instances, Stoks's application of his cluster of site characteristics predicted the exact rape location. Stoks's effort is impressive ecological research. Its success strongly encourages both efforts aimed at independent validation of its accuracy and continued applied utilization of its microspatial findings. The potential application and extension of the fruits of this empirical effort may be even further potentiated if given a theoretical base of relevance to both its conceptualization and its hypothesis-deriving richness. We recommend prospect–refuge theory first developed in a Darwinian context (Appleton, 1975) and later applied to school vandalism (Pablant & Baxter, 1975), burglary (Taylor & Nee, 1988), and crime on college campuses (Fisher & Nasar, 1992). The latter authors comment:

> Appleton (1975) proposed the prospect-refuge theory as an explanation for human environmental preferences. He argued that prospect and refuge offered an evolutionary advantage such that humans favor places...that afford prospect (an open view) and refuge (protection)....Such places aid survival from animate hazards by offering an observation point to see, to react, and if necessary to defend, as well as a protective space to keep oneself from being harmed. (p. 37)

Fisher and Nasar (1992) assert, and we strongly concur, that prospect–refuge theory constructs have marked potential for aiding our understanding of microspatial findings such as Stoks's (1982), and for advancing their further development and conceptualization.

THE BAR

Perhaps better than most examples, aggression occurring in or near bars or taverns illustrates well the person–environment transactional antecedents of such behavior. Drinking alcoholic beverages *does* facilitate aggressive behavior. MacDonald's (1961) review of relevant studies indicates that in over half of the murders analyzed, the perpetrator had been drinking before the crime. Holcomb and Anderson (1982) and Sorrells (1977) report similar results in, respectively, separate analyses of adult and juvenile murderers. Alcoholic intoxication has also been identified as a major antecedent or concomitant of assault (Myers, 1982), wife abuse (Gayford, 1975), and rape (Johnson, Gibson, & Linden, 1978). Even more indicting of the role of alcohol in aggression is Bushman and Cooper's (1990) meta-analytic review of 30 existing *experimental* studies of the alcohol–aggression relationship, from which causation may appropriately be inferred, an analysis from which they conclude that alcohol does indeed facilitate aggressive behavior. In barroom settings, the alcohol–aggression sequence appears to be mediated by person variables, place variables, and especially person-by-place interactions.

The ingestion of substantial quantities of alcohol appears to lead to a series of reliable intraindividual consequences, regardless of the individual's setting or context. These may include a number of perceptual and cognitive changes. The perceptual field narrows and a more restricted range of cues is responded to:

> When a person's perceptual field is narrowed to the point at which his perception of the situation is based on a few environmental cues, random fluctuations can mean drastic changes in his perception of the situation. This can lead to misunderstanding and conflict. Actions by others may appear inconsistent and arbitrary to the intoxicated person because he does not have a full view of the context in which they are taking place. (Gibbs, 1986, p. 140)

Conceptual impoverishment and decline in abstracting ability may occur under the influence of alcohol, "which decreases the likelihood of use of coping devices that go outside the immediate situation and thus cut down the probability of alternative acts" (Pernanen, 1976, p. 416). Such impoverishment and heightened concreteness may also result in inaccurate assessment of the intentions of other persons and reduced capacity to evaluate risk. Add to these perceptual and cognitive sequelae the purported changes in arousal level, emotional lability, reduction in anxiety, and, McClelland, Davis, Kalin, and Warner (1972) suggest, heightened concern with power, and it seems appropriate to conclude that the heavy drinker is often a fight waiting to happen. What he or she may need for its actual occurrence is a facilitating location, of which many contemporary bars are a prime example.

Gibbs (1986) proposes that:

> The atmosphere of the bar shapes the style of drinking and proper comportment while under the influence of alcohol. It also regulates the amount of aggression that can be expressed and determines which expressions of aggression are appropriate. Some bars feature more structure than others for interpreting and reacting to conflict situations. (p. 145)

Such structure may include formal rules (e.g., no gambling on darts or pool for stakes higher than a drink), informal rules (e.g., silence and a step back from the table when an opponent is shooting pool), or conflict resolution mechanisms (e.g., a shared understanding that the bartender is the final arbiter of a conflict, or that customers not involved in a dispute should avoid taking sides). In contrast to such a structure of formal and informal rules and implicit understandings are the "skid-row aggressive" bars observed at length by Graham, LaRocque, Yetman, Ross, and Guistra (1980):

> This environment was characterized by very permissive decorum expectations, unpleasant, unclean and inexpensive physical surroundings, higher percentages of...unkempt patrons than in other bars, a tense atmosphere, patrons drinking rapidly and becoming highly intoxicated, downtown location, poor ventilation;...people talking loudly to themselves, tables crowded together in rows and unfriendly bar workers....Patrons tend to be in and out of the bar all day....For many of the patrons, this bar is one of the circuit of bars they visit during the day....There are few limits on acceptable behavior and little pressure on patrons to behave "normally." (p. 146)

These two barroom descriptions more or less anchor the endpoints of a continuum of drinking-place facilitation–inhibition of overt aggression. What occurs when person characteristics and place characteristics interact? Johnson (1986) suggests that a "situational self" emerges, one relatively "free of the moral restraints which under normal circumstances inhibit violence" (Gibbs, 1986, p. 111). Such freedom from, or reduction of, moral restraint "granted" by the relaxed expectations of the barroom setting lies at the heart of other person-by-place analyses of alcohol-caused aggression. MacAndrew and Edgerton (1969), for example, describe drinking situations as culturally agreed-upon "time-out" periods, during which it is permissible to blame deviant behavior "on the bottle."

Toch (1986) appraises bars as venues for "self-image promoting"; Campbell (1986) similarly speaks of such settings as arenas for impression management. Her interview study of 200 bartenders revealed that their refusal to serve a patron was the single most frequent reason for a dispute, a finding clearly related to concerns with image promotion and management of impressions. Alcohol-driven aggression growing from person–place interaction, in this instance from a routine activity theory perspective, is also evident in Felson, Baccaglini, and Gmelch's (1986) analysis of barroom brawls:

> Bars may create the opportunity for conflict because they bring together in one location young adult males, a violence prone population. This explanation is consistent with the routine activity approach to crime [according to which] the probability that a violation will occur at any time and place might be taken as a function of the convergence of likely offenders and suitable targets in the absence of capable guardians. (p. 153)

Consistent with this view, Felson et al.'s (1986) analysis of aggressive incidents in American and Irish bars revealed that the average age of the patrons was the single best predictor of both verbal and physical aggression: the older the patrons, the fewer the aggressive incidents.

Not only, in routine activity theory terms, does the bar thus provide *offenders*, but it also provides *targets*. Patrons in, and coming to and from, the bar are likely to have cash and may become intoxicated—both of which enhance their suitability as targets of assault and robbery. So, too, the barrooms themselves are accessible, public, vulnerable, cash-on-hand targets. Targets for aggression and crime related to bars may extend beyond the bar itself, the bar serving as a draw to the block or neighborhood of offenders who reach out to what they perceive as other nearby, suitable targets. Roncek and Maier (1991), replicating an earlier evaluation of bars as crime-associated neighborhood "hot spots" by Roncek and Bell (1981), found that in the city of Cleveland, for the two-year period studied, there were 112,142 index crimes on the city's 4,396 blocks, an average of 25.51 crimes per block for the study period. On the 499 city blocks on which there was a bar, there were 21,099 index crimes, or an average of 42.28 crimes per block. Other such crime-associated hot spots exist—high schools (Roncek & Faggiani, 1985), shopping centers and fast-food restaurants (Brantingham & Brantingham, 1991), and convenience stores (D'Alessio & Stolzenberg, 1990)—so it is not alcohol or alcohol intoxication per se that is of causative relevance here. Nonetheless, bars are aggression-associated and, in a person–environment sense, aggression-contributing locations.

In summary, a comprehensive person-by-place view of a typical aggressive incident, in or near a barroom, would consist of young males drinking to a point of constricted perceptual field and reduced conceptual and abstracting capacity; oriented toward displays of prowess, manliness, and power; in a permissive working-class or lower-class atmosphere with much heavy, rapid, asocial drinking; and with little interaction not only with other patrons, but also with the bar's personnel—until the aggression-releasing "last straw" of further drink refusal. Beyond such intoxication-associated aggression, crime-associated aggressive acts are apparently made much more likely in the vicinity of the bar by its "hot spot" capacity to draw together offenders, targets, and diminished guardianship.

THE CAR

By name, by advertising image, by use, and by abuse, the automobile and its roadway surroundings join home, street, and bar as prime microsites for concrete forms of aggressive behavior, which are many and varied. Parry (1968) surveyed a sample of 17- to 24-year-old British motorists, who collectively reported frequent use of rude signs at other motorists, chasing other drivers, feeling like injuring another driver, fighting with other drivers, trying to edge another car off the road, driving at other vehicles in anger, and making excessive use of the horn. Turner, Layton, and Simons (1975) obtained similar results among Salt Lake City drivers. McAlhany (1984) conducted a further such survey in Texas. The most frequent expressions of aggression were tailgating, rude gestures or shaking fists, deliberate blinding by high headlight beams, deliberate preventing of passing or changing lanes, being sworn at, being blocked from leaving a stop sign or traffic light, the throwing of an object, and, predictive of more of the same to come later, the showing of a weapon. Novaco's (1991) more recent typology of automobile aggression, reflecting the march in America toward higher and more lethal levels and types of aggression, includes roadway shootings, throwing of objects, assault with a vehicle, sniper or robber attacks, drive-by shootings, suicide or murder crashes, and roadside confrontations. Novaco (1991) summarizes the current situation accurately:

> Both cars and trucks are often used by their drivers as instruments of dominance, and the road serves as an arena for competition and control. Moreover, roadways in metropolitan areas have become contexts where aggressive scripts (mental programming of antagonistic behavior) are activated by driving circumstances. The disposition for aggression, otherwise subdued by the restraining contingencies, palliatives, and gentilities of societal living, becomes engaged behind the wheel, being easily provoked by traffic and the behavior of other drivers. The roadway, whether freeway or surface street, whether urban or rural, is a context where aggressive behavior is potentiated precisely because of multiple disinhibitory influences. (p. 254)

Who are the aggressive drivers, and what are their demographic and personality characteristics? In the Parry (1968), Turner et al. (1975), and McAlhany (1984) driver surveys described above, aggressive acts were more common for younger than older drivers, males more than females, and non-college graduates than graduates. Michalowski (1975) found that a significant proportion of those drivers committing vehicular homicide had prior histories of violent criminal behavior. Tillman and Hobbs (1949) studied high-accident-frequency taxi drivers and found that, compared to those with low accident rates, they showed greater levels of childhood aggression, family disharmony, AWOL rates when in the armed services, and, when driving, higher levels of irritability, distractibility, horn honking, competitiveness, and lack of concern about the mechanical limitations of their taxis. Other studies have suggested that highly aggressive–high-accident drivers, compared to low-aggression–low-accident controls, are more competitive (Macmillan, 1975), are more extroverted (Fine, 1963), show greater disregard for social mores (Rommel, 1959), and are both more impulsive and have more likely experienced recent major stressful events in their lives (Williams, Henderson, & Mills, 1974).

Our major theme throughout this book is that aggressive behavior is a result of combined person and environment characteristics. The sparse literature on qualities of chronically aggressive drivers has been presented above. A modest amount of field research has begun to point to setting features and events which, when experienced by such individuals, tend to lead to overt aggression. Doob and Gross (1968) created a frustrating circumstance for drivers by arranging to have a car, stopped at a traffic light, fail to move when the light changed. In one research condition, the stopped vehicle was a high-status automobile (a new black Chrysler Imperial). In the low-status condition, a rusty old Ford station wagon or an equally decrepit Rambler was used. Backed-up drivers honked their horns more, and more quickly after the light change (the two study measures of aggression), when stopped behind one of the older vehicles than they did behind the Chrysler. Consistent with the survey data noted earlier, male drivers honked their horns more and with less latency than did female drivers. Deaux (1971), but not Chase and Mills (1973), found that both male and female drivers honked more and more quickly when the driver of the stopped auto was female.

In another context, Berkowitz and LePage (1967) have shown that the mere presence of a gun can, under certain circumstances, have a cuing, aggression-arousing effect on those exposed to it. Is the same effect evident under driving conditions? Turner et al. (1975) used a pickup truck in their stopped-vehicle experiment and tested the possible impact on driver behavior of such potential aggressive cues by placing or not placing a rifle on a gun rack visible behind the stopped driver, as well as a bumper sticker that said, "Vengeance," or "Friend." Both the presence of the rifle and the rifle plus the "Vengeance" bumper sticker combination resulted in higher rates of horn honking compared to the control conditions. A final stopped-vehicle experiment, conducted by Kenrick and MacFarlane (1986), also employed horn honking as the aggression index. Their concern was the effect, if any, of atmospheric conditions on such behavior. Both ambient temperature and a humidity discomfort index proved to be linearly related to the frequency, latency, and duration of horn honking—particularly for drivers who had their windows open. Rather than employing a stopped vehicle, Hauber (1980) sought to create driver frustration by having a pedestrian enter a crosswalk in front of a moving vehicle at a point which would cause the driver to stop or slow down. The response of one quarter of the drivers was classified by the experimenters as aggressive, e.g., fist shaking, cursing, and horn honking. Younger drivers (male and female) were more aggressive than older drivers; driver aggression was twice as frequent when the crossing pedestrian was male; and aggression was substantially more frequent in the afternoon than in the morning.

Horn honking at stalled cars, a rude gesture, and a shouted curse are each unpleasant low-level manifestations of overt aggression. In the United States today, aggression in and by use of the automobile has not infrequently taken much more ominous forms. Intentional crashing, fights between drivers, objects thrown at cars, roadside snipers, carjack-ings, and drive-by shootings are the almost daily fare of the popular press. A growing minority of drivers carry a gun in their car (Clifford, 1989). Novaco's (1991) study of traffic-school participants revealed that 44 per cent had been chased by another driver, 36 per cent had had an object thrown at them while driving, 13 per cent had been bumped or rammed, 8 per cent had had a physical fight with another driver, 4 per cent had been threatened with a gun, and 5 of his 412 respondents had actually been shot at while driving. The growing frequency and lethality of such automobile-sited aggression have made it all the more vital that an understanding of the psychological mechanisms underlying such be-havior be identified and examined. Novaco (1991) has provided a major contribution in this regard. He speaks of four interrelated processes which, acting in combination, may substantially enhance the likelihood of roadway aggression.

Anger arousal. As research by Berkowitz (1989) and Novaco (1986) has shown, anger is an especially common antecedent of overt aggression. Further, emotional arousal of a nonangry type may combine with anger arousal to potentiate aggressive behavior. As Novaco (1991) observes:

> Driving an automobile involves many conditions of arousal activation. Merely driving a car is arousing. Passing, braking, turning, attending to other cars, unexpected occurrences, etc., are even more potent activators of arousal. The research which Stokols and I have conducted with regard to chronic exposure to traffic congestion has found highly significant increases in baseline blood pressure, lowering of frustration tolerance, increases in negative mood and aggressive driving habits to be associated with traffic exposure in long distance commuting. (p. 306)

Impedance stress. Impedance, in the context of auto travel, may be generally defined as "behavioral constraints on movement and goal attainment" and, concretely, as the amount of traffic congestion, the number of road exchanges, the number of freeways, the amount of time and miles traveled, the commuting duration, and similarly aversive indices. Novaco, Kliewer, and Broquet (1991) compared the effect on mood and conflict at home in samples of low- versus high-impedance commuters. Low-impedance drivers were in the bottom 20 per cent of the total sample's distribution of commuting time and distance. They traveled 7 miles or less to work, on a commute taking 20 minutes or less. The high-impedance sample, constituted of the upper 20 per cent of this distribution, traveled 20 to 64 miles to work and spent 50 minutes or more doing so. Study results found clear group differences on the home mood measures, with the high-impedance group showing significantly more negative, more dysphoric levels. Again, in Novaco's (1991) words:

> Elevations of arousal, negative mood, and impatience work against restraints on aggression, which are further weakened by the anonymity of roadways and the escape potential provided by the automobile. (p. 311)

Deindividuation. The anonymity, sense of diminished accountability, and possibility of escape, each of which is associated with high-speed freeway driving, may contribute to a process of losing one's sense of individuality, a phenomenon usually discussed under the term *deindividuation.* A series of investigations combine to suggest that a deindividuated state is indeed facilitative of aggressive behavior (Diener, 1976; Prentice-Dunn & Rogers, 1980; Zillman, Bryant, Cantor, & Day, 1975; Zimbardo, 1969). Though much of this research has examined deindividuation as a characteristic of mob or other collective behavior, its applicability to the driving context seems clear.

Cognitive scripts. Cognitive scripts are schemes or routines developed by the individual for representing and organizing information. Such scripts, when depicting roadway aggression, may derive both from the models of such behavior one observes on the road and from media portrayals and newspaper accounts of roadway violence. Novaco (1991) comments:

> The concept of an aggressive script then is that of a mental programming of antagonistic behavior in a particular context whereby situational cues activate various subroutines for an actor's responses. Automobile driving is indeed impregnated with cues linked to aggressive scripts. (p. 312)

Novaco's (1991) conceptualization of mechanisms likely to underly aggression on the road is a valuable first step, all the more so in view of the very minimal attention paid thus far by the behavioral sciences to such situated behavior. Given the sheer magnitude of automobile ownership and traffic in the United States and, as we have seen, the frequency with which cars are also a microlevel site for aggression, much more such attention is well deserved.

THE STORE

Routine activity theory, as noted earlier, seeks to explain criminal behavior by asserting it to be a function of the convergence in time and space of potential offenders, suitable targets, and diminished guardianship. The retail store, or at least certain types of stores in certain types of locations, are an especially frequent microlevel site for such convergence. Convenience stores, for example, have proven to be an especially vulnerable crime target, especially those located (1) close to major transportation routes, (2) on streets with small amounts of vehicular traffic, (3) next to vacant lots, and (4) in areas with few other stores or commercial activity (Duffalo, 1976). Note in regard to each of these locational characteristics its relevance to supplying potential offenders (factor 1), or to increasing target suitability and reducing likely guardianship (factors 2, 3, and 4). D'Alessio and Stolzenberg (1990) identified four additional ecological features of convenience-store location, operation, and design which proved to be vulnerability-relevant, namely, parking-lot size, hours of operation, gas service, and degree of social disorganization. Increased parking-lot size and a flow of gas-purchasing customers each increase the level of surveilling guardianship and thus are associated with lessened levels of victimization. Later hours and siting in an area of social disorganization have an opposite association with regard to severity of victimization. Hours open proved of significance because more than 50 per cent of the convenience store robberies occurred between 10 P.M. and 12 midnight (and especially on Fridays, Saturdays, and Sundays). Social disorganization, according to D'Alessio and Stolzenberg (1990), is pertinent because:

> Social disorganization theory assumes that the social and communal bonds that normally exist in a neighborhood disintegrate as members of the community become more mobile. A steady influx of alien people into a community extinguishes any sense of attachment with one's neighbors. Because individuals in these highly transient communities lack the communal bonds necessary to participate actively in protecting their neighborhoods, crime increases in these areas. (p. 265)

Jeffery, Hunter, and Griswold (1987) and Clifton and Callahan (1987) report reduced vulnerability to robbery—in fact, three times less frequency—when the store cash register is in the middle of the store and visible through the window to be seen by passing "guardians," than when it is off to a side and less open to such surveillance. Also strongly associated with reduced likelihood of victimization is staffing the store with two clerks, rather than one. Convenience stores do indeed appear to be convenient crime sites also. Clifton and Callahan (1987) report that over a five-year period in the Gainesville, Florida, area, 96 per cent of all 47 convenience stores were robbed, in contrast to the analogous rates for the area's 67 fast-food establishments (36 per cent), 71 gas stations (21 per cent), and 44 liquor stores (16 per cent). In response to convenience-store robbery rates such as this, and anticipating our later examination of environmental design interventions to reduce such outcomes (see Chapter 8), Crow and Bull (1975) examined two sets of 60 convenience stores each, matched on a variety of characteristics including number of previous robberies and degree of target attractiveness as rated by robbery ex-offenders. The 60 experimental-group stores instituted a variety of environmental design changes hypothesized to impact favorably on robbery rate: improved lighting, improved visibility (removal of all window advertisements), blocking of possible escape routes, and so forth. No such changes were made in and near the 60 control-group stores. Over an eight-month observation period, robberies decreased by 30 per cent in the altered, but not in the control-group, convenience stores.

Convenience stores are one common shopping microsite in the United States today. Shopping malls are another. As Brantingham, Brantingham, and Wong (1990) point out, at least certain groupings of stores have been particularly attractive locations for criminal activity in the past, e.g., London's "rookeries" in the nineteenth century (Mayhew, 1861); Chicago's commercial district in the early twentieth century (Shaw & McKay, 1931); and so, too, the modern shopping mall. Simply stated, when a location attracts large numbers of people, some proportion of them will be criminally motivated, more so or less so—as we will see below—depending upon the specific location and its relevant characteristics.

Four types of shopping malls have emerged in the United States. Neighborhood malls often have a supermarket as their major store, tend according to Brantingham et al. (1990) to serve populations up to about 40,000, and are usually located on a busy local street. Community malls serve larger populations, perhaps 40,000 to 100,000; feature a large, inexpensive chain store; and are typically located on main arteries. Regional malls have a still larger clientele, usually have two department stores and a substantial number of specialty shops, and are sited at major highway intersections. A small number of what might be termed *megamalls* have also been recently constructed in the United States. These consist of a very large number of stores, several department stores, several movie theaters and restaurants, and, in one instance, an amusement park!

Brantingham et al. (1990) note that malls first developed in the suburbs, typically in middle- to upper-income areas. At least some categories of criminally motivated individuals (e.g., those without automobile transportation available to them) had reduced opportunities to seek out such sites. As malls moved cityward, added movies (making them more attractive to teenagers) and bars (making them more attractive to drinking populations), and came closer to public transit stops (making them more accessible to low-income individuals), criminal motivation and target suitability increasingly converged. Crime increased both in and near such malls. Arcades and food fairs are especially crime-prone within-mall areas; apartment houses nearby, with their occupants off to work during the day (low level of guardianship), proved to be especially vulnerable near-mall crime locations (Felson, 1987; Sherman, Gartin, & Buerger, 1989).

Two novel and thus far largely underutilized approaches to the understanding of business and related crime locations have emerged in recent years. One is the study of the location and distribution of *physical resources* within a geographic area (O'Donnell & Lydgate, 1980); the other, touched upon earlier in this chapter, is the examination of crime-occurrence *hot spots* (Sherman et al., 1989). O'Donnell and Lydgate (1980) developed a land-use coding system to categorize the physical resources within Honolulu police beats. Examples of the coding categories developed included retail goods, eating places, alcohol consumption, entertainment, permanent residences, transient residences, recreation, warehouses, and commercial offices. Offenses reported to the police during a four-year period were then correlated with these physical resource data. Study findings varied by type of crime. Vandalism was most highly associated with only one resource, permanent residences, which the investigators suggest best reflects the number of adolescents—a high-vandalism group—at the type of location. Assault, weapons offenses, disorderly conduct, and other violent crimes were most associated with retail goods, eating places, alcohol consumption, and entertainment.

A study of crime hot spots was conducted in Minneapolis (Sherman et al., 1989). It revealed, perhaps even more dramatically than common observation would have estimated, that crime scenes are very far from randomly or even widely distributed. Over half (50.4 per cent) of all police calls for which cars were dispatched were sent to only 3.3 per cent of all possible locations. The top 5 per cent of all locations generated an average of one call every two weeks. Business establishments requiring the greatest number of calls during the one-year study period included a large discount store in a low-income neighborhood (810 calls), a large department store (686), and a corner with both a bar and a convenience store (607). The investigators further report that all of the 4,166 robbery calls were located at only 2.2 per cent of all sites in Minneapolis; all 3,908 auto thefts at 2.7 per cent; and all rapes at just 1.2 per cent of all locations. Ninety-five per cent of all the city's locations were free of these three crimes for the study year. The authors note:

When the three general offense types are combined in the same places, there are 230 hot spots with five or more of any of the three offenses, and 54 locations with at least 10. There is also a high conditional probability of an additional offense once one has occurred. Under the simple Poisson model, each place in the city has only an 8% chance of suffering one of these crimes. But the risk of a second offense given the first [is] 26%. Once a place has had three of these offenses, the risk of recurrence within the year exceeds 50%. (p. 39)

Though the present section focuses on the occurrence of aggression and criminal activity at stores and other business microlevel sites, it should be noted that this same investigation revealed that all of the Minneapolis assaults during the study year occurred at 7 per cent of all possible locations, and that 9 per cent of all locations proved to be the hot spots for domestic disturbances. Further analysis revealed that hot spots for these diverse felonies are often related. Ninety per cent of all calls of all types occurred on seven main thoroughfares. The investigators conclude:

Like the criminology of individuals, a criminology of place could fall prey to the facile notion that getting rid of the "bad apples" will solve the problem. Neither capital punishment of places (as in arson of crack houses) nor incapacitation of the routine activities of criminal hot spots (as in revocation of liquor licenses) seems likely to eliminate crime. But since the routine activity of place may be regulated far more easily than the routine activity of persons, a criminology of place would seem to offer substantial promise. (p. 49)

THE SCHOOL

For decades, it seemed, school was neutral turf. Aggression in the community and in near proximity to the school generally remained there, and school problem behaviors were largely of the throwing-spitballs or talking-out-of-turn variety. As the levels and lethality of aggression in the United States continued to grow, and as home, street, and mass media continued to flood the lives of schoolchildren with literally thousands of direct and vicarious experiences of (often successfully employed) aggressive behaviors, schools themselves became major venues for violence and vandalism. As one besieged classroom teacher put it, "The streets have come to the school."

AGGRESSION TOWARD PERSONS

In 1975, the Bayh Senatorial Subcommittee issued its Safe School Report. This survey of 750 school districts indicated that in America's schools between 1970 and 1973, homicides had increased by 18.5 per cent, rapes and attempted rapes had increased by 40.1 per cent, robberies had increased by 36.7 per cent, assaults on students had increased by 85.3 per cent, assaults on teachers had increased by 77.4 per cent, burglaries in school had increased by 11.8 per cent, drug and alcohol offenses had increased by 37.5 per cent, and the number of weapons confiscated by school personnel (pistols, knives, nunchaku sticks, and even sawed-off shotguns) had increased by 54.5 per cent. The National Association of School Security Directors reported that, in 1974, there were 204,000 assaults and 9,000 rapes in American schools. Matters had gone a very long way from spitballs and turn taking. There were 18,000 assaults on teachers in 1955, 41,000 in 1971, and 63,000 in 1975; by 1979, the number of such attacks had risen to 110,000. The situation has not improved since. In the 1988–1989 school year, compared to the preceding year, school crime had increased 5 per cent, and in-school weapons possession had risen 21 per cent in California's public schools (Goldstein, 1992b). In a similar comparison, the New York City public school system reported a 35 per cent increase in assaults on students and school staff, a 16 per cent increase in harassment, a 24 per cent increase in larceny, and an overall crime-rate increase of 25 per cent. Noteworthy is the fact that the greatest increase in crime rate occurred at the elementary-school level (Goldstein, 1992b). The level of assaults on teachers in America's public schools is sufficiently high so that the vocabulary of aggression has been expanded to include what Block (1977) has called the "battered teacher syndrome": a combination of stress reactions including anxiety, depression, disturbed sleep, headaches, elevated blood pressure, and eating disorders.

The seriousness of these attacks on teachers notwithstanding, it must be remembered that most aggression in America's schools is directed toward other *students*. Victimization data from 26 major American cities surveyed in 1974 and 1975 indicated that 78 per cent of personal victimizations in schools (rapes, robberies, assaults, and larcenies) were students (McDermott, 1979). Ban and Ciminillo (1977) report that in a national survey the percentage of principals who report "unorganized fighting" between students had increased from 2.8 per cent in 1961 to 18 per cent in 1974. Examining many of the data on the correlates of aggression toward students, Ianni (1978) reported that seventh-graders are most likely to be attacked and twelfth-graders the least likely; at about age 13 the risks of physical attack tend to be greatest. Fifty-eight per cent of such attacks involve victims and offenders of the same race; 42 per cent are interracial. It has also been demonstrated that the smaller the size of a minority group in school, the more likely it is that its members will be victimized by members of other racial groups.

The 1989 annual school crime report from the School Safety Council reports that almost 3 million students, faculty, staff, and visitors were crime victims in American schools in 1987. Two and a half million of these crimes were thefts. During the first half of 1990, approximately 9 per cent of all students, age 12 to 19, were crime victims in the United States: 2 per cent of violent crimes and 7 per cent of property crimes. Fifteen per cent said their schools had gangs. Sixteen per cent claimed their school had had an actual or threatened attack on a teacher (Goldstein, 1992b). Siegel and Senna (1991) add that "although teenagers spend only 25 percent of their time in school, 40 percent of the robberies and 36 percent of the physical attacks involving this age group occur in school" (p. 43).

A 1990 report, aptly titled *Caught in the Crossfire* (Center to Prevent Handgun Violence, 1990), fully captures the central role of firearms in the more recent surge of school violence. From 1986 to 1990, 71 people (65 students and 6 employees) were killed by guns in American schools. Another 201 were seriously wounded, and 242 were held hostage at gunpoint. Older adolescents were most frequently perpetrators, as well as victims. Such school gun violence grew from gang or drug disputes (18 per cent), longstanding arguments (15 per cent), romantic disagreements (12 per cent), fights over possessions (10 per cent), and accidents (13 per cent). An estimated 270,000 students carry handguns to school one or more times each year. The American School Health Association (1989) estimates that 7 per cent of boys and 2 per cent of girls carry a knife to school every day.

AGGRESSION TOWARD PROPERTY

School vandalism, defined as acts that result in significant damage to schools (Greenberg, 1969), has been characterized, in terms of perpetrator motivation, as predatory, vindictive, or wanton (Martin, 1961) and, in terms of perpetrator perception, as acquisitive, tactical, ideological, revengeful, playful, or malicious (Cohen, 1971). Across motivational or perceptual subtypes, vandalism viewed collectively is an expensive fact of American educational life. Though estimates for some years show not inconsiderable variability, several reports lead to a consensus view that, in more-or-less direct parallel to incidence statistics for aggression toward people in schools, aggression toward property increased substantially in the several years ending in the mid-1970s and then generally leveled off at what is best described as an absolutely high level (Casserly, Bass, & Garrett, 1980; Inciardi & Pottieger, 1978; Rubel, 1977; *New Jersey Commissioner's Report to the Education Committee*, 1988; Wetzel, 1989). In 1969, $100 million of such school vandalism is reported to have occurred; in 1970, $200 million; in 1973, $260 million; in 1975, $550 million; and in 1977, $600 million. As the National Education Association's (1977) report indicates, as these years passed and vandalism costs grew, approximately half of such costs were directly due to property damage incurred, and the remaining half represented indirect vandalism costs associated with hiring and supporting a security force, the use of security devices, and so forth. These total vandalism-cost figures typically have not included one additional and major hidden cost of such property destruction: insurance.

Matters have worsened in subsequent years. Los Angeles County reports a 14-year vandalism expenditure in its schools of $52 million from property damage, $32 million as a result of arson, and $25 million due to theft and burglary of school property (Los Angeles County Office of Education, 1988b). By 1991, 1 of 8 teachers and 1 of 9 students in America's schools had reported incidents of stealing within any given month (Miller & Prinz, 1991). Others report concurring data regarding continuing high levels of in-school theft (Harris, Gray, Rees-McGee, Carroll, & Zaremba, 1987; Hutton, 1985). Arson, a particularly dangerous form of vandalism, perhaps deserves special comment. Whereas window breaking is the most frequent single act of aggression toward property in schools, arson is clearly the most costly, typically accounting for approximately 40 per cent of total vandalism costs annually.

In addition to the several reports we have presented thus far on the high levels of *in-school* violence and vandalism, there now are emerging data on a parallel pattern of *near-school* aggression. In both San Diego (Roncek & Lobosco, 1983) and Cleveland (Roncek & Faggiani, 1985), residences on blocks adjacent to public high schools had significantly higher crime-victimization rates than did residences in areas even a single block further away from the schools, even after controlling for an array of demographic, social, and housing characteristics of the residential areas compared. This replicated result, again consistent with a routine activities perspective, perhaps further illustrates the meshing of school and community and, complementing the observation cited at the beginning of our school discussion, might be stated as evidence that "The school has come to the streets."

CAUSES AND CORRELATES

The nature of leadership and governance in a school can be a major correlate of violence within its walls. A firm, fair, consistent principal-leadership style, for example, has been shown to be associated with low levels of student aggression. High levels of arbitrary leadership and severe disciplinary actions tend to characterize schools experiencing high levels of aggression. In contrast, a school climate shaped by active student participation in the school's decision making has been found in four separate studies to be associated with low levels of violence and vandalism (Feldhausen, 1978; Howard, 1978; Newman, 1980; Wiatrowski, Gottfredson, & Roberts, 1983).

School size is a further correlate of school violence: The larger the school, the more likely its per capita occurrence (Weeks, 1976; Wiatrowski et al., 1983). Such a relationship, it has been proposed, may grow from the easier identification of students and by students with the school in smaller schools, as well as such consequences of larger schools as nonparticipation in governance, impersonalness, and crowding. Further, as Garbarino (1973) observes:

> As schools increase in size, student objections to strict controls, the lack of choice...and uniformity rather than individual attention are very likely to increase as well. As an adaptation to an unresponsive environment, many students (and staff) will become passive and uncommitted to school; others will react with anger or frustration. The marginal or unsuccessful student is particularly likely to experience the negative effects of the large school and, as increasing numbers of such students are compelled to remain in school, the likelihood of their "finding" one another and forming educationally and socially deviant peer groups is enhanced. As school size increases, administration becomes more centralized, bureaucratic, and inflexible. Large educational bureaucracies and the accompanying proliferation of rules also decreases innovation, responsiveness, and adaptation, a fact which has important implications for school crime. Controlling crime in the school requires not only a personalized social climate, but considerable flexibility and responsiveness to the need for change. (p. 28)

Precise, optimal numbers are difficult to establish. Stefanko (1989) asserts that over 2,000 students is too large. Turner and Thrasher (1970) suggest 700 to 1,000 as appropriate; Rosenberg (1975) proposes 400 to 500 as an optimal range. Whatever the specific number, a clear consensus favoring smaller schools as aggression-reducing is apparent.

Crowding is a particularly salient school-violence correlate, as aggressive behavior in fact occurs more frequently in more crowded school locations—stairways, hallways, and cafeterias—and less frequently in classrooms themselves. Other often-chronic "causality zones" include lavatories, entrance and exit areas, and locker rooms. Student violence is most likely during the time between classes and, for reasons that may have to do with "spring-fever effects," during the month of March. With a number of exceptions, school violence also correlates with the size of the community in which the school is located. The proportion of American schools reporting serious levels of aggressive behavior is 15 per cent in large cities, 6 per cent in suburban areas, and 4 per cent in rural areas. Public school students were slightly more likely to be victimized than were private school students.

Greenberg (1969) reports that school vandalism rates tend to be highest in schools with obsolete facilities and equipment and low staff morale. These also tend to be schools which are poorly maintained, poorly lit, and poorly supervised (Downing & Bothwell, 1979; Tygert, 1980). Howard (1978) found that the age of the school per se was not a vandalism correlate, but its rated appearance was. Such vandalism-prone schools are, in Stefanko's (1989) terms, "Rigid, uninspired buildings with cheerless, square rooms and bleak hallways, surrounded by asphalt and chainlink fences [which] foster perceptions of a rigid, harsh authoritarian environment" (p. 7). Leftwich (1977) found a similarly strong relationship between high teacher-turnover rates and level of vandalism. Mayer and Sulzer-Azaroff (1991), in their research on school "setting events" which appear to influence, or at least covary with, the occurrence of high levels of school vandalism, point to an overly punitive school environment, characterized in particular by (1) overuse of punitive control methods, (2) inadequate clarity of school and classroom rules and disciplinary policies, (3) inconsistent or weak administrative support and follow-through, and (4) inadequate attention and responsiveness to individual differences among students regarding both academic matters and behavior management approaches. In contrast, vandalism has been found to be unrelated to teacher–student ratios, to the proportion of minority students in the school, or to the percentage of students whose parents are on welfare or unemployed (Casserly et al., 1980).

We have focused thus far in this section on costs and correlates of school vandalism. It is also instructive to note factors associated with *low* levels of aggression toward property in schools. These include informal teacher–teacher and teacher–principal interactions, high levels of teacher identification with the school, and low student-dropout rates (Goldman, 1961). The Safe School Study (Bayh, 1975) also reported vandalism to be lower when school rules were strictly but evenhandedly enforced, parents supported strong disciplinary policies, students valued teachers' opinions of them, teachers avoided use of grades as disciplinary tools, and teachers avoided use of hostile or authoritarian behavior toward students.

The human and economic costs of aggression toward people and property in America's schools is very substantial. After decades of what, at least in retrospect and probably in reality, seem like negligible incidence rates, both types of aggression increased precipitously during the late 1960s and early 1970s, held steady for a period, and subsequently continued to climb to higher and higher levels. There are several reasons to suspect that even these apparent current levels may be serious underestimates. Inconsistent and imprecise definitions of violence and vandalism, inaccurate or nonexistent record keeping, unwillingness to report acts of aggression, fear of reprisal, wide variance in reporting procedures, and school administrator concern about appearing inadequate may each lead to markedly under-

estimated and underreported incidence statistics. In fact, it has been estimated that actual levels of school violence and vandalism may be as much
as 50 per cent higher than those generally reported (Ban & Ciminillo, 1977).

Home, street, bar, car, store, and school are each significant microsites
for the enactment of aggressive behavior and are instances of a level of
ecological analysis layered or nested within and both influencing and
influenced in turn by mesolevel neighborhood and macrolevel regional
causes and correlates of such behavior. These latter levels of analysis are
the domains of concern focused upon in the two chapters which follow.

CHAPTER 3

MESOLEVEL: THE NEIGHBORHOOD

Neighborhood is both a physical and a psychological concept, a place and a state of mind. Traditionally, it is first of all a physical location. Typically, its area falls somewhere between the *microneighborhood*, defined by Altman and Zube (1987) as "the next door neighborhood, the person in the next apartment, or the most immediate set of adjacent households" (p. xviii), and the *walking-distance neighborhood*, usually specified as the elementary school district (Morris & Hess, 1975). The residential block, or a small cluster of such blocks, in most instances is the physical definition of neighborhood (Keller, 1968; Rivlin, 1987). Sheer proximity is its physically defining characteristic. Its interpersonal implications, as Cohen (1983) notes, exist even before members of its population meet, as characteristics of setting often help to segregate people with similar personal characteristics—especially by social class, ethnicity, and lifestyle.

As a state of mind, the sense of belonging to a neighborhood may be intense. Proshansky, Fabian, and Kaminoff (1983) speak of place identity, Rivlin (1987) of place attachment, and Seaman (1979) of one's phenomenological sense of connection to a place. Though on average Americans move once every five years (Rivlin, 1987), local social ties, physical amenities and familiarity, individual household characteristics, and the perceived rewards of remaining in rather than leaving the neighborhood may lead to a positive emotional bond between individuals and their residential environment. The strength of such person–environment bonding may be influenced not only by the perceived positive features of the neighborhood, but also by the perception of shared threat directed at the neighborhood's population. Suttles's (1972) notion of the defended neighborhood is relevant here. He proposes that an area's physical characteristics and its residents' beliefs, expectations, fears, and, more generally, their cognitive map combine under certain circumstances (e.g., poverty, ethnic differences, high levels of anonymity, or high levels of criminality) to create a defended neighborhood.

TAXONOMIES OF NEIGHBORHOOD

Warren (1980) has provided a taxonomy of neighborhoods, employing interaction, identity, and connections as his organizing criteria. Six patterns constitute his schema:

1. The integral neighborhood. This area has high levels of face-to-face contact, as well as norms and values supportive of the larger community. This is a highly cohesive neighborhood, with such features as block associations and wide participation in both within-neighborhood and outside organizations.
2. The parochial neighborhood. This neighborhood is high in within-neighborhood interaction but low in outside-neighborhood connection. It is protective of its own values and tends to filter out values in conflict with its own.
3. The diffuse neighborhood. This neighborhood has little informal social participation. Though local organizations may exist, their leadership, which is indigenous, does not represent the local residents' values.
4. The stepping-stone neighborhood. This neighborhood is made up of residents with little commitment to the area and strong connections outside it. Within-neighborhood interaction tends to be formal.
5. The transitory neighborhood. This area is low in interaction, participation, and identity. It is a neighborhood of urban anonymity, characterized by high population turnover.
6. The anomic neighborhood. This type of neighborhood lacks participation or identification with either the local or the larger community. Warren (1980) describes it as a completely disorganized and atomized residential area.

Other neighborhood typologies have been suggested and, as we shall see, are aggression-relevant. Davidson (1981) contrasts city-center, industrial-commercial, inner-city, and suburban neighborhoods for their assault and crime opportunity potentials, in much the same manner as did Shaw and McKay (1931) and other early ecological sociologists and criminologists. Dunn (1980) contrasts neighborhoods he descriptively labels Central,

Ethmix, Worksub, Hiwealth, County, Singleman, Medprob, Medsuburb, and Hiprob. He finds significantly lower levels of assault in those described as Worksub, Medsuburb, County, and Singleman. Schuerman and Kobrin (1986) examined how neighborhoods evolve into high-crime areas and offered a developmental taxonomy consisting of emerging, transitional, and enduring crime-impacted neighborhoods. Demonstrating, as we will time and again throughout this chapter, that person and environment reciprocally influence one another, that physical and social ecology cannot exist without one another, these latter authors note, based on their 20-year study of Los Angeles neighborhoods, that

> neighborhood deterioration precedes rising crime early in the cycle but that, as neighborhoods move into the later enduring stage, rising crime rate preceded neighborhood deterioration. Among the changes signaling neighborhood deterioration and rising crime rates were a shift from single- to multiple-family dwellings; a rise in residential mobility, unrelated individuals and broken families, the ratio of children to adults. (p. 67)

A different but overlapping taxonomy, in this instance not of neighborhoods but of neighboring behavior, is suggested by Keller (1968):

> There is the *tribal pattern*, where neighbors are enmeshed in a diversified round of exchanges and contacts; the *intimate pattern*, where families are involved with only a few of their neighbors; the *casual pattern*, where a series of overlapping contacts link many families to one another indirectly; the *clique pattern*, where there is a dominant group and many isolated families; the *ring-around-the-rosie pattern*, in which every family has one or two contacts but there is no direct network linkage among them; and finally the *anomie pattern*, in which isolation of families from neighbors and neighborhoods is the rule. (p. 40)

The pattern that emerges, according to Keller, is a complex function of such physical and psychological factors as the density of residences, the distance between dwelling units, the economic well-being of the inhabitants, the degree of cooperation demanded or permitted among residents, and the general trust placed by individuals in nonrelatives.

Unger and Wandersman (1985) have also sought to determine what constitutes neighboring. First, they suggest a social component comprising personal and emotional support, instrumental assistance, informational support, and social network linkages. Second, they propose a cognitive component. This consists of (1) cognitive mapping, which helps individuals identify safe people and safe places within the neighborhood, and (2) symbolic communication, embodied in things that personalize or otherwise demarcate the entire neighborhood or subareas within it, for example, rows of plants, gates, walks, changes in texture of walks, graffiti, and so forth. Finally, they posit an affective component, consisting of a sense of mutual aid, a sense of community, and an attachment to place.

Note that in each of these definitions, in each of these taxonomies, it is people and their behavior as it occurs in particular places ("neighborhoods") which is the central theme. Here, as in most environment-oriented criminological research, as Rand (1984) notes, the theorist or investigator

> has utilized geographical locations only as proxies for social characteristics of the area, such as economic status, family status, racial status, etc. These characteristics vital to researchers' concepts of delinquent subcultures were presumed to be correlated with criminal behavior. The locations per se, however, we deemed of no value for criminological inquiry. Consequently, the role of spatial organization of urban areas was overlooked as a factor contributing to the opportunities for and constraints on illegal behavior. (p. 1)

NEIGHBORHOOD SOCIAL ECOLOGY

Stated otherwise, a great deal of criminological research is *social ecological* in thrust. Examined for their predictive or associational utility are places defined by their collective social, not physical, characteristics. Thus, extensively investigated in literally hundreds of primarily sociological studies and theoretical statements, as well as implicated for their apparent relevance to criminal behavior, have been such person–population characteristics as social disorganization (Bursik, 1986; Rand, 1984; Shaw & McKay, 1931); social inequality (Sampson, 1983; Sullivan, 1989); income inequality (Sampson, 1985; Townsend, 1974); unemployment (Bullock, 1955; McGahey, 1986); differential economic opportunity (Greenberg, 1986; Mayhew, 1862; Rand, 1984); lower socioeconomic status (Dunn, 1980; Gordon, 1967; Michalowski, 1975); percentage black (Bensing & Schroeder, 1960; Dunn, 1980; Schmid, 1960); percentage Spanish-speaking (Worden, 1980); percentage foreign-born (Dunn, 1980); percentage minority (Bullock, 1955; Worden, 1980); percentage unmarried (Michalowski, 1975); percentage male (Michalowski, 1975); percentage female-headed households (Sampson, 1983); population turnover (Bursik, 1986; Sampson, 1983); intra- and intercity mobility (Savitz, 1970); and family and business outmigration (Reiss & Tonry, 1986).

Research on and theoretical concern with this array of population and individual characteristics have been reflected in an on-again, off-again, still-ongoing 150-year-long sorting process aimed at identifying variables relevant to causation, constructing mediating chains of effect, and seeking to determine percentages of outcome variance accounted for. Most of the variables cited do appear to be relevant to crime, often aggressive crime. Their relevance is most frequently correlational, sometimes causal. Some of the revealed connections are isolated empirical findings; others are

theory-driven and theory-building. The viability and utility of this broad
social ecological effort continues.

NEIGHBORHOOD PHYSICAL ECOLOGY

Having thus set the crime and aggression environment stage, and
given its social ecological thrust its due, we wish now to turn to our major
neighborhood concern, one thus far playing a less active role in the person–environment duet, namely, the physical ecological perspective. In this
effort, we concur with Taylor and Gottfredson (1986), who comment:

> Physical environments do not directly cause or prevent crime except in the case
> of security hardware. They influence crime by way of their influence on resi-
> dents' and offenders' perceptions and behaviors. (p. 412)

In this mediating spirit, a number of neighborhood physical features
have been examined, some minimally, others more extensively. They
include the neighborhood's housing: its structures (Dunn, 1974); its age
(Lebeau, 1978); its density (Reiss & Roth, 1993); its inclusion of large-scale
public housing enclaves (Reiss & Tonry, 1986) or its adjacency to such
housing (Roncek, Bell, & Francik, 1981); building size, height, and accessibility (Newman & French, 1980); the number of single versus multiple
dwellings (Greenberg, Rohe, & Williams, 1982); the number of rundown
or abandoned structures (Wilson & Kelling, 1982); the neighborhood's
streets—their number (Greenberg et al., 1982), their width, traffic patterns,
ease of access (entrances and exits), and ease of internal circulation (Taylor
& Gottfredson, 1986), and the number and pattern of one-way and two-way
restrictions (Brown & Altman, 1981); the neighborhood's opportunities,
given its buildings and streets, for residential surveillance, an opportunity
also influenced by such physical features as gaps between houses, blind
alleys, extensive shrubbery, and quality of lighting (Newman, 1975, 1979);
boundary permeability, distance from main roads, enclavization or insularity, real or symbolic barriers, and signs of beautification or other territorial signage (Taylor & Gottfredson, 1986); the proportion of
neighborhood land devoted to nonresidential use (Greenberg et al., 1982),
to bars and taverns (Davidson, 1981), to other commercial establishments,
and to playgrounds (Wilson & Kelling, 1982); the neighborhood's closeness
to the city's main business district (Davidson, 1981); and its degree of
gentrification (McDonald, 1986). There are two additional features of
neighborhood physical ecology, incivilities and density, which we wish to
consider in depth as examples of variables receiving the level of research
and theoretical attention we believe is deserved by the pool of other

crime—relevant physical neighborhood characteristics we have just enu-merated.

INCIVILITIES

Physical incivilities are concrete ecological features which serve as both reflections of and impetus for neighborhood disuse, disdain, decay, and deterioration. They include trash and litter; graffiti; abandoned or burned-out stores, houses, and automobiles; dirt; vacant lots; broken win-dows and streetlights; ill-kept buildings; vandalism of diverse sorts; and similar expressions of a cycle of decline. Physical incivilities are accompa-nied by social incivilities, in an often dramatic display of person–environ-ment reciprocal influence. Such social incivilities may include increased presence of gangs, drug users, prostitutes, "skid row" alcoholics, and bench or street sleepers; increased presence of drug purveyors and drug users; increased crime by offenders and increased fear of crime by neigh-borhood residents; and increased panhandling, harassment, chronic loiter-ing, gambling, and drinking. In addition to "incivility" (Hunter, 1978), these physical and social neighborhood characteristics have been labeled "prelude to trouble" (Skolnick & Bailey, 1966), "urban unease" (Wilson, 1968), "non-normal appearances" (Goffman, 1971), "early signs of danger" (Stinchcombe, Adams, Heimer, Scheppele, Smith, & Taylor, 1980), "signs of crime" (Skogan & Maxfield, 1981), "soft crimes" (Reiss, 1985), and "cues to danger" (Skogan, 1990). Gates and Rohe (1987) and Skogan and Maxfield (1981) have reported that neighborhood incivility level appears to be a correlate of such sociodemographic indices as race, income, neighborhood cohesion, prior victimization, and neighborhood crime level. Higher levels of incivility are reported by African-Americans and Latinos, people with low income levels, people criminally victimized previously, and people living in high-crime neighborhoods, and in neighborhoods with less cohe-sion or sense of control. Another correlate of incivility is more incivility (Lewis & Salem, 1986), in what appears to be a contagious downward-spi-raling process. LaGrange, Ferraro, and Supanic's (1992) interview survey of 1,100 persons in widely distributed neighborhoods revealed a strong association between the level of both physical and social incivility on the one hand, and both the perception of risk and the fear of victimization on the other. This latter finding replicates earlier demonstrations of the inci-vility–fear association (Rohe & Burby, 1988; Taylor & Hall, 1986).

Does the level of incivility relate to, and perhaps actually help cause, the level of neighborhood crime? Taylor and Gottfredson (1986) reported a correlation of .63 between incivilities and crime rates, though both appeared on further analysis to grow from the neighborhood's sociode-mographic characteristics. Wilson and Kelling (1982) hold that incivility does in fact progress to serious levels of crime and disorder. As Skogan (1990) notes:

> According to Wilson and Kelling, disorder undermines the process by which communities ordinarily maintain social control. Where disorder problems are frequent and no one takes responsibility for unruly behavior in public places, the sense of "territoriality" among residents shrinks to include only their own households; meanwhile, untended property is fair game for plunder or destruc-tion. Further, a neighborhood's reputation for tolerating disorder invites out-side troublemakers. Criminals are attracted to such areas because they offer opportunities for crime. Where disorder is common and surveillance capacities are minimal, criminals will feel their chances of being identified are low, and may be confident that no one will intervene in their affairs. (p. 10)

Skogan (1990) describes a parallel sequence of decline from disorder to serious crime. Its components are citizen withdrawal from community involvement, heightened fear, outmigration of families and inmigration of unattached and transient individuals, diminished sense of mutual respon-sibility, and weakened informal social control. At its incivilities' nadir:

> Uncollected litter blows in the wind. In cold weather, men gather around fires in trash cans. Unattached males, the homeless, and the aimless live in seedy residential hotels and flophouses. Abandoned buildings serve as "shooting galleries."...Vacant lots are filled with the rubble. Residential and commercial buildings stand scarred by arson. (pp. 13–14)

Skogan's (1990) own investigation in this domain gathered informa-tion regarding incivilities and their consequences from an average of 325 people in each of 40 different neighborhoods in the United States. In his appropriately titled report, *Disorder and Decline*, he found strong evidence that perceived crime, fear of crime, and actual level of crime victimization were each a function of neighborhood physical and social incivility.

Incivility does relate to crime, and it is likely to do so in a cause-and-effect manner. The mediating processes connecting the two may be conta-gion (Lewis & Salem, 1986), an array of sociodemographic neighborhood characteristics (Taylor & Gottfredson, 1986), diminished sense of control (Janowitz, 1975), neighborhood residents' sense of "unworthiness" (Rain-water, 1966), and/or the reduced interactions and surveillance associated with the perception of the neighborhood as first, an inhospitable, and, later, a dangerous place (Skogan, 1990). Whatever its mediation of crime, incivil-ity appears to be a significant physical ecological characteristic of many problem neighborhoods and thus is worthy of further inquiry and exami-nation.

DENSITY

It is important that we begin this section with a definition of terms, making clear what density is and is not, since both research and explanation in this domain have in the past suffered from a confusion of both theoretical and operational meaning. Density is a physical description of people in relation to amount of space, often confused with crowding, which is a subjective feeling that one has less space than one desires (Stokols, 1973). Density is the number of people in a given place divided by the amount of space available. It is an objective assessment of number of persons and amount of space. Crowding is a psychological response, a motivational state, which *may* occur under conditions of high density. It is the sense that one needs more space, and it is likely to occur when a condition of high density is associated with restriction of movement, competition, or other bases for desiring reduced contact. As Holahan (1982b) notes, "Density is the direct perception of available space, while crowding is a subjective evaluation that the perceived amount of space is inadequate" (p. 199).

Pertinent to our concern here with the relevance of density to crime and aggression is the distinction which has been drawn between social and spatial density:

> If the discomfort [crowding] is seen as arising from the presence of too many other people (social density), the individual may blame those other people for interfering with his or her good feelings, and react to them with antagonism. In contrast, if the discomfort is viewed as a product of too little space (spatial density), the individual may blame the environmental arrangement for his or her discomfort. (Holahan, 1982b, p. 200)

In addition to the social/spatial distinction and, as we shall see, also relevant to criminal behavior are such further subcategories of density as internal or inside density (the number of persons per room or per residence), structural density (the number of housing units per structure), building density (the number of buildings per acre or other spatial unit), and external or outside density (the number of persons per square mile or per census tract) (Michelson, 1970; Gillis, 1974). Various combinations of these density subtypes can lead to quite different appraisals of crowdedness. Suburban neighborhoods, for example, are typically low in both inside and outside density, i.e., in both people per room or residence and people per external spatial unit. Rural areas more frequently consist of high inside density, but low outside density, whereas urban luxury areas reverse this combination; i.e., there are relatively few persons per room or residence, but the building may be several stories high and there may be several high structures per unit of space. The urban ghetto, in contrast to all of the above, is often characterized by high inside and outside density.

In addition to density and crowding, there are two other spatial concepts relevant to our discussion, personal space and territoriality, both of which are boundary-regulating notions. Personal space is the person's characteristically preferred interpersonal distance, employed for purposes of maintenance of an intrusion-resistant zone around oneself. It is an invisible boundary that moves with the person as the person moves. Territoriality is the personalization, ownership, and defense of areas or objects. It typically involves a visible area with a stationary location (Holahan, 1982b; Stokols, 1978). Russell and Ward (1982) point out that the term *personal space* has also been employed to mean the particular distance that a person chooses to keep from another person at a particular time, as well as the amount of space between two persons that a particular culture defines as appropriate. *Territory* has been further defined "as achieving and exerting control over a particular segment of space" (Proshansky, Ittleson, & Rivlin, 1970), as "defending an exclusive preserve" (Ardrey, 1966), and as "an area controlled [and defended] by an individual, family, or other face-to-face collectivity" (Sommer, 1969). Goffman (1971) distinguishes between fixed, situational (temporary), and egocentric (moving with the claimant) territories. Lyman and Scott (1967) offer a taxonomy of four territorial forms (body, interactional, home, and public) and also distinguish three types of territorial encroachment: violation (unwarranted use of the territory), invasion (the physical presence of an intruder within the territory), and contamination (rendering a territory impure with respect to its definition and usage).

With the terms of relevance thus defined, we may turn to the person–environment research examining the influence of such spatial phenomena on human criminality and aggression. The methodological challenges of such an investigation are not minor. Much of the research that does implicate density or crowding as antecedent to or concomitant with aggression or crime consists of laboratory studies in which, as Epstein (1981) notes,

> ...crowding is usually engendered by placing a relatively large number of people in a relatively small room for short periods of time. Unlike residential environments, crowding is not usually engendered in laboratories by creating a scarcity of resources or a reduction in desired levels of privacy. Thus, at first glance, there is little resemblance between crowded homes and crowded laboratory rooms. (p. 135)

In addition to generalization difficulties in the leap from laboratory to field, a not insignificant portion of the relevant data and their interpretation suffers from the ecological fallacy (drawing conclusions about indi-

viduals from aggregate data) (Krupat, 1985), implying causation from
correlational results (Krupat, 1985), failure to be sufficiently responsive to
cultural differences in the meaning and perception of spatial qualities, and
perhaps a too-ready assumption that crowding is necessarily a negative
condition under all circumstances (Baldassare, 1979).

Nonetheless, given these methodological concerns, a considerable
amount of reasonably reliable information is available about the relevance
to crime and aggression of density, crowding, and other spatial phenomena, information we now wish to consider. Early, largely observational
research examining the consequences of density on the behavior of nurs-
ery-school children suggested that as numbers of children increased (with
space held constant), aggressive interactions also increased (Hutt & Vaizey,
1966; Jersild & Markey, 1935; McGrew, 1972). Perhaps presaging the inconsistent results in this domain which were to follow, Price (1971) found no
such facilitative effect in his density–aggression study. Also working with
nursery-age youngsters, Smith and Connolly (1976) found that substantially reduced available space did increase aggressive behavior, though
Rohe and Patterson's (1974) effort in this domain suggested it was not space
per se, but the concomitant reduction in available play resources, that was
the causative factor. In their research, high density coupled with low play
resources did increase aggressive interaction, but the same high density
with high resources did not. This early finding is but one of many to follow
which make clear that the question, "Does density influence aggression?"
is far too simple. As we shall see, "Under what person–environment
conditions does density influence aggression?" will prove to be a considerably more appropriate question to ask.

Also working with young children, two other studies have shown
aggression to increase with density, but the effect moderates or disappears
when the available space is formally divided by either partitions (Rohe &
Nuffer, 1977) or the assigning of spaces (Fagot, 1977). In company with
such effects, but now reflecting the person component of the person–environment mix, both Loo (1972) (with children) and Freedman, Levy, Buchanan, and Price (1972) (with adults) found social density to influence
aggression in males—higher in adults, lower in children—but no such
effects in females. Early studies have also implicated other person variables, in addition to gender, as effect mediators. For example, both Hutt
and Vaizey (1966) and Loo (1972) have shown the density–aggression
sequence to be especially pronounced in anxious, impulsive, and behav-
ior-disordered youngsters.

These early microlevel studies were matched by broader-scale sociological inquiry into the effects of both internal and external density on
various manifestations of "social pathology," including juvenile delin-

quency and adult criminality. A substantial density–criminality connection was proposed by Shaw and McKay (1931) working first in Chicago, and then in several other U.S. cities. Schmidt and Keating (1979), using the external density measure, population per acre; Gillis (1974), using the building-density measure, proportion of multiple dwellings; and Galle, Gove, Miller, and McPherson (1972), using the internal density measure, persons per room—each confirmed this finding, although Winsborough (1965) did not. Choldin and Roncek (1975) also found internal density to relate to criminality, in this instance violent crime. Levy and Herzog (1974) reported that person per kilometer accounted for 30 per cent of the variance in juvenile delinquency in their Dutch sample. Although such density–aggression effects were moderately consistently found, some of these same investigators suggested that the sociodemographic variables for which density may be a proxy—income, educational level, ethnic background, and the like—are likely themselves to be an even more potent determiner of crime and aggression.

Between the laboratory and the macrolevel field setting are a host of intermediate physical venues—home, school, and prison—which also have been examined to discern whether and when density may influence or covary with crime and aggression. In the home, an investigation by Walden, Nelson, and Smith (1981) reported higher peer ratings of aggression for young children from crowded, rather than less crowded, homes. Cohen, Poag, and Goodnight (1982) speculated that such a finding might reflect greater levels of physical punitiveness in crowded homes, a notion in fact subsequently demonstrated by Booth and Edwards (1976). These latter investigators also found a small positive effect of household social density, but not external density, on the level of sibling quarrels. It may well be, as these several researchers propose, that the apartment or home crowded with people is also replete with such possible aggression instigators as heightened physiological arousal, intrusions, diminished privacy, interpersonal encounters, and inadequate surveillance and supervision of children. Living on higher floors in a multiple-family dwelling may be more aggression-engendering than residence on equally dense lower floors, perhaps because of the lesser "ease of escape" (Mitchel, 1971; Newman, 1976). This may be but one example of the sense of control which has been shown to function as a major mediator of whether or not density (and other environmental stressors such as noise and temperature) in fact lead to aggressive behavior. MacDonald and Oden (1973), for example, demonstrated that young adult residents of a crowded dorm were not negatively affected by its social density if control of escape therefrom was perceived by them to be in their hands. We will examine further this positive mediating role of perceived control later in this section. It may well be that perceived control was also the operative psychological process in the school density studies by Fagot (1977) and Rohe and Nuffer (1977) cited earlier, in which density did increase aggression, but such aggression was shown to be reducible by, respectively, the use of space assignments or partitions.

Examinations of student density in school settings and its consequences have also suggested a reliable density–aggression relationship (Goldstein, 1992a). Such a relationship may be mediated by the greater anonymity, impersonalness, and nonparticipation in governance and other school-based activities in densely populated schools. It is also relevant to the density–aggression relationship to note that it is the more crowded school locations, such as stairways, hallways, and cafeteria, and much less so in the classrooms, in which student–student and student–teacher aggression strongly tends to take place (Bayh, 1975; Goldstein, Harootunian, & Conoley, 1994).

Does density influence or covary with aggression in prison settings? Before examining the relevant research, it is worth reemphasizing the basic person–environment thrust of this book by noting that while home, school, and prison are indeed three very different *physical* locations, their occupants—family, students, and prisoners—are equally very different *social* "locations." Any and all density–aggression findings which emerge are, ipso facto, physical-by-social, person-by-environment findings.

Megargee (1977) found that prisoner assaults covaried inversely with spatial density: The less the space per inmate, the higher the number and rate of violations. Nacci, Teitelbaum, and Prather (1977), examining social density, reported that overcrowding (the ratio of average population to capacity) was significantly associated with assault rates in 37 federal prisons. Again highlighting a person–environment reality in such results, the density–aggression relationship appeared to be especially evident for young offenders. McCain, Paulus, and Cox (1980) reported archival data indicating that increases in prison population not accompanied with increases in person housing availability produce substantial increases in disciplinary infractions as well as deaths by violence. Jain (1987) confirmed this finding, but Atlas (1982) failed to find a density–aggression effect, perhaps, he suggested, because the presence of large numbers of people may act as an inhibitor—a novel notion following from the fact that most of the assaults which did occur in his study prison took place in lightly traveled areas such as stairwells and other "niches." Gaes and McGuire (1985) examined the effect of density on assault rates in 19 federal prisons and found a significant relationship across three different assault indices: assault against staff without weapons, assault against inmates without weapons, and assault using a weapon against other inmates.

From the macrolevel neighborhood location to the microlevel site, density variously defined and measured appears to be a generally consistent but moderate influence upon and correlate of aggressive behavior. A wide variety of explanations have been put forth suggesting possible intervening processes mediating this relationship. Density, a physical-spatial description, is held to lead to aggression, an overt behavior, through a process of crowding stress, a subjective psychological state experienced when and if the individual experiences the crowding as competition (Epstein & Karlin, 1975; Jain, 1987) or scarcity of resources (Wicker & Kirmeyer, 1977); invasion of privacy (Altman & Chemers, 1980b); behavioral constraints (Proshansky et al., 1970); stimulus overload (Baum & Valins, 1979; Milgram, 1970); or some other facilitator of a sense of either loss of control over one's own decision-making (Baum & Valins, 1979; Rodin, 1976) or interference with one's goal-directed behavior (Schopler & Stockdale, 1977). Also purported to be operative are negative mood (Epstein & Karlin, 1975), physiological arousal (Evans, 1978), lowered frustration tolerance, learned helplessness (Stokols, 1978), and such situation-specific variables as familiarity with the other persons present and the type of activity involved (Weinstein, 1979). Further, Zimbardo (1969) has suggested that anonymity and deindividuation—and the associated reduced accountability for one's actions—may lead from density to crowding to aggression. Whatever are the mediating factors, they are likely to act in sequence and in concert. Epstein (1981) notes:

> When an environment becomes crowded, resources may become scarce, activities of one person may interfere with the activities of another person, unavoidable interpersonal interaction may distract the individual or...prevent the individual from attaining his or her personal goals, while violations of spatial norms may increase arousal and discomfort....If an alternative path to the goal...is unavailable, then the individual may perceive that he or she lacks control over his or her environment. (p. 127)

Neighborhood as place may be densely populated, contain incivilities, and in other ways be physically criminogenic. Crime and aggression in neighborhoods may also be facilitated by the opportunities for such behaviors created or abetted by the flow of people and activities contained within its boundaries, as our next section seeks to explicate.

NEIGHBORHOOD AS CRIMINAL OPPORTUNITY

ROUTINE ACTIVITY THEORY

In recent years, growing support has emerged for a view of criminal behavior based not, as are most such theories, on characteristics of offenders in isolation, but, instead, jointly on offender, victim, location, and temporal factors as they combine to present criminal opportunities. One such view was Hindelang, Gottfredson, and Garofalo's (1978) lifestyle exposure model linking the likelihood of victimization to the timing and location of an individual's daily movements. It is a perspective developed and evaluated most fully in the context of what has been termed *routine activity theory* (Cohen & Felson, 1979; Cohen, Kleugel, & Land, 1981). The theory's primary features are summarized well by its developers:

> Rather than emphasizing the characteristics of offenders, with this approach we concentrate upon the circumstances in which they carry out predatory criminal acts. Most criminal acts require convergence in space and time of *likely offenders, suitable targets*, and *absence of capable guardians* against crime. (Cohen & Felson, 1979, p. 588)

In this context, it is worth stressing the central shift in thinking that such theorizing represents from the usual criminological focus on criminogenic motivation (a person characteristic) to criminogenic opportunity (a person–environment characteristic). Felson and Cohen (1980) observe:

> One can estimate for a community the number of violations expected to occur during a given time period by tallying the frequency with which three criminogenic circumstances [offenders, targets, and lack of guardians] converge in time and space. This calculation contrasts with many conventional criminogenic treatments because we take as our starting point the concrete circumstances allowing illegal tasks to be accomplished rather than emphasizing the inclinations to perform these tasks. (p. 392)

Several evaluations of routine activity theory have been conducted. Reppetto (1974), Pope (1978), Rengert and Wasilchick (1985), and White (1990) each studied the crime of burglary from an opportunity perspective, focusing on such opportunity-relevant matters as how residents supervise their neighborhood (capable guardians), how residents limit the access of possible offenders, neighborhood permeability (number of access streets from traffic arteries), and how the rhythms of the neighborhood, the physical characteristics of the dwellings within it, and the visibility of potential crime sites influence the rate of victimization. Cohen and Felson (1979) showed a broad correspondence between national living and labor trends over a 30-year period which reflected diminished capable guardianship (e.g., increased labor force participation by single individuals), increased target suitability (e.g., as electronic and other products became more portable and hence more "stealable"), and increased rates of robbery, assault, rape, and homicide. Roncek (1981) found that a substantial number of San Diego's most crime-ridden residential blocks were directly adjacent to public high schools. He later sought to explain this finding in routine activity theory terms by noting that the presence of nonresidential land use increases crime in subareas of cities. One explanation for this effect is that such uses draw additional people to an area. The greater the number of people using an area, the larger the number of potential victims and offenders can be. Also, the effectiveness of informal social control can depend on the number of people using an area. Where many people use an area, distinguishing who is present for legitimate reasons and who is not can be difficult. (Roncek & Lobosco, 1983)

Sampson (1986) studied the relationship of both theft and violent crime to residential-living, work, and marital-status patterns and found substantial support, as had Felson and Cohen (1980), for the routine activity theory assertion of

the importance of family activity patterns in determining the opportunity structure of predatory criminal behavior. They [Felson & Cohen, 1980] note that the proportion of primary individual households (e.g., singles, nonrelatives) is an overall indicator of guardianship. Those who live alone (e.g., single women) are more likely to be out alone (e.g., going to work, restaurants) than married persons and are thus more vulnerable to personal crimes (e.g., rape, robbery). Also, leaving the home unguarded during the day (and night) increases the risk of household crimes. Therefore, a community with a high proportion of primary individual households presents a more attractive environment for crime than areas with a strong family orientation. (p. 28)

Much of the testing of routine-activity-theory predictions has focused on theft and burglary, and Miethe, Stafford, and Long (1987) have asserted that violent crime is largely a spontaneous act of passion and have held it to be unrelated to routine activity patterns. But two investigations suggest otherwise. Kennedy and Forde (1990) found assault victimization to be strongly predictable from the routine activity patterns of, especially, the young unmarried males they studied who go to bars, movies, work, or otherwise are out of their homes walking or driving around. Messner and Tardiff (1985) extended the evaluation of this opportunity perspective to the occurrence of homicide in New York City. They hypothesized that both the location and the type of homicide would be systematically associated with an array of sociodemographic (age, sex, marital, and employment status) and temporal (time of day, week, and year) characteristics because such are the factors which structure and determine the nature of an individual's routine activities and "in so doing, affect both the location of potential victims in physical space and the pool of personal contacts from which offenders are ultimately drawn" (p. 243). As predicted, because they are at home more, homicides of the married and the unemployed more frequently occur at home. Also as predicted, males are more likely than are females to be killed by strangers and away from home. Very young and very old murder victims were much less likely than those in other age groups to be killed beyond 10 blocks from their residences. Victimizations occurring on weekends were more likely to occur at home and somewhat less likely to occur beyond 10 blocks from home, than was true of weekday victimizations. A similar weekend effect emerged for murders of family members, whereas stranger homicides were relatively more common on weekdays. Each of these findings is consistent with and can be derived from the particulars of routine activity theory. How people live and work in their neighborhoods, whom they routinely meet, what they do in work or play, where they do it, and when they do it all influence target suitability, the presence of likely offenders, the nonavailability of capable guardians, and thus the potential for possible victimization.

THE JOURNEY TO CRIME

There is one additional neighborhood-level concern of relevance to criminal behavior which has been examined: the journey to crime. Felson (1987) asserts that the principal of least effort, which holds that "people find the shortest route, spend the least time, and seek the easiest means to accomplish something" (p. 913), also applies to criminal acts. Carter and Hill (1980), in their work on "area-images," speak of the planning phase of criminal acts being a time during which an "opportunity-matrix" is constructed by the offender-to-be. Since knowledge of criminal opportunities decreases as a function of distance, the journey to crime from offender residence to crime occurrence should generally be both short and pass through familiar territory. In fact, a number of investigations have found a distance–decay function, in which the number of offenses declines with increasing distance from the residence of the offender. Bullock (1955) found this effect for the crime of homicide in Houston (where offender and victim most frequently lived on the same block); Capone and Nichols (1976) report it for robbery in Dade County, Florida; and Turner (1970), in Philadelphia, and Phillips (1980), in Lexington, Kentucky, did so for juvenile offenders. Although this distance–decay relationship generally holds, actual journeys to crime distances have been shown to vary somewhat by both type of crime and type of offender. Distances involved in violent crimes are shorter than those involved in property crimes (Reppetto, 1974; Capone & Nichols, 1976). Rand (1984) also found a strong association between the distance traveled and the value of the property stolen in burglaries: The greater the value, the greater the distances. In aggravated assaults, armed offenders travel, on average, almost twice as far as those without weapons. The findings of this investigation, in addition, replicated the distance–decay phenomenon noted earlier. Of total offenses committed, 47 per cent took place within one-half mile of the offender's residence and 70 per cent within one mile. Perhaps because of their frequent spontaneity, homicide and rape showed the highest degree of localization, confirming in many cases the same-block (and even the same-residence) finding reported earlier by Bullock (1955). Victims and offenders lived at the same location in 28 per cent of the rapes and 18 per cent of the homicides, but in only 4 per cent of the robberies and 3 per cent of vehicle thefts. Similar type-of-crime distance effects have been found by Baldwin and Bottoms (1976), who report violence and sex crimes to be the most localized and fraud and auto theft to be the least localized. Phillips (1980) found a distance progression, with increasingly long journeys to crime as one moved from assault to vandalism to petty larceny to drug offenses.

The journey to crime, as we have urged to be true of so many dimensions of criminal and aggressive behavior, is also very much a person–environment event. Reppetto (1974) and Baldwin and Bottoms (1976) both report that younger offenders were more likely to commit their crimes in their own neighborhoods than were older offenders, a finding confirmed by Nichols (1980), who reported that the journey to crime of older offenders was twice the distance of that for younger offenders, and Phillips (1980), who also found journey length to increase with age. Also, in Nichols's (1980) research, males traveled further than females and, as Petersilia (1987) also found, white criminals travel further than do non-whites. Phillips (1980), too, found whites and males to make substantially longer journeys to crime than blacks or females. Though such offenders' characteristics thus appear relevant to the criminal journey they undertake, across offenders Brantingham and Brantingham (1991) found the offense rate to be higher at the periphery or margins of the neighborhoods studied compared to their centers. Consistent with an opportunity theory perspective, and especially that of routine activities, Davidson (1981) suggests that the Brantinghams' findings indicate that motivated offenders will travel far enough to minimize the risk of identification (i.e., they will seek a minimum of capable guardians) but not so far that it will be difficult informationally to identify suitable targets.

NEIGHBORHOOD AS SUPPORT NETWORK

Neighborhoods are frequent venues for crime and aggression, and their structures, traffic patterns, land use, incivilities, and density may each contribute to such antisocial qualities. But neighborhoods can also be prosocial places, where much that is good and affirming about human behavior transpires, and does so in ways that reduce the potential for violent acts and criminal transgressions. Neighborhoods can function to foster the development of social networks, and to promote the offering of social support.

SOCIAL NETWORKS

In the context of neighborhood functioning, a *social network* has been defined as "the linkages that a neighbor develops with particular individuals both within and outside neighborhood boundaries" (Unger & Wandersman, 1985, p. 146). More generally, it is "an individual's relatives, friends, and associates, the set of people with whom an individual is directly involved" (Fischer, 1982, p. 2), and, most generally, a social network is "the social relations in which every person is embedded...the chains of persons with whom a given person is in actual contact and their interconnection" (Boissevain & Mitchell, 1973, p. 24). A social network may be categorically defined or ego-defined. The former kind consists of a set of persons distinguished by a shared characteristic or type of relationship, for instance, an extended family, the students in a given class, or a particular gang. The ego-defined social network, according to Fischer (1977), is defined with respect to a particular individual and includes only those who are actually linked to that person in a particular way, for example, the people with whom an adult plays cards or the subgroup or clique with whom a particular gang youth hangs out.

NETWORK CHARACTERISTICS

Network characteristics and their relational, communicative, and other implications have been the focus of substantial inquiry in both sociology and community psychology (Albrecht & Adelman, 1987; Fischer, 1977, 1982; Furman, 1989; House, Umberson, & Landis, 1988). As will be noted, some of these properties are dyadic (concerning the relationship between the focal person and one network member) and others are network variables (characterizing the focal person's relationship with two or more network members). A comprehensive listing of social network characteristics includes the following:

1. Density or integration: the extent to which members of a network are interconnected. The more a person's associates are associates of one another, the more dense is that person's network.
2. Multistrandedness: also known as *role multiplexity*. This network characteristic is the number of different ways a focal person is linked to another network member.

3. Links: the connections between two or more network members. Links may vary in intimacy, frequency, duration, source, and role multiplexity.
4. Size or range: the number of persons constituting the network.
5. Reciprocity: the degree to which the products of the network, such as social support, are reciprocally available and exchanged.
6. Symmetry: the degree of balance of power, attraction, or other network product within a link.
7. Intensity: the degree of commitment within a link.
8. Homogeneity: the degree of similarity of network members on given salient characteristics.
9. Reachability: the average number of links needed to connect two members by the shortest route.
10. Clustering: the extent to which the total network is divided into distinguishable cliques.
11. Dispersion: the range of sources from which network membership is drawn.
12. Dominant source: the single source or context from which most network membership is drawn.
13. Level: the comprehensiveness of relationships within the network. Interactional, dyadic, group, and global levels of social network relationships have been distinguished.
14. Facets: alternative ways of "carving up" network relationships. They include degree of support, degree of conflict, distribution of power, and the relative status of the particular relationship within the individual's more encompassing social network.
15. Perspective: the alternative views that different persons (e.g., insiders, participants, observers, outsiders) may have of an interaction, relationship, group, or network.

Two theoretical frameworks have been offered to account for social network formation and functioning. Rogers and Shoemaker (1971) have described a convergence model, in which a central role is given to the creation and sharing of meaning as network members communicate with one another. The second perspective, Hammer, Gutwirth, and Phillips's (1981) social feedback model, relies on notions of reciprocal influence and reduction of uncertainty via interactive feedback processes.

Social networks may be for better or worse. Social networks may yield not only social support and its concomitants, but also social burdens. As Fischer (1982) puts it, "Our friends and relatives not only support us, they also require us to support them. They can give pain as well as pleasure" (p. 135). House et al. (1988) refer to such network-associated burdens as relational demands and conflicts, and Shinn, Lehmann, and Wong (1984) describe an array of social exchange costs. The actual or potential role of such costs in social network functioning has often been ignored and should not be—especially considering the possible value and relevance of social network theory and research for the prevention and reduction of crime and aggression.

SOCIAL SUPPORT

Definitions

Recently, there has been an explosion of academic interest in the construct of social support. Perhaps the interest is due largely to its purported stress-buffering, health-enhancing potency in an era in which American society in general and community psychology in particular have been greatly concerned with stress, stress reduction, and the facilitation of wellness. Caplan (1974), an early social support theorist, defined this construct as the provision, in time of need, of information, cognitive guidance, tangible resources, and emotional sustenance. Cobb (1976) defined it more generically as "information leading the subject to believe that he/she is cared for and loved, esteemed and valued, that he/she belongs to a network of communication and mutual obligation" (p. 300). House (1981) saw social support as "an interpersonal transaction involving one or more of the following: (1) emotional concern (liking, love, empathy), (2) instrumental assistance (goods and services), (3) information (about the environment), or (4) appraisal (information relevant to self-evaluation)" (p. 3). Thoits (1982) called social support "the degree to which a person's basic social needs are gratified through interaction with others" (p. 147). According to Albrecht and Adelman (1987), "Social support refers to verbal and nonverbal communication between recipients and providers that reduces uncertainty about the situation, the self, the other, or the relationship, and functions to enhance a perception of personal control in one's life experience" (p. 19).

Shumaker and Brownell (1984), Lin (1986), and Heller, Swindle, and Dusenbury (1986) each placed special emphasis in their definitions on social support *as perceived*, especially by its recipient. Thus, social support is "an exchange of resources between at least two individuals perceived by the provider or the recipient to be intended to enhance the well-being of the recipient" (Shumaker & Brownell, 1984, p. 17). Again, social support is defined as "the perceived or actual instrumental and/or expressive provisions supplied by the community, social networks, and confiding partners" (Lin, 1986, p. 9). Finally, "a social activity is said to involve social support if it is perceived by the recipient of that activity as esteem enhancing or if it involves the provision of stress-related interpersonal aid (emotional support, cognitive restructuring, or instrumental aid)" (Heller et al., 1986, p. 467).

Social support is alive, well, and growing as a focus of professional interest, even if there is substantial diversity in beliefs about what it is. Barrera (1986) suggests that the core ingredients across these diverse definitions are (1) social embeddedness, or a sense of connectedness; (2) the perception of support or assistance; and (3) the actual delivery of such support or assistance. Kahn and Antonucci (1980) see the key elements of social support as affect (expressing liking, admiration, respect), affirmation (expressing agreement or acknowledgment), and aid (giving such assistance as information, labor, time, or money). Vaux (1988) seeks to resolve the definitional diversity by asserting that social support is best viewed as a higher order metaconstruct comprising a number of legitimate and distinguishable subconstructs (definitions). According to Vaux, these subconstructs, or core definitional streams, include support network resources, supportive behavior, and subjective appraisals of support.

Some aspects of the definition of social support seem clear and are generally agreed upon: its informational function, its affective implications, its perceptual basis, and its assistance content. Shinn et al. (1984) and Vaux (1988) also clearly distinguish between social networks, discussed earlier, and social support. As Shinn et al. note, the two are frequently confused. The mere presence of others with whom one is in a close relationship may yield support; alternatively, however, "other people can be sources of conflict, they can strew obstacles in one's path instead of helping one overcome them, or their well-intentioned efforts can backfire if they do not fit one's situation" (p. 56).

Perhaps this examination of contemporary definitions of social support can best be summarized in the following final perspective, one that conveys especially well the sense, the spirit, the essence of this elusive construct:

You are the wind beneath my wings—Henley and Silbar

> The line above...captures in a subtle but powerful image the role that social support plays in our lives. Our family and close friends, mentors and workmates, acquaintances and neighbors are always there—a social medium through which we pass. Like the wind, their presence is so ordinary as often to go unnoticed. Yet like the wind beneath a bird's wing, they are an essential part of our flight—holding us up, carrying us along, providing life, allowing us to soar and to glide, giving us location and identity.... Social support has to do with everyday things—sharing tasks and feelings, exchanging information and affection. (Vaux, 1988, p. 1)

Expressions of Social Support

An understanding of what social support is, and of the manner in which it functions, will be further enhanced by a survey of its diverse expressions or concretizations. People may enact social support by listening, expressing concern, showing affection, sharing a task, caretaking, lending money, giving advice, making suggestions, and socializing (Vaux, 1988). They may provide behavioral assistance, feedback, guidance, information, comfort, intimacy, services, or lay referrals (Shumaker & Brownell, 1984). Social support is expressed through concern, assistance, valued similarity, positive interaction, and trust (Brim, 1974); emotional support, cognitive guidance, tangible assistance, and social reinforcement (Hirsch, 1980); help in mobilizing resources, managing emotional problems, sharing tasks, and providing material and cognitive assistance (Caplan, 1974); and provision of attachment, social integration, reassurance of worth, reliable alliance, guidance, and opportunity for nurturance (Weiss, 1974). Social support may be, as Berndt (1989) suggests, esteem (or emotional) support, informational support, instrumental support, or companionship support. Its avenues of expression are many and varied indeed. Which avenue is employed in a given instance appears to depend not only on the particular circumstances but also on age, gender, kinship, socioeconomic status, culture, and kindred factors relating to person, person–environment, and relationship-centered considerations (Belle, 1989; Feirling & Lewis, 1989; Vaux, 1988; Weisner, 1989).

Consequences of Social Support

Social support provision has been held to protect individuals from the diverse negative effects of stressful circumstances (the stress-buffer model) or to act directly to enhance a sense of well-being, independently of stressful circumstances and experiences (the direct effect model). It can offer, according to Nietzel, Guthrie, and Susman (1990), (1) protective direct action, (2) inoculation, (3) appraisal guidance, (4) diversion, (5) problem-solving assistance, and (6) palliative emotional support. Social support has been held to promote satisfaction; a feeling of being cared for, respected, or involved; and a sense of attachment, belonging, or reliable alliance (Vaux, 1988). Sandler, Miller, Short, and Wolchik (1989) suggest that it may protect self-esteem by both preventing the occurrence of esteem-threatening events and moderating the negative effects of stressful events on self-esteem.

Other consequences of social support may be less beneficial and perhaps even harmful. Dependency on others may be promoted, and self-reliance and tolerance for dealing with discomfort may be diminished

(Brownell & Shumaker, 1985). Negative consequences may also befall the support giver: The cost of providing support may be too great when, as Vaux (1988) observes, the need for support is chronic, the relationship is not reciprocal, or the demand for support is high.

We have included in this chapter an exploration of theory and research on social networks and social support for their potential relevance to the reduction of neighborhood crime and aggression and to the facilitation of prosocial alternatives. Are there programs or research attesting to such neighborhood-functioning relevance? Neighborhood Watch and Block Parenting programming are two of the more prominent neighborhood efforts anecdotally tying crime and aggression reduction to networking and support, and we have suggested further possible connections in our speculations regarding networking and support among members of delinquent gangs (Goldstein, 1992a). However, the bulk of aggression-relevant networking and support theory and research lies in the domain of child abuse. Tietjen (1980) observes that social networks may influence family functioning in a number of ways—providing social support, providing information, enforcing social norms, and offering opportunities for stress reduction. Bronfenbrenner (1977) and Doyle (1984) point to similar positive consequences. Yet it is one of the most reliable findings in the child abuse literature that abusive parents tend to be especially socially isolated and bereft of a social network and its attendant support-offering and other benefits (Garbarino & Sherman, 1980; Milner & Wimberley, 1980; Pancoast, 1980; Roth, 1986; Shorkey, 1980). Garbarino and Stocking (1980) comment:

> The principal theme that emerges from an ecological analysis of parent-child relations is that the ability of parents to successfully raise their children depends in large part on the *social* context in which families live. It depends on the extent to which parents and children have enduring connections with others outside the home. (p. 5)

> What transforms individual risk into abuse? The ecological perspective argues that it is the social context in which families live. More specifically, it is social and economic deprivation in the environment of families. Investigations repeatedly have demonstrated that social isolation is a correlate of child maltreatment....Parents who maltreat children prefer to solve problems on their own. They have few relationships outside the home, and they are likely to discourage outside involvements on the part of their children. They tend to be transient...lack enduring roots in their environments. And they tend to have a life long history of avoiding activities that would bring them into contact with other adults. (p. 7)

Thus, social isolation, insularity and even hostility—quite the opposite of a functioning social network offering supportive benefits—clearly appear to be associated with, and likely contributory to, child abuse. Social networks and social support have been shown to be positive neighborhood forces in the lives of participants. Their weakness or absence can be harmful and may function to the detriment of those isolated from such involvement.

Our examination of mesolevel, neighborhood phenomena and their role in the physical and social ecology of aggression is complete. In the chapter which follows we seek to explore parallel influences at the macrolevel region and nation.

CHAPTER 4

MACROLEVEL: THE REGION

We have examined site- and neighborhood-level antecedents and correlates of crime and aggression and, in both instances, found not insignificant locational contributions to such behaviors. The present chapter extends this inquiry to larger geographic areas: cities, counties, states, regions, and entire nations. This broader level of inquiry, the largest portion of which has been regional, has its roots in the "cartographic" or "geographic" school of criminology, which began first in France, and then in Belgium, the Netherlands, and England, in the early 1800s.

REGIONAL COMPARISONS

Guerry's (1833) pioneering cartographic examination of the distribution of crimes against persons and property in France initiated this macrolevel approach. He found a per capita overrepresentation of property crimes in the north of France, and of crimes against persons in the south. In fact, though the southern region had half the population of the north, it had twice the number of crimes against persons. Quetelet (1833) reported a similarly disproportionate (to population) level of crimes against persons in the southern areas of Belgium and the Netherlands. Guerry and Quetelet were not only cartographic criminologists, but social ecologists too. They speculated that such regional crime differences grew from regional differences in income, education, density, and ethnicity. Parent-Duchatelet (1837), Fragier (1840), Robriquet (1841), and Buret (1842) were other, similarly minded European criminologists of the era. Rawson, Fletcher, and Mayhew each brought this perspective to England. Rawson (1839) examined the distribution of crime across England, comparing metropolitan, manufacturing, mining, and agricultural regions, finding metropolitan areas to have the highest rates, and mining areas the lowest. Fletcher (1849, 1850), in his studies of "moral statistics," was able to demonstrate an association between the educational levels of regions in both England and Wales, on the one hand, and their levels of "more serious offenses against the person and malicious offenses against property" (1849, p. 37) on the other. Mayhew's (1861, 1862) cartographic comparisons led him to reject poverty, education, and density as explanations for cross-regional differences and to emphasize instead differential criminological socialization. Mayhew's (1862) linking of the incidence of crime within regions to the number and location of taverns and lodging houses credits him as one of criminology's first opportunity theorists.

In the United States, early geographic criminological efforts were—with one major exception—primarily neighborhood-focused. Park and Burgess (1916), Shaw (1929), and Shaw and McKay (1931), as well as other representatives of what came to be knows as the *Chicago School of Human Ecology*, conducted landmark studies of intracity crime distribution, yielding patterns which they sought to explain largely on the basis of social disorganization and the cultural transmission of criminal motivation. Comparative regional concern emerged toward the end of this early period and focused almost exclusively on seeking to establish and explain purported South versus non-South differences in rates of criminal behavior. Such differences in crime differentials, with substantially higher rates in the South, in fact emerged in the initial studies of this phenomenon by Hoffman (1925), Brearly (1932), Lottier (1938), and Porterfield (1949). Brearly's (1932) data indicated a southern homicide rate more than 2.5 times higher than for the United States as a whole, leading him to characterize the South as "that part of the United States lying below the Smith and Wesson line" (p. 117). Lottier (1938) replicated Brearly's findings and added that the homicide rate for each of the 11 ex-Confederate states exceeded that of any of the nonsouthern states. These early findings reflect crime data of the 1920s. Though some reduction in the disparity has taken place in recent years, with rare exceptions (e.g., Erlanger, 1975; Greenberg, Carey, & Popper, 1987), aggression and violent crime differentials favoring the southern United States have been a frequently replicated finding over subsequent decades (Doerner, 1975; Harries, 1990; Hawkey, 1983; Myers, 1980; Pettigrew & Spier, 1962; Shannon, 1954; Smith & Parker, 1980). Homicide and assault each show this regional differential pattern.

Two broad explanations have emerged seeking to explain these patterns. As we shall see, and as is generally the case for as complexly determined a behavior as aggression, in several respects both explanations appear to be correct. The first rationale to emerge was the subculture-of-violence thesis. It held that more than a century's series of experiences had shaped southern attitudes and behaviors in ways decidedly facilitative of the enhanced likelihood of aggression. Such thinking emerged as early as 1880, in Redfield's book *Homicide, North and South* (1880), in which he noted murder rates for the South 10 times greater than for northern states. Both he and Franklin, in his *The Militant South: 1800–1861* (1956), sought to explain such disparities in terms of already-established cultural traditions: much greater incidence of gun ownership and use, dueling as an accepted means of dispute resolution, vigilante groups, local militia, military training, military titles, and the several ways in which the South much more fully than the North could still be described as a frontier society. Lunde (1975) notes that "then, as now, the South lagged behind the rest of the county in industrialization, economic prosperity, educational level, and other factors thought to be associated with the crime rate" (p. 22). Other qualities have also been suggested as further constituting a southern subculture of violence. Cash (1941) speaks of the "ideal of honor" and its violent protection, a feudal pattern of land ownership, and the institution of slavery. Defeat in the Civil War, accompanied by a "siege mentality" and defensive southern pride, was suggested by Hackney (1969). Reed (1971) found that southerners, compared to nonsoutherners, were more likely to own a gun, more likely to disapprove of restrictions on gun ownership, and more likely to approve of corporal punishment. (At the present time, 28 American states still permit corporal punishment in their schools, including almost all of the states in the southern United States.) Others advancing the subculture-of-violence explanation of South–non-South violent disparities include Cash (1941), Rosenfeld (1986), and, perhaps most prominently, Hackney (1969) and Gastil (1971). Hackney's view of the spirit of such a subculture is captured well in his description and affirmation of Cash's (1941) book *The Mind of the South*:

> Violence was an integral part of the romantic, hedonistic, hell-of-a-fellow personality created by the absence of external restraint that is characteristic of a frontier. The cult of honor, with its insistence on the private settlement of disputes, was one manifestation of the radical individualism of the South, but there were other influences at work. The plantation…reinforced the tendency toward violence that had been initiated by the absence of organization. (p. 920)

Hackney (1969) continues:

> In various guises, the image of the violent South confronts the historian at every turn: dueling gentlemen and masters whipping slaves, flatboatmen indulging in rough-and-tumble fights, lynching mobs, country folk at a bearbaiting,…brutal police, panic-stricken communities harshly suppressing real and imagined slave revolts, robed night riders engaged in systematic terrorism, unknown assassins, church burners, and other less physical expressions of a South whose mode of action is frequently extreme. (p. 906)

Gastil (1971) concretized his view of the southern subculture of violence by developing a "Southernness index," a series of weights assigned to each state based upon the proportion of the state's population having southern origins. His national analysis by state revealed that "state homicide rates grade into one another in rough approximation to the extent to which Southerners have moved into mixed states" (p. 415), leading him to conclude "that high homicide rates in the United States today are related primarily to the persistence of Southern cultural traditions developed before the Civil War and subsequently spreading over much of the country" (p. 412).

Loftin and Hill (1974) challenged the subcultural perspective, asserting that both Hackney and Gastil had employed biased procedures when estimating cultural effects. Instead, conducting their own regression analyses by region and across an array of demographic variables, Loftin and Hill (1974) proposed that South versus non-South violent criminal differences were *structural*, not *subcultural*. Featured in their structural view were socioeconomic levels, as reflected in their "Structural Poverty Index." There is, they asserted, "strong evidence that socioeconomic variables are closely correlated with state homicide rates" (p. 722). Smith and Parker (1980) subsequently replicated this finding, but only for primary homicide rates (family or friend victims), and not for nonprimary homicides (stranger victims). Other structural correlates showing relationships to state homicide level, though less strongly than economic deprivation, were infant mortality rate, percentage of the population with less than five years of education, percentage of inductees who failed the armed-forces mental test, and percentage of children living with one parent. Additional structuralist challenges to the subcultural view were conducted by Bailey (1976) and Humphries and Wallace (1980). Bailey reported that "when poverty and income inequality are controlled, there is only a chance relation between region and homicide for 1960 and 1970" (p. 146). And, as Harries (1990) notes:

> Humphries and Wallace (1980) viewed crime as a product of withdrawals of capital leading to the out-migration of higher paid workers and the "marginalization" of those remaining, leading in turn to distress in the inner city and conflict over scarce resources. They felt able to conclude that "we can dismiss explanations such as the Southern culture of violence thesis...on the grounds that urban violence is not a function of region!" (p. 72)

We have urged elsewhere (Goldstein, 1988) that *all* acts of aggression derive from multiple causality, and that it is both a gross oversimplification and unproductive vis-à-vis intervention, to champion single-source or unidimensional antecedents. Concretely, we proposed:

> When Johnny throws a book at his teacher (or draws a knife), it is unproduc-
> tive...to explain such behavior as caused by Johnny's "aggressive personality"
> or "economic disadvantage," or other single causes. Johnny's aggressive act, as
> well as all other acts of aggression, grow from an array of societal and individual
> causes. [These include] physiological predisposition, cultural context, immedi-
> ate interpersonal environment, immediate physical environment, person [per-
> petrator] qualities, disinhibitors, presence of means, presence of potential
> victims. (p. 293)

So, too, with regional difference in potential and actual aggression.
South and non-South, in our view, have demonstrated reliable crime
differentials for *both* cultural and structural reasons. Such a multiplicity of
causes is supported by the work of Huff-Corzine, Corzine, and Moore
(1986), who found both a socioeconomic marker (Loftin & Hill's 1974
Structural Poverty Index) and cultural markers (percentage born in the
South and Gastil's 1971 Southernness Index) to be significantly predictive
of state variations in homicide rate. Combined person–environment causality is also central to the findings of Nisbett (1993), who reports that for
small, but not large cities, South versus non-South violence comparisons
can still be reliably demonstrated and that, in addition to such place
characteristics, southern respondents in this research were significantly
more likely than nonsouthern respondents to (1) own a gun for purposes
of protection, (2) believe that a violent response to an insult is highly
justified, (3) make use of spanking as a means of discipline, (4) more readily
interpret another's behavior as an insult, and (5) more quickly experience
anger as a result of such perceived provocation. Yet, Nisbett's results
notwithstanding, it is important to note that cultural and structural forces
are not uniquely regional phenomena; they operate also on a supraregional
basis. There is a growing consensus that South and non-South are converg-
ing—both culturally (via mass media and other "global village" influences)
and structurally (via mass marketing, national companies, and similar
across-region economic influences)—and, thus, it should not surprise us
that so, too, are the interregional crime rates. Odum (1936) had earlier
predicted such "growth of generalism" and "steady eroding of regional
differences," and McKinney and Bourque (1971) showed this to in fact be
occurring in comparisons of South versus non-South urbanization, industrialization, occupational distributions, and educational levels. Parallel
convergence appears to have been (and to be) taking place regarding
regional crime differentials. Jacobson (1975) comments:

> At the outset of the 1950s, crime rates for the South are consistently and
> significantly higher than those in the non-South. Murder rates stand out in this
> respect—two and one-half times the like figure for the non-South. Similarly
> large differentials are apparent for aggravated assaults, burglaries, and auto
> theft. By 1960, the unequivocally high rates of Southern crime of the previous

decade have changed notably. Grand larcenies and auto thefts in the non-South now exceed like figures for Southern cities. Overall, person crimes for the South and non-South are nearly identical....by 1970, the convergence pattern initiated in the 1950s is nearly complete. [There are] no significant differences between the South and non-South for rape, burglary, larceny, person and property crimes....By 1970, only three of the nine separate offenses have retained a statistically significant difference, and for one of these—murder—the difference between the South and non-South appears to be narrowing over time. (p. 234)

Such regional convergence, and the forces supporting it, was further demonstrated by Myers (1980), who found South–non-South homicide rate differentials disappearing for those southern counties which had become most urbanized and industrialized (i.e., most like the non-South), but not for those remaining most structurally unchanged.

Convergence in regional crime rates, ideally, would mean that higher rate regions experience a diminution in the frequency of murder, assault, and other mayhem, to a level approaching that of lower rate regions. Unfortunately, in the United States, "convergence" has had quite an opposite meaning. South and non-South are reaching toward criminal parity not because the South is less crime-ridden but, instead, because crime rates in the non-South have escalated to meet southern levels. As Harries (1990) notes, "Convergence in this sense is a negative phenomenon, since...no pronounced behavioral change has occurred in the South, but violence has steadily increased elsewhere" (p. 81). The "elsewhere," increasingly, seems especially to be the American West. Kowalski, Dittmann, and Bung (1980), Greenberg et al. (1987), and Weiner and Wolfgang (1985) have each documented such "Westward movement"—in murder, assault, and rape. Having learned from the long and energetic investigative saga focused on the nature and bases for South versus non-South violent crime differentials, perhaps we will see in future research and speculation regarding West versus non-West differentials such qualities as greater complexity, multi-causality, and deeper insights into regional characteristics and their crime-relevant associations.

NATIONAL COMPARISONS

A second instructive macrolevel arena for aggression is the nation, and the nation to consider first is one of the world's most aggressive, the United States. Whether viewed relative to that of other countries (which we will do shortly) or in comparison to its own earlier levels, aggression in America is high and growing. For example, for that particularly aggression-prone group, youths under age 18, between 1981 and 1990 all categories of violent crime increased substantially: murder and nonnegligent manslaughter (60.1 percent), forcible rape (28.2 percent), aggravated assault (56.5 percent), and an overall violent crime increase of 29.1 percent (Federal Bureau of Investigation, 1990). Of those persons in the United States arrested for violent crimes in 1990, 23,060 were under age 15, and 1,270 were younger than 10. Anecdotal evidence strongly suggests that this broad increase in youth violence is occurring for both males and females (*New York Times*, 1991). One of every ten American youngsters who died in 1987 was killed with a gun. In both 1988 (1,538) and 1989 (1,897) new records for firearm murders of youths 19 and under were established in the United States, dramatic increases which hold when adjusted for population growth (Center to Prevent Handgun Violence, 1990). Teenagers in America were, at minimum, at least four times as likely to be murdered than were their counterparts in 21 other industrialized countries. In this context it is worth noting that there are approximately 200 million privately owned guns in the United States. In 1990 alone, 1.8 million pistols and revolvers were manufactured in the United States, and 683,000 handguns were imported (*New York Times*, 1992).

The American home is no stranger to physical aggression. A nationwide survey conducted in 1968 for the National Commission on the Causes and Prevention of Violence (Mulvihill, Tumin, & Curtis, 1969) revealed that 93 per cent of survey respondents reported having been spanked in childhood; 55 per cent had been slapped or kicked, 31 per cent punched or beaten, 14 per cent threatened or cut with a knife, and 12 per cent threatened with a gun or actually shot at. Domestic violence is visited not only upon children; spouses—particularly wives—are also frequent targets of physical abuse. Strauss (1977) estimated that approximately 25 per cent of wives were targets of physical aggression by their husbands, an estimate generally reaffirmed in subsequent analyses (e.g., Stark & Flitcraft, 1988). An equally grim picture emerges for elderly citizens. In 1990, the United States House of Representatives Subcommittee on Health and Long-Term Care reported that 1.5 million elderly Americans, or 5 per cent of all elderly United States citizens, are physically abused each year, most by their own children. In 1980, the comparable estimate was 1 million (Marin & Marycz, 1990).

The recent history of child abuse in the United States has followed a parallel path. As recently as the mid-1960s, the terms *child abuse* and *battered child syndrome* were not part of either public or professional awareness. Largely through the efforts of such persons as Gil (1970), Helfer and Kempe (1976), and Kempe, Silverman, Steele, Droegemueller, and Silver (1962), significant consciousness raising has occurred. The nation is now keenly aware of child abuse. The number of child abuse incidents is quite substantial, reported in 1984 to be 1.7 million, an increase of 17 per cent from 1983 and 158 per cent from 1976, the first year such data were systematically collected (American Humane Society, 1986). Subsequent years continue to show a steady rise in the number of children reportedly abused: 1.9 million in 1985, 2.0 million in 1986, 2.1 million in 1987, 2.2 million in 1988, and 2.4 million in 1989 (Federation of Child Abuse and Neglect, 1990).

In addition to street and home, the third major American setting for the expression of unremittingly frequent and varied aggression is its mass media: newspapers, books, comics, radio, movies, and especially television. The impact of contemporary mass media on behavior is immense. One manifestation of this impact has been an increase in violence. This assertion is still disputed in some quarters, but a reading of the combined evidence about the influence of television viewing (in particular, on overt aggression) leaves little room for doubt or equivocation (Comstock, 1983). The very heavy diet of violence offered by television appears to contribute substantially to both the acquisition of aggressive behavior and the instigation of its actual enactment.

Prime-time television in the United States during 1992 showed an average of 9.5 acts of violence per hour. The comparable figure for 1982 was 7 such acts per hour. Saturday morning cartoons now portray 32 violent acts per hour. By age 16, the average adolescent—who views approximately 35 hours of television programming per week—will have seen 200,000 acts of violence, 33,000 of which are murders or attempted murders (National Coalition on Television Violence, 1990). No wonder a substantial minority of viewers will engage in actual copycat violence.

The pernicious effects of television violence go further, extending to the substantial decrease in sensitivity, concern, and revulsion toward violence among the general viewing audience. Higher and higher levels of violence become more and more tolerable. These and other aggression-enhancing and aggression-tolerating effects of television have been documented in many sources (Baker & Ball, 1969; Comstock, 1983; Feshbach & Singer, 1971; Howitt & Cumberbatch, 1975; Lefkowitz, Eron, Walder, & Huesmann, 1977; Liebert, Neale, & Davidson, 1973; Slaby, 1992).

The historical bases for such dramatically high and growing levels of violence in a broad array of American venues—street, home, mass media, and the several categories of high-violence neighborhoods and sites examined in earlier chapters—grow from national traditions and experiences as old as the country itself.

A HISTORICAL PERSPECTIVE

The United States was born in the crucible of individual and collective violence, a relationship which has persisted with but infrequent interruption for over two centuries. Its Revolutionary War lasted over seven years and succeeded in its goal of a new and independent nation. It was also, as we shall see, but one of many examples of an instance in which aggression rewarded is aggression continued. The Revolutionary War, in particular, can be viewed appropriately as the beginning of America's long love affair with the gun, with the "right to bear arms." The new nation lay strung out along the eastern coast of a 3,000-mile-wide unexplored continent—a continent of buffalo and other game to kill, of native American Indians to displace, of a frontier to conquer. Each era in U.S. history helped shape the particular forms of aggression that occurred. As the nation began moving westward in the late 1700s, frontier settlements and a frontier mentality prevailed. Independence, self-reliance, and impatience with the still poorly formulated victim and criminal laws of the nation were all characteristic. Justice was often "frontier justice," which meant "taking the law into one's own hands" by groups of local citizenry. Hanging for horse thievery, "riding undesirables out of town," and similar unorganized group aggressiveness may be viewed as the informal beginnings of what, especially immediately after the Civil War, became the vigilante movement. Frontier living, its purported glamour in the mass media notwithstanding, was often very difficult economically, giving rise not only to criminal gangs, bank robbers, counterfeiters, and other early crime in America, but also to aggressive behavior by many of its noncriminal rural citizens. Shays's Rebellion in Massachusetts (1786–1787), the Whiskey Rebellion in Pennsylvania (1794), and a series of similar incidents initiated by such groups as the Grangers, the Greenbackers, and the Farmers' Alliance are examples of the several economically engendered agrarian uprisings characteristic of the day.

Beginning in the early 1800s, and peaking during 1830–1860, a major new feature was added to the American scene, and to aggression in the United States. This was a lengthy period of great immigration, as thousands and then millions of persons from diverse national, religious, and ethnic backgrounds migrated to the United States. The ingredients in this great human melting pot often mixed poorly, and high levels of individual and collective aggression were the frequent result—particularly in America's cities.

The Civil War took place in the United States in 1861–1865, pitting Northerner against Southerner and, at times, neighbor against neighbor and even cousin against cousin in bitter, lethal conflict. Its price was high, and well beyond the actual war casualties (617,000 dead and 375,000 injured), for out of this war grew forces which engendered new and virulent forms of aggression throughout the country. During the postwar Reconstruction period, and often stemming from war-related animosities, feuding, lynching, and high levels of vigilante activity occurred. The feud, primarily a phenomenon of the southern mountain states, was a type of interfamily or interclan guerrilla warfare. Much more malignant in its effects was lynching. Here, unorganized, ephemeral mobs, in a deindividuated expression usually of antiblack aggression, would capture and hang typically guiltless black persons. It is the shame of America that 4,950 recorded lynchings occurred during the period 1882–1927.

Vigilante aggression became more organized. Its targets included blacks, but also many other (usually minority) groups. Among the 326 known vigilante groups recognized as having existed, perhaps the most infamous were the Ku Klux Klan, the Bald Knobbers, and the White Cappers. Cowboy gangs, romanticized in book and movie, also became prominent during this post–Civil War period. Their specialties, train and bank robberies, while consistently portrayed as flamboyant derring-do by the media, were plain and simple acts of criminal violence.

The Industrial Revolution came to America's burgeoning cities during the late 1800s. It was progress and brought with it hope, modernization, and economic growth. But not infrequently it also involved economic exploitation and management–labor violence. Strikes and boycotts grew to become riots, some of them among the bloodiest events in American history. The railroad strike in Pittsburgh in 1877 and the strife in the Pennsylvania coal fields around the Molly Maguire movement at about the same time are two prime examples. Industrial conflict continued at high levels as workers sought to unionize, and especially violent strikes occurred in the Colorado mining industry (1913–1914) and throughout the auto industry during the 1930s. During this extended period, there were 160 separate times in which state or federal troops were called out to intervene in industrial violence.

As was found to be true in other nations, the level of individual and collective violence within the United States diminished in the 1930s. Perhaps both the major events of that decade, war and depression, engendered a sufficient sense of being joined against a common enemy, or at least of being caught in similar circumstances, so that within-nation–outgroup hostility diminished.

In the middle of the 20th century, while labor violence, feuding, vigilante groups, lynching, and the aggression of the frontier West all became largely events of the past, America's affinity to violence continued in new forms. Crime, especially by juveniles, grew in both its sheer amount and its level of aggression. While conservative forces less frequently, or at least less obviously, initiated collective violence, radical forces took their place. In the 1960s, the United States was rocked time and again with student, racial, and antiwar riots, as well as a small number of terrorist events.

The litany of America's violent history would be much less than complete without mention of perhaps its saddest chapter. Starting in Tidewater, Virginia, in 1607 and ending in 1890 at Wounded Knee, South Dakota, nearly 300 years of intermittent aggression was perpetrated against the American Indian. It is a history which can never be undone but, hopefully, is partially being redressed in the America of today.

INTERNATION COMPARISONS

Given the firm historical roots of violence and its currently high and growing incidence, it should not surprise us that as Reiss and Roth (1993), speaking for the National Research Council, report:

> Homicide rates in the United States far exceed those in any other industrialized nation. For other violent crimes, rates in the United States are among the world's highest....Among 16 industrialized countries surveyed in 1988, the United States had the highest prevalence rates for serious sexual assaults and for other assaults including threats of physical harm. (p. 3)

This same report contrasts the American homicide mortality rate for 1981–1986 of 8.3 per 100,000 population, to that of the next highest country (Spain, 4.3), and to the average European rate of between 1 and 2 per 100,000. Forcible rape and assault rates, as noted, were highest in the United States, followed by Canada, Australia, and West Germany. Fingerhut and Kleinman (1990) more recently compared national homicide rates for 21 countries. The U.S. rate was four times the next highest rate (Scotland). Japan and Austria had the lowest homicide rates. Three quarters of the homicides in the United States were caused by firearms, in contrast to less than a quarter of all the homicides in the 20 comparison countries. Again, young males (age 15–24) appear to be the most frequent perpetrators of such violence, and here again the internation comparisons are dramatic (for 1987): United States, 4,223 such homicides; Canada, 62; France, 59; West Germany, 49; England and Wales, 48; Japan, 47; Australia, 34; Scotland, 22; New Zealand, 17; Sweden, 14; Israel, 13; Norway and Finland, 11 each; Switzerland, 7; and Denmark, 4.

In addition to the several historical forces described earlier as characteristics of the United States, such disparities in internation individual and political violence levels have also been attributed to a combination of economic inequality and the cultural legitimization of violence in the United States (Unnithan, 1983); a combination of residential mobility (low community stability) and income heterogeneity (high relative deprivation)

(Krause, 1976); the joint influence of economic inequality, land inequality, and regime repressiveness (Robinson, 1990); and both such more macrolevel indices as world-system position and transnational corporate penetration (London & Robinson, 1989) and the more individual microlevel index of opportunity for father–child contact (Segall, Dasen, Berry, & Poortinga, 1990).

One of the most informative cross-national studies regarding aggression and its comparative levels and bases was conducted by Archer and Gartner (1984). These investigators successfully undertook the formidable task of gathering comprehensive crime and violence data from 110 countries and 44 major cities for the years 1900–1970. Their primary investigative interest was to discern whether participation in wars increased the level of violence in a country after the war was over. Earlier lore, anecdote, and qualitative research had implied such a relationship to be the case. Nevins (1924) pointed to an upsurge in highway robberies and horse theft after the American Revolution. Others asserted similarly increased violence levels in the diversely "appropriate" form for each era, following the Franco-Prussian War (Durkheim, 1933), the Civil War (Abbott, 1927), World War I (Exner, 1927), World War II (Lunden, 1963), and the Vietnam war (Gurr, 1981). Archer and Gartner's (1984) analysis of violent crime following a large series of wars for the war-involved and control countries represented in their data base also revealed this outcome, and further revealed that although the comparative increase emerged for both victorious and defeated nations, it did so to a greater degree for the former. It was also greater for nations experiencing heavy combat losses. These several authors have nominated a diversity of bases for such an effect, including modeling; the lionization and decoration of war "heros" to reward their prowess at killing; the cheapening of values; the loosening of family ties; weakened respect for law, life, and property; social disorganization; increased mobility; disruption of community life; the existence of special crime opportunities (due to blackouts, bombed-out houses, and unguarded property); and the creation by wartime circumstances (e.g., rationing) of new types of crime. Based on both these speculations and their own findings, Archer and Gartner (1984) suggest seven possible theoretical models to explain the war–violent-crime-increase relationship, centered around (1) demographic artifacts, (2) social solidarity, (3) social disorganization, (4) economic factors, (5) catharsis, (6) violent veterans, and (7) legitimization of violence. Their data analysis provided substantial support only for the last of this series, for which they offer the following mediating processes:

> If wars do legitimate violence, it is interesting to speculate about the ways in which this effect could be mediated....Huggins and Strauss (1975) have shown

that fictional violence in children's literature reaches a maximum during war years. Wars also may produce changes in depictions of violence in movies, news stories, ads, and propaganda. Since most homicides grow out of disputes between relatives or close acquaintances, perhaps wars simply increase the probability that violence will be regarded as a justifiable means of resolving such disputes. Wars could affect individual behavior simply through the awareness that violent homicides (in the form of soldiers killed in combat) are occurring— sometimes in staggeringly large numbers....War involves homicide legitimated by the highest auspices of the state...as praiseworthy and heroic. (p. 94)

We view their findings regarding the potency for individual acts of aggression of cultural legitimization of such behaviors as yet one further addition to a broad conclusion regarding the influence of the ecology of aggression upon its enactment—in this instance on an internation comparative basis.

CITY COMPARISONS

The final macrolevel venue we wish to consider comparatively is the city. Much of the ecology-of-aggression speculation and investigation which has been put forth focuses on city life, reflecting the immense increase in urban population in the United States. In the late 1700s, 3 per cent of the 3 million American population lived in cities; by 1976, the comparable figure was 70 per cent, with an estimate of 90 per cent for the year 2000 (Fischer, 1981). Much of the theorizing about this urbanizing phenomenon and its aggression-related concerns grows from one of three theoretical perspectives:

The oldest approach, *determinist theory*, states that urban settings act directly on their inhabitants and that certain characteristics of cities [e.g., stimulation, noise, smells, and density] can lead to social and personality disorders and to deviant behavior. According to this theory, cities *cause* certain social pathologies. A more recent position, *compositional theory*, hypothesizes that urban settings do not directly affect social behavior. Rather, the crucial factor affecting behavior is the ethnic, national, or other qualities of subgroups in cities. Hence, crowding, city size, and other physicalistic variables are not as important to the quality of urban life as are culture, family organization, and neighborhood social structure. The third approach, *subcultural theory*, is an integration of the two preceding theories. (Altman & Chemers, 1980a, p. 240)

In our own person (i.e., compositional)–environment (i.e., determinist) view, the combinational, multiply based subcultural view makes greatest theoretical and empirical sense at this stage in the onward development of physical and social ecological theory and research. Given this view, first promulgated vis-à-vis cities by Fischer (1981), we need to look to both person and environment characteristics, especially as they reciprocally interact, in order to assert a sound basis for any intercity crime and aggression differentials which may be demonstrated. Such differentials have, in fact, been reliably reported. Byrne (1986), working from the same interactional perspective—combining "personal characteristics of population aggregates and physical characteristics of cities" (p. 79)—examined 1975 census and crime data for 910 American cities with a population of at least 25,000. He found, for each of the four index crimes studied, that the person–environment combination just described held the strongest degree of crime association. He also found, as have a number of others (Harries, 1976; Hoch, 1974; Webb, 1972), a strong positive association between city size and both violent and property crime. This last finding, regarding city size, has most recently been reconfirmed by the 1993 National Research Council's crime survey (Reiss & Roth, 1993). The Aggregate Uniform Crime Report (Federal Bureau of Investigation, 1991) violent crime rates from 1973 to 1990 reveal a rate of 359 such crimes per 100,000 residents for cities with less than 10,000 population to a rate of 2,243 per 100,000 for cities with 1 million or more residents. Weiner and Wolfgang (1985) found similarly. Cities with populations greater than 250,000 experienced substantially higher volent crime rates than did those with populations of less than 10,000—6 times more homicides, 4–6 times more rapes, 15–25 times more robberies, and 2–3 times more assaults. Interestingly, Archer and Gartner (1984), in their analysis of violent crime in 44 major international cities, suggest that it is the relative (to other cities in *that* country) city size, not its absolute population, that is violent-crime-associated:

> The determinant of a city's homicide rate is therefore not the absolute size of the city, but its size *relative* to its contemporary society. We believe that this interpretation explains why homicide rates do not necessarily increase as a city grows. Large cities have always had relatively high homicide rates because they have always been more urban than their national environments. (p. 116)

These and other intercity crime comparisons (Ogburn, 1935; Schuessler & Slatin, 1964; Harries, 1976) have put forth—as was true for internation comparisons—a wide array of person, environment, and person–environment causative and correlational explanations. Cities differ in their levels of violent crime, it has been asserted, because of the substitution of indirect secondary relationships for direct, face-to-face primary contacts (Park and Burgess, 1916); their size, density, heterogeneity of population, and segmentation of human relationships (Wirth, 1939); anonymity (Cohen, Poag, & Goodnight, 1982; Lofland, 1973); overload (Milgram, 1970); income, density, and minority population (Beasley & Antunes, 1974); income inequality (Carroll & Jackson, 1983; Sampson, 1985); residential instability (Harries, 1976); stress (Glass & Singer, 1972); unemployment (Brenner, 1976); and, underscoring a dual person–environment perspective, a combination of such physical characteristics as lighting, layout, and police surveillance with such person variables as belief in the efficacy of police, feelings of personal vulnerability, and community spirit (Krupat, 1985).

We have considered theory and research at diverse macrolevel venues as they bear upon the causes and correlates of crime and aggression.[*] We close this consideration with the awareness that, though examined separately, people live in a nested set of such environments. As Harries (1990) has noted in his discussion of the "geography of violence," "Each person exists in an extraordinarily complex environment of layered interacting stimuli, at the household, neighborhood, urban, metropolitan, regional, national, and even international levels" (p. 102). The task of discerning the aggression-relevant impact of each of these levels acting alone is under way. The task of identifying their joint action has barely begun.

TEMPERATURE

There remain other, quite different ecological characteristics of macrolevel environments—be they cities, regions, or nations—which have been examined in some depth. These features may appropriately be described as atmospheric in character and include lunar cycle, barometric pressure, noise, air pollution, and temperature. Phase of the lunar cycle (Campbell, 1982; Sharfman, 1980), barometric pressure (Mills, 1942), noise (Glass & Singer, 1972; Holahan, 1982b; Kalt & Zalkind, 1976; Page, 1977), and air pollution (Rotton & Frey, 1985) have—with occasional exceptions— each rather consistently been demonstrated to be unrelated to the occurrence of criminal or aggressive behavior, popular lore notwithstanding. Temperature, however, is another evidential matter, although, even here, its demonstrable influence upon such behaviors appears to occur more predictably when high ambient temperature is part of a cluster of aggres-

---

[*] Because they are relatively uncommon, there are a series of additional macrolevel environments whose relation to aggressive behavior we have not considered. However, initial person-environment research involving such settings has been conducted, and is cited here for the reader interested in their further exploration. We refer to studies of aggression among persons isolated in arctic (Moran, 1979) or desert (Suedfeld, 1987) settings, astronauts (Bluth, 1980), aquanauts (Radloff & Helmreich, 1968), serving as Peace Corps members in foreign nations (Pallanick, 1968), or as members of mapping expeditions in uncharted territories (Tikalsky, 1982).

sion-promoting stresses acting in concert, such as crowding, diminished resources, alcohol consumption, unoccupied time, and regional location, e.g., the warmer South versus the cooler non-South. As early as the 1700s, the Abbé du Bos attributed criminal behavior to unusually high Roman summertime temperatures (Koller, 1937). Guerry (1833) noted such a summertime peaking in France, as did Champeneuf for 1821–1835 (Lewis & Alford, 1975). A temperature–crime connection had become sufficiently well accepted in the 19th century so that Quetelet (1833) described the association as the "thermic law of delinquency." Such a view was confirmed further, in the United States, by Dexter (1904), who examined, month by month for eight years, the incidence of assaults in New York City early in the 20th century, as they related to ambient temperature. He found a strong and consistent relationship as one moved from January to July each year, but, importantly and consistent with similar curvilinear associational findings on these variables to emerge much later, assault increased to a maximum in the 80°F to 85°F maximum daily temperature range (27°C–29°C) and then decreased substantially as temperatures rose still further.

In particular, Ellsworth Huntington (Oliver, 1973), one of the leading figures during this era of environmental determinism, came to be associated with the championing of this thermic connection. Environmental determinism more generally was energetically attacked during the late 19th and early 20th centuries as too unidimensional, yet this particular deterministic finding (variously explained, as we shall see) has subsequently been oft-replicated and has thus endured. Cohen (1941) demonstrated the temperature–crime association on a national (U.S.) level, by comparing Uniform Crime Report data for the 1930s to temperature levels and found the predicted seasonal peaking. An association between temperature and aggression need not be limited to individual acts of violent crime. Major political uprisings, rebellions, and revolutions have also commenced during the hottest months of the year. As Goranson and King (1970), O'Neal and McDonald (1976), and the United States Riot Commission (1968) have observed, considerable descriptive historical evidence stands in support of such a collective-violence association with temperature levels.

The reliability of any behavioral science finding is augmented not only by its frequency of occurrence, but also by the diversity of the data bases from which it emerges. The temperature–crime or aggression connection has been reported by field investigators working in numerous, different locales and time periods, and employing differing sets and types of criminal justice statistics. Although the results of laboratory studies of this connection have been inconsistent, even a substantial portion of this body of work concurs in reporting this relationship. Lewis and Alford (1975) examined monthly assault rates for the 56 U.S. cities with populations of at least 250,000 during 1969–1971. Their thermic law predictions were well supported. During January and February, 90 per cent of the cities had assault rates below the national mean monthly rate. In March and April, the assault rate began to climb, first in the Southeast and then in the Northeast. They continue, "May marks the beginning of the violent season....The incidence of assault climbs again in July and the peak in violence is reached in August when the whole country is dominated by high assault rates" (p. 215). The rate, they indicate, then declined in September and October and "collapsed" in November and December. An analogously robust temperature–assault association has also been reported by Feldman and Jarman (1979) for Newark; Harries and Stadler (1983) for Dallas; Rotton and Frey (1985) for Dayton; Cotton (1986) for Des Moines; Perry and Simpson (1987) for Raleigh; Michael and Zumpe (1986), who analyzed 27,000 reports of abuse against women from 23 shelters in five U.S. cities; and these same investigators (Michael & Zumpe, 1986) for the rate of rape in 16 dispersed U.S. locations. The analogous temperature-associated data for homicide are somewhat more mixed, with some investigators reporting such a positive association (Anderson, 1987; Brearley, 1932; Cohen, 1941; Lester, 1979; Michael & Zumpe, 1986; Perry & Simpson, 1987; U.S. Department of Justice, 1988) and others failing to do so (Cerbus, 1970; Cheatwood, 1988; DeFronzo, 1984; Feldman & Jarmon, 1979; Pokorny, 1965; Wolfgang, 1958).

The combined studies across manifestations of aggression lead appropriately to the conclusion that as Anderson (1989) has stated after his own review of this domain:

> Clearly, hot temperatures produce increases in aggressive motives and tendencies. Hotter regions of the world yield more aggression....Hotter years, quarters of years, seasons, months, and days all yield more aggressive behaviors such as murders, rapes, assaults, riots, and wife beatings, among others. (p. 93)

Why should this be the case? Some have suggested that the finding is largely artifactual and due—for example, in the case of summer-month peaking—to the increased exposure to risk, increased social contact and free time, increased beer drinking, and longer periods of daylight during July and August. Yet Lewis and Alford (1975) note that such theoretically facilitative conditions largely exist in the Deep South and the Southwest during winter months also, and these regions, too, show the summer peaking. Besides, as Boyanowsky, Calvert, Young, and Brideau (1981–1982) have found, aggression in laboratory contexts increases not only when subjects are made uncomfortably hot, but also when they are made uncomfortably cold. Anderson (1989) identifies five alternative explanatory models. In the *negative affect escape model* (Baron & Bell, 1975), low to moderate levels of negative affect instigate aggression, but at higher levels of such affect, escape tendencies predominate. Thus, as noted earlier, according to this view, "fight" builds in probability to about 85°F under most circumstances, and as temperatures rise beyond that point, escape "flight" becomes increasingly probable. Removing the escape probability component yields the second perspective, the *simple negative affect model*. Anderson (1989) notes, "This model is similar to the intuitive ideas passed down for generations. When people are hot [or cold], they are in bad moods" (p. 76). Zillman's (1983) *excitation transfer/misattribution of arousal model* is the third perspective on the temperature–aggression association. It is a perspective which assumes that sympathetic-nervous-system excitatory reactions are largely nonspecific and thus are subject to misattributional labeling. As Anderson (1989) notes, "Arousal produced by excessive temperature may be misattributed to anger at some provoking individual" (p. 76). A sister position, the *cognitive neoassociational model* (Berkowitz, 1983), holds that aggressive thoughts are linked to and can be primed by a variety of aversive experiences. Misattribution is not a necessary component here. Instead, aversive experiences, such as uncomfortably hot temperatures, may directly instigate such priming effects and thus influence the individual's interpretation of the situation in such a manner that aggression becomes more probable. Finally, the *physiological-thermoregulatory model*, described by Anderson (1989) and as yet largely hypothetical, is offered in response to beginning suggestions of a temperature–aggression link in a small series of studies of neural and hormonal systems and their possible interactions.

Anything approaching definitive data is far from available to array these models authoritatively in terms of their explanatory potency. In Anderson's (1989) view (but not in a contrary analysis by Bell, 1992), the negative-affect escape model has been soundly contradicted by empirical evidence, but the four other perspectives have barely begun to receive experimental scrutiny. Noteworthy, however, is the degree to which all five are intraindividual models, centering on one or another person-characteristic attributions made, affects experienced, cognitive associations transpiring, and neural and hormonal processes. The temperature–aggression linkage is a person–environment event. These several "in the skin" processes are very likely a consequential part of the event, but only a part.

PART III

SOCIAL ECOLOGY

CHAPTER 5

MICROLEVEL: THE VICTIM

Persons age 12 or older, living in the United States, experienced 34.7 million crimes in 1991, according to the National Crime Victimization Survey (Bureau of Justice Statistics, 1992). Approximately 6.4 million of these victimizations consisted of violent crimes, such as rape and assault. Also in 1991, there were approximately 22,000 murders in the United States, 2.2 million estimated instances of spouse abuse, and 2.8 million estimated occurrences of child abuse. In many of these victimizations, the distinction between perpetrator and victim seems quite clear. A woman returning to her car in a suburban shopping center one evening, arms full of packages, is attacked and assaulted by a stranger. A motorist driving at 40 miles per hour in an area with a 45 mile per hour speed limit is honked at, gestured at, and cursed by a teenage driver who passes him at 60 miles per hour. A young woman agrees to go out to a movie with a date, and later that evening, although she actively resists his sexual advances, she is raped by him. The perpetrator–victim distinction is not infrequently less sharp in the context of other instances of violence, for example, the situation of a child behaving oppositionally who is smacked in the face by his frustrated father. In still other instances, who is perpetrator and who is victim is quite ambiguous. Two men are drinking at a bar in a low-income neighborhood. One goads the other about his appearance, criticizes something he said, and challenges the other to "do something about it," and the other drinker responds by smashing his fist into the provocateur's nose. A husband demeans his wife repeatedly, threatens to harm her, and at the height of an episode of rage charges toward the bedroom yelling that he is going for his revolver to shoot her. She grabs a kitchen knife and stabs him to death.

Webster's (1984) defines two terms which are relevant to these scenarios:

1. Contribute—To give or supply in common with others, to play a significant part in bringing about an end result (p. 285).
2. Culpable—Guilty, meriting condemnation or blame, as "wrong or harmful" (p. 314).

There are six perpetrator–victim pairs in our examples. It is our position that all six perpetrators are both contributors and culpable, but that the victims vary considerably in these regards. All six are contributing, in that in each instance one or more victim characteristic or behavior helped in lesser or greater degree to set the stage for the aggressive act. To assert contribution is most definitely *not* to "blame the victim." Blame, as we have seen, is a matter of culpability, not contribution. Only the goading, challenging drinker and the threatening, gun-seeking husband seem to us to be culpable victims. Each could easily have become the incident's perpetrator; each shares at least equally with the perpetrator major and wrongful blame for the unfolding sequence of events.

We seek to draw the crucial distinction between contribution and culpability here because we do believe that aggression is a dyadic, transactional event, whose transactional nature has been stressed far too little, perhaps in part because contribution and blame have too frequently been used transitively. The shopper can park where and when she wishes; the motorist at 40 miles per hour is driving both safely and appropriately; the date-raped young woman agreed to attend a movie but thereby signaled nothing more; and the child behaving oppositionally may be acting thusly for healthy, identity-establishing reasons. Each of these persons, because aggression is a transactional event, contributes to his or her own victimization; none are responsible or culpable for it.

Toch (1980) captures our position well:

> violence is at least a two-man game. Even where the victim does no more than appear at the wrong time and place, his contribution is essential for the consummation of his destruction....Common sense and law are attracted to the image of passive victims mauled by spontaneously malevolent aggressors. In the world of violence, however, the situation is rarely that simple....To understand violence it is necessary to focus on the chain of interactions between aggressor and victim, on the sequence that begins when two people encounter each other, and which ends when one harms, or even destroys, the other. (p. 6)

Simon (1991), in accord with this view, adds:

> The idea of analyzing violent behavior in terms of the relationship between the victim and the offender stems from the awareness that violent behavior does not occur in a vacuum, and that the escalation of an altercation from the realm of the verbal to the realm of the violent often involves the behavioral contribu-

tion of both the victim and offender....In fact, the interest in victim-offender relationships began with the knowledge that victims of violent acts may not only contribute to the altercation but may, in many cases, actually initiate the violence. This reciprocal contribution by both sides suggests that the victim and offender have, at times, almost interchangeable roles, and that designation of victim and offender roles may, in some cases, be determined by chance. (p. 19)

Taking a finer grained position, some writers have sought to specify extended, continuumlike degrees of victim contribution. Mendelsohn (1963), building upon the earlier work of von Hentig (1947), suggested a degree-of-guilt typology consisting of victims who were (1) completely innocent, (2) having minor guilt, (3) as guilty as the offender, (4) more guilty than the offender, and (5) most guilty. Fattah (1967), in a similar effort, distinguished (1) nonparticipating victims, (2) latent or predisposed victims, (3) provocative victims, (4) participating victims, and (5) false victims. Also at least implying a degree-of-victim-contribution notion, Sparks (1982) observes that the substance of victim contribution may variously consist of impunity (qualities of the victim make the crime easy to get away with), attractiveness (as in an affluent-appearing house), opportunity, vulnerability, facilitation, and precipitation.

Others have also taken the transactional stance espoused here (Block, 1981; Gottfredson, 1989; Patchen, 1993; Silverman, 1974), and Baumgartner (1993) has even extended it to social network "others" (e.g., in-laws, siblings, and friends) beyond the protagonists themselves. Campbell (1986) correctly criticizes prevailing behavioral science for continuing to search so frequently for the antecedents of aggression in static intrapersonal attributes such as perpetrator hostility level, or ego-strength. The victim is a player, often a very major player, in the social ecology of every aggressive act.

CHILD ABUSE

The child victim contributes to his or her own abuse. This assertion of contribution, well supported as we will see by empirical findings, and in no degree suggesting responsibility or culpability, is a central feature of a number of broadly ecological theories of child abuse. Bronfenbrenner (1977) implies it in his conceptualization of child maltreatment as a result of influences operating at the individual, family, community, and cultural levels. Belsky (1978), building on Bronfenbrenner's perspective, makes explicit the notion that child abuse grows jointly from "psychological disturbances in parents, abuse-eliciting characteristics of children, dysfunctional patterns of family interaction, stress-inducing social forces, and abuse-promoting cultural values" (p. 17). This integrative focus accords well with our own perspective. No single source—parent, child, family, community, or culture—is seen as overriding; each (in combination) is viewed as contributing importantly to the abusive act.

Such a viewpoint, especially with regard to the eliciting role of abusee characteristics, is but a recent perspective. For much of the history of mental-health concern with the welfare of children, the child was viewed as a passive, acted-upon victim who brought naught but his or her presence to the victimization event. It was not uncommon, at least with some treatment perspectives, even to leave the disturbed or maltreated child literally at home while the apparent "sole source" of the youngster's difficulties, the parent, received the intervention. That perspective has changed, and changed considerably. Kadushin and Martin (1981) capture well this alternative view of parent–child reciprocal influence:

> Traditionally, and until quite recently, parent-child relationship research, theorizing and prescriptive advice was [sic] based on the presupposition of unidirectionality. It was assumed that the parent is invariably the active agent, the child the passive recipient of influence efforts. Traditional child guidance axioms exemplify the unidirectional orientation that the parent is always cause, the child always effect....Parent-child relationships are more accurately characterized as the result of simultaneous, reciprocal, dynamic transactions. Both parties in the transaction act to stimulate response, and act in response to stimulation....The child is shaped by the behavior of others while, at the same time, shaping the behavior of others. In doing so, the child modifies, regulates the conditions of parental behavior—creating, in some measure, his own environment. Bidirectionality, as opposed to a unidirectional orientation, views the child as an active partner in the process. (p. 48)

Bell and Harper (1977) and Culbertson and Schellenbach (1992) are among the several investigators urging this transactional, reciprocal view of parent–child influences. It also lies at the core of the coercive-family-process research of Patterson (1982) and his research group, Gelles and Straus's (1979) integrative model of child abuse etiology, and Garbarino's (1977) ecological framework. What are the specific child characteristics posited to be or demonstrated to be contributory toward the abuse process? They appear to be of several types: demographic, physical, and behavioral. Note as these are described that in no instance is it the child characteristic per se that is abuse-eliciting, since it is the case that most youngsters displaying the given quality are *not* abused. The characteristic's "victimogenic potential" (Kadushin & Martin, 1981) lies, instead, in its transactional relationship to parental inconveniences, annoyance, rejection, anger, and so forth.

Demographic Characteristics

Abused, as compared to nonabused children, tend more frequently to be unplanned, born to very young and unmarried parents (Smith &

Hanson, 1975) following a difficult pregnancy and delivery (Lynch, 1975). Average age at the time of abuse is 7.4 years (Wolfe, 1987). Abuse in the form of neglect is more common in infancy and toddlerhood and declines with age. Abuse in the form of physical assault yields its most frequently fatal consequences among younger children, especially when the parents are also young (Jason & Andereck, 1983). Males are more likely to be killed or injured in this manner than are females. Sexual abuse, in contrast, tends to be visited upon older female children (Knutson, Schartz, & Zaidi, 1992). Wolfe (1987) found similarly that 85 per cent of sexually abused children were female. Racial (nonwhite) and socioeconomic (lower-social-class) demographic markers associated with child abuse have also been reported (Pelton, 1978; Spearly & Lauderdale, 1983) but are suspect as possible artifacts associated with both initial reporting differences and availability or unavailability of alternative means of resolving abuse accusations.

PHYSICAL CHARACTERISTICS

Premature birth has frequently been cited as a common antecedent of subsequent abuse, purportedly as it places difficult demands on parenting skills (Lamb, 1986; Maden & Wrench, 1977; Martin & Beezley, 1974). Specifically implicated here are such prematurity-associated child and interactional characteristics as illness, fragility, high-pitched cry, distorted head-to-body ratio, wizened appearance, diminished opportunity for parent–child contact and bonding, and, not infrequently, a congenital defect and associated handicapping condition. Kadushin and Martin (1981) comment:

> A difficult beginning risks inauguration of a negative relationship between mother and child. The child is unplanned, the pregnancy is unwanted, the child is unwelcome, and the child's parent-child interaction is off to a bad start. The child's very existence imposes a burden on the parent(s) for which they are unprepared, makes demands which can be met only with considerable difficulty, and interferes with the possibility of achieving alternative life goals and expectations. The child is, of course, not to blame for the inconveniences and the punishments which an unplanned pregnancy might impose; for the physical pain of a frequently difficult delivery; or the financial, social and emotional sacrifice demanded by the need to involuntarily accept the role responsibilities of parenthood. Nevertheless, it is because of the child that the parent encounters all this, so that while it is unjust, it is understandable that the parent attributes the source of a sequence of problems to the child. (p. 66)

Whether or not connected to prematurity, handicapping conditions have been shown to be a not-uncommon companion to child abuse, including one or another neurological dysfunction (Martin & Beezley, 1974), orthopedic impairment (Ammerman, Cassisi, Hersen, & Van Hasselt,

1986), deafness (Schlesinger & Meadow, 1972), and other disabilities (Garbarino, Brookhouser, & Authier, 1987). Lynch (1975) found that abused children had significantly greater health problems during their first year of life, and Sherrod, O'Connor, Vietze, and Altemeier (1984) report the differences in illness frequency to continue as the child grows older.

BEHAVIORAL CHARACTERISTICS

In comparison to who the child *is* (demographic and physical characteristics), child abuse also appears to be substantially associated with what the child *does* (behavioral characteristics). It is in this behavioral realm, in particular, that the transactional nature of child abuse becomes clear, as youngster behaviors respond to, initiate, impinge upon, and are impinged upon by parental actions and reactions, in what Patterson (1982) has called a chaining sequence. Abused children tend to display early temperamental qualities of irritability and fussiness (Gil, 1970); feeding difficulty (Hansen, 1977); failure to reciprocate parental actions, such as hugging and verbalizing (Emde, 1980); withdrawal and lethargy (Solnit & Provence, 1979); or, contrastingly, overdemandingness and overdependency (Elmer & Gregory, 1967) and hyperactivity (Terr, 1970). They may be depressed (Zalba, 1967), fearful (Lukianowicz, 1971), and display a variety of social-emotional deficits (Kaufman & Cicchetti, 1989).

Of special relevance to our primary theme, the social ecology of aggression, is the oft-demonstrated reciprocal relationship between parental and child aggression. Abused children frequently behave in an aggressive manner themselves (Burgess & Conger, 1978; George & Main, 1979; Patterson, 1982). It is, of course, quite difficult in the chaining of parental and youth aggression to deconstruct its sequencing and point to who initiates and who responds. The very notion of an aggressive behavior chain implies an ongoing stimulus–response–stimulus sequence whose point of origin may be temporally remote and unidentifiable. A midchain segment taken from what is very likely a typical behavior sequence leading to abuse is described by Kadushin and Martin (1981):

> The specific behaviors related to abuse varied with the age of the child....Behavior included truancy, stealing, fighting, lying, enuresis, prolonged crying, failure to do chores, persistent disobedience, unacceptable habits, exit-entrance behaviors....Parents' first reaction to incidents...was in general a low-level noncorporal response—an admonition, threats, scolding, discussion, repetition of the requests or a demand for a modification of the child's behavior, time out, etc. The child's behavior in response to the parent's initial intervention stimulated escalation of the subsequent parental response in the direction of greater punitiveness. Children talked back, ignored...challenged...failed to re-

spond....[The parent] feeling frustrated by the child's response...the interaction escalated toward abuse. (p. 250)

Libbey and Bybee (1979) studied a series of physically abused adolescents and report that in 91 per cent of the cases, parental abuse was immediately preceded by the youngster arguing or disobeying the parent. Feshbach (1970) and Culbertson and Schellenbach (1992) have observed similar parent–child patterning. Patterson's (1982) findings regarding the presence of such a "coercive family process" in instances of child abuse similarly demonstrate its underlying interactive sequencing. He comments:

...much of each member's ongoing behavior is jointly determined. A given event partially reflects the prior behavior of the other person, as well as his own immediately prior behavior. An extended coercive interchange may then be said to be the outcome of a bilateral exchange. As the interchange unfolds, both members of the dyad alter each other's reactions. (p. 193)

It thus seems appropriate to conclude that child abuse is very much an interactive event. We have held the parent culpable, the child only contributory. In this context, we concur with Snyder and Patterson (1987), who assert that "the child is both a victim and an architect of his own environment" (p. 237).

RAPE

The distinction we have drawn between victim contribution and culpability is equally relevant as our focus shifts from child abuse to another major manifestation of aggression, rape. Such a distinction was not nearly as evident as recently as 20 years ago. Amir (1971), reflecting the greater proclivity to "blame the victim" characteristic of that era, wrote at length about "victim-precipitated rape":

The term "victim precipitation" describes those rape situations in which the victim actually, or so it was deemed, agreed to sexual relations but retracted before the actual act or did not react strongly enough when the suggestion was made by the offender(s). The term applies also to cases in risky situations marred with sexuality, especially when she uses what could be interpreted as indecency in language and gestures, or constitutes what could be taken as an invitation to sexual relations. Of the 646 forcible rapes in this study, 122 have been found to fit the previous definitions as victim-precipitated (VP) rape cases. (p. 266)

Thus hypothesizing that there exist "characteristics of certain potential victims which may actually bring about the offense" (p. 253), Amir reported that such VP rape was more common for older than younger victims, when the victim had "a bad reputation," and when victim and offender either met in a bar or had previously known each other well. Amir more generally proposed that victim precipitation could consist of acts of either commission or omission. The former might consist of such behaviors as agreeing to have a drink, or to ride with a stranger; the latter he illustrated as failing "to react strongly enough to sexual suggestions and overtures" (p. 261).

A number of investigators have shown that males and females differ substantially in their proclivity to hold the rape victim responsible for her victimization. Feild (1978) provided evidence that men, more than women, believe that rape victims precipitate their own victimization by both their appearance (clothing, makeup) and behavior. Calhoun, Selby, Cann, and Keller (1978) and Rumsey and Rumsey (1977) report similar male–female attributional differences. Divorced victims are held at greater fault than married victims (Jones & Aronson, 1973); women who knew the perpetrator, whether casually or long term, were seen as more blameful than those with no prior acquaintanceship (Feild, 1978); and findings regarding the role of the victim's physical attractiveness are mixed. Calhoun et al. (1978) found greater attractiveness to be associated with greater blamefulness; Seligman, Brickman, and Koulack (1977), contrariwise, found the physically unattractive victim to be seen as more provoking.

So pervasive has been the view that in many instances the rape victim "brings on" or "provokes" the rape incident, a view often expressed explicitly or implicitly by the courts, police, press, emergency room staff, and victims' husbands or boyfriends, that many rape victims themselves come to share this causality belief. It is no wonder, as Morokoff (1983) puts it, that "many victims feel it is they who are on trial and not the defendant" (p. 104).

In both law and shared belief, America has come some distance from this earlier accusatory stance. At least overtly and, we believe, to a considerable degree also privately, the rape victim's role in the rape incident is increasingly viewed as, in a feminist perspective, solely that of the person acted upon or, as in a systems perspective, as contributing to the event but sharing no responsibility for it—rather than the earlier, finger-pointing, blame-sharing, culpability perspective. The systems view focuses largely on matters of communication and miscommunication:

> If women and men interpret dating behaviors differently, there may be serious repercussions. A woman may ask a man out, meaning only that she wants to go out with him, or she may go to his apartment "to talk," meaning only that she wants "to talk to him." If the man interprets such activities as a sign that she wants sex, he may feel led on if he finds that she does not want sex. Unfortunately, many males regard being led on as justification for having sex with the woman against her will—in other words, as justification for rape. (Muehlenhard, 1989, p. 242)

Muehlenhard, Friedman, and Thomas (1985) found that men are more likely to assume that the woman wants sex if she allows the man to pay all dating expenses than if she pays her own, if she asks the man out rather than if he asks her out, if they go to his apartment rather than a movie, and if the man drives his car. Also clearly relevant to the rape consequences of miscommunication and differing male–female interpretations of the same event are instances of female views of petting as petting, versus a male perspective of petting as a prelude to intercourse (Goodchild & Zellman, 1984; Lundberg-Love & Geffner, 1989), and of the offering of resistance as declining further escalation versus a token attempt at impression management (Check & Malamuth, 1983).

What is a woman to do? A substantial literature has emerged, much of it of a "how-to" nature, suggesting a broad array of rape-victimization-minimizing techniques. Some are of the "apparent escort" type, proposing one or another means for not being, or appearing to not be, alone in the eyes of potential perpetrators: asking a male fellow employee to walk oneself to one's car; walking close to a group of walking people; seeking out a male friend, or giving the impression of being accompanied by displaying a pipe, a man's hat or other such "male evidence" nearby or on one's car seat; and leaving no materials in one's car indicating it to be a "woman's car." Other techniques, which Gardner (1990) describes as "profaning the self in the name of safety," are manipulation of manner or dress to appear "too repulsive a target for approach." "Making a scene" also falls in this category. Anticipatory preparation and high vigilance describe the third set of techniques: carrying a weapon and a whistle; concern about where and when one walks here, stands there; choosing paths in part for their escape route potential; and showing care in one's dress, grooming, and the like. In all, these approaches impose a heavy and offensive burden of victimization-avoidance procedures. While the need to consider and use such measures may at times be prudent, individually and collectively they are yet another type of victimization. Until "contribution" more fully replaces "culpability," and until "no" means "no," and "stop" means "stop," such measures may regretfully need to continue to be employed.

ASSAULT AND MURDER

Notions of victim precipitation and such related constructs as the "duet frame of crime" (von Hentig, 1947), "reciprocal determinism" (Bandura, 1973), "circular causality" (O'Leary & Murphy, 1992), and "bidirectionality" (Powers, 1986) have also emerged in examinations of those manifestations of aggression culminating in assault or homicide. Gelles

(1972), in an article relevantly titled "It Takes Two," points out in the context of spouse abuse that

> victims of these violent acts are not simply "hostility sponges" or "whipping boys" for their violent partners. On the contrary, the role of the victim in intrafamily violence is an important or active one. The actions of the victim are vital intervening events between the structural stresses that lead to violence and the violent acts themselves. (p. 155)

O'Leary and Murphy (1992) urge an even stronger assertion of victim contribution:

> Systems-oriented theorists believe that causality is circular rather than linear. Whether one is seen as victim or as abuser depends upon the point at which a sequence of interpersonal events is punctuated....At one point in an argument, the wife may have seemed like the perpetrator (e.g., the wife moved close to her husband who was seated in a chair reading the paper and verbally demanded that the husband address an issue), whereas only minutes later, the wife may have seemed like the victim (the husband disagreed with the wife, got angry at her for even addressing the issue, jumped out of his chair, and slapped her). (p. 31)

The fictitious illustrations embedded in this quotation come very close to common reality in instances of spousal assault. As Gelles (1972) has demonstrated, in the majority of instances examined by him, the victim's contribution to the escalating sequence ending in her or his victimization were most typically verbal, not physical, expressions of aggression by her or him. As will be described later in this section, in contrast to assault, it is more frequently the case in homicide that the victim's bidirectional contribution to his or her own demise is a physical expression of aggression. Such verbal assaultiveness, suggests Gelles (1972), frequently takes the form of nagging, arguments about drinking or gambling, cursing, criticism of the spouse's sexual performance, bringing in an array of past issues and arguments ("kitchen-sinking"), and, in one or another way, tormenting the other. Such verbal behaviors can be particularly inflammatory in a marital context in which

> prolonged interaction, intimacy, and emotional closeness of family life expose the vulnerability of both partners and strip away the facades that might have been created to shield personal weaknesses of both husband and wife. As a result, couples become experts at attacking each other's weaknesses and are able to hurt each other effectively with attacks and counterattacks. (Gelles, 1972, p. 164)

Victim precipitation in the context of homicide, as suggested earlier, may more frequently involve physical aggression on the part of the ultimate victim. Wolfgang (1967b), in fact, defines victim precipitation in this culpability-assigning sense:

> The term *victim-precipitation* is applied to those criminal homicides in which the victim is a direct, positive precipitator of the crime. The role of the victim is

characterized by his having been the first in the homicide drama to use physical force directly against his subsequent slayer. The victim-precipitated cases are those in which the victim was the first to show and use a deadly weapon, to strike a blow in an altercation… (p. 72)

Using this more stringent definition, Wolfgang (1967b) reported that of the 588 criminal homicides in Philadelphia in the period he examined, 150 or 26 per cent were designatable as victim precipitated (VP). Wolfgang's comparisons between the VP and non-VP homicides are of interest. Forty-three (29 per cent) of the 145 VP homicides, compared to 45 (11 per cent) of the 438 non-VP murders were males slain by females. VP homicides are also proportionately more likely to be husband-wife murders, to involve the use of alcohol by the victim (but not the offender) just prior to the altercation, and to involve victims with a previous police record.

Felson and Steadman (1983) examined victim behavior in a series of homicides compared to that displayed by a comparable number of assault victims. The homicide victims were more likely to have displayed or actually used some type of weapon than were assault victims. Consistent with Wolfgang's (1967b) result, murder victims were more likely to have been intoxicated with alcohol or drugs. Homicide victims were generally more aggressive themselves than were the assault victims—more threats, more identity attacks, more physical attacks. The victim behaviors noted appear to have functioned additively. Those victims who both used a weapon and engaged in an actual attack on the second party were killed in 87 per cent of such instances. Those who attacked without a weapon were killed 63 per cent of the time. None of the victims who displayed a weapon but did not engage in an actual attack were killed. Such outcomes, Felson and Steadman (1983) suggest, imply a quid pro quo retaliation process, in which "the successive behaviors of a participant are more a function of the antagonist's behaviors than they are of his or her own earlier actions" (p. 69). Luckenbill's (1977) description of the interactional sequence leading to homicide as a "character contest" accords well with this retaliatory perspective.

In addition to the behavior of victims, their sheer number also has been shown to influence the outcome of the assaultive event. King (1992), for example, notes that multiple victims facing a lone offender possess increased possibility of overpowering the offender, a perception which may in fact enhance the likelihood of weapons use by the offender, and hence the possibility of turning what began as a robbery or assault into a homicide. King (1992) helps further in clarifying the interactionist pattern of offender–victim progression to assault or homicide by examining the notion of "balance of resources." The number of offenders and of victims; the weaponry displayed and/or used by either or both; the degree of victim resistance or passivity; the gender, age, and apparent physical condition of offender(s) and victim(s); and characteristics of the microenvironment in which the event unfolds—each influences the offender–victim balance of resources, and thus the ultimate outcome of the incident.

OTHER CONTRIBUTORY VICTIMIZATIONS

We have examined the role—sometimes contributory, at other times culpable—of victim behavior and characteristics in child abuse, rape, assault, and homicide. Other evidence exists, of several diverse types, further bolstering the perspective on victimization which assigns at least a contributory role to the victim. These include athlete targets of aggression (Russell, 1991), staff in psychiatric (Sheridan, Henrion, Robinson, & Baxter, 1990) and penal (Rice, Harris, Varney, & Quinsey, 1989) institutions, psychotherapists (Eichelman, 1991), bar patrons (Felson et al., 1986), bullied schoolchildren (Olweus, 1991), motorists (McAlhany, 1984), and police (Toch, 1985). For at least certain of these victims, evidence points to a number of their concrete behaviors and characteristics which are victimization-associated. For example, the review provided by Rice et al. (1989) indicates that in psychiatric institutions, staff behaviors and characteristics contributing to patient aggression toward staff include the demand for activity (Depp, 1976), imposing limits or refusing patient requests (Quinsey & Varney, 1977), imposing sanctions (Ochitill & Krieger, 1982), inexperience (Bernstein, 1981), and authoritarianism (Edwards & Reid, 1983). Staff wearing uniforms are also more likely to be assaulted than are those in "civilian" clothing (Rinn, 1976).

Victimized police officers are a useful second source of additional specific victimization-connected qualities. Toch (1985) observes:

> Goals [of police officers] such as the need to demonstrate manhood, propensities such as callous manipulativeness, perspectives such as readiness to take instant offense are preludes to confrontations....The point is that each person in a violent encounter can become a precipitant stimulus or can present a catalytic situation for the other person(s) involved. (p. 114)

We noted earlier, in the context of our discussion of child abuse, Snyder and Patterson's (1987) assertion that "the child is both a victim and an architect of his own environment." Apparently, it is also true that husbands, wives, hospital staff, police, competing athletes, bullied schoolchildren, and many others—including citizens strolling America's streets—may also find themselves to be both the victims and the architects of their own victimization.

CHAPTER 6

MESOLEVEL: THE GROUP

Whether they are gangs; clans; tribes; ethnic, religious, or regional groups; or nation-states, groups in conflict not infrequently escalate in a spiral of animosity which culminates in overt aggression. At all spatial levels—street, neighborhood, regional, and national—such violence may be both intense and enduring and may grow, at least in large part, from what Volkan (1988) aptly labeled, "the need for allies and enemies." In the present chapter we seek to explore in depth the roots of such us-versus-them thinking, motivation, and behavior. We will do so by recourse to relevant research from both field and laboratory.

REALISTIC-GROUP-CONFLICT THEORY

Competition between groups in the real world—nations, tribes, athletic teams, gangs, ethnic groups, and others—is a pervasive and enduring phenomenon, a phenomenon of major social and political salience and significance. As Forsyth (1983) observes:

> The simple hypothesis that conflict is caused by competition over valued but scarce resources has been used to explain the origin of class struggles (Marx & Engels, 1947), rebellions (Gurr, 1970), international warfare (Streufert & Streufert, 1979), and the development of culture and social structures (Simmel, 1950; Sumner, 1906). (p. 377)

The resources competed for may be power, prestige, territory, status, or wealth. Among the several psychosocial consequences of such competition, heightened attachment to one's own group and heightened antagonism toward the outgroup are regularly observed. To better understand the sources of such consequences and the conditions under which they may

97

be promoted or ameliorated, a number of social scientists have sought to
re-create and examine such intergroup competition under more controlled
circumstances. Chief among these investigations of realistic group conflict
are the seminal studies conducted by Muzafer Sherif and his research
group (Sherif, Harvey, White, Hood, & Sherif, 1961).

In each of these geographically dispersed field experiments, which
have come to be known as the *summer camp studies*, approximately 24 white,
middle-class 11- to 12-year-old boys participated. From the boys' perspective, their participation involved simply attending a summer camp for a
three-week period. The camp was staffed by the researchers, whose study
design planned three stages of camp programming: group formation,
intergroup conflict, and conflict reduction. In the first stage of the experiments, the boys were transported to the camp in two separate groups.
These groups were matched on an array of psychological and physical
qualities and were constituted in such a manner that most pairs of boys
who were friends before the two groups were formed were assigned to
different groups, thus minimizing the preexperimental level of within-
group attraction. Upon arrival at the camp, the two groups were situated
in widely separated locations, out of possible contact with one another.
During the week this first phase of the experiment lasted, each group of
boys engaged in athletics, hiked, camped, swam, and, as a concomitant of
such interaction, developed a group structure with its associated norms
and roles. Within each of the two groups, now self-named and self-deco-
rated the Rattlers and the Eagles, high levels of cohesiveness and positive
in-group attitudes were well evidenced. Toward the end of this first week,
boys in each group began to realize that they were sharing the camp
facilities with another group and began referring to "those guys" in increasingly comparative, competitive, and rivalrous ways. This minor aspect of the Sherif et al. (1961) studies—i.e., initiation by the group of
comparative in-group favoritism in the absence of not only overt competition with the other group but without even having met them—will loom
large later in this chapter as we examine the potent influence of mere
categorization into groups on diverse in-group and out-group biases.

The researchers welcomed the boys' requests for competitive, between-group opportunities, for this is precisely what the research plan
called for at stage two. A tournament was announced, to last four days, of
baseball, tug-of-war, tent-pitching competition, cabin inspections, and
other contests:

> At first, the tension between the two groups was limited to verbal insults, name
> calling, and teasing. Soon, however, the intergroup conflict escalated into
> full-fledged hostilities. After losing a bitterly contested tug-of-war battle, the
> Eagles sought revenge by taking down a Rattler flag and burning it....A fist fight

[followed]. Next, raiding began, as the Rattlers sought revenge by attacking the Eagles' cabin during the night. The raiders...swept through the Eagles' cabin tearing out mosquito netting, overturning beds, and carrying off personal belongings. During this period, the attitudes of each group toward the other became more and more negative, but the cohesiveness of each became increasingly stronger. (Forsyth, 1983, pp. 375–376)

Indeed, each group's rapid march from friendly rivalry to overt hostility was accompanied by widely evidenced increases in within-group favoritism. Such heightened cohesiveness, attraction, and solidarity, for example, emerged in a series of miniexperiments (within the larger camp experiment) disguised as games. One such game was a bean toss in which a large quantity of beans was scattered in the grass. Each group had a fixed amount of time to pick up as many beans as possible. Later, the experimenters projected a picture of what was purported to be each boy's pickings, and all boys had to estimate the number of beans displayed. In reality, the amount was the same in every instance, arranged in diverse configurations. Boys' estimates showed a highly consistent bias favoring their own group members. Such favoritism, as a second example, was also fully reflected in the youths' sociometric choices. When asked to indicate their best friends, over 90 per cent of the boys in both groups chose someone in their own group even though, it will be recalled, less than two weeks earlier their (then) best friends had been placed in the other group.

Having succeeded so fully in engendering both types of bias—in-group favoritism and out-group discrimination—the experimenters in the project's third phase sought to examine whether such attitudes and behaviors could be eliminated or at least reduced. Arranging largely unstructured opportunities for members of the two groups to meet and interact, have contact, and get to know one another better appeared to have little ameliorative effect. Contacts between the groups' leaders, who then might pass along the benefits of such contact, also seemed of scant value. Preaching and admonishments similarly fell on largely unhearing ears. What did appear to work, however, was the imposition of positive interdependency, that is, conditions in which each needed the other for the attainment of some mutually desired objective. The superordinate goals thus created by the experimenters included the groups' pooling their money to rent a movie that both groups wanted to see but neither could afford alone, jointly coming to the rescue of the camp's water truck when it had apparently got stuck and required the muscle power of both groups to pull it out of the mud, and similar interdependency scenarios. The result of this sequence of events, creating as it were one larger, superordinate group, was—on several criteria—a reduction of both in-group favoritism and out-group hostility.

In quite a different experimental context, Blake and Mouton (1961, 1986) sought to replicate and extend the Sherif et al. (1961) findings, in this instance with adults. Participants were management-level employees of various industrial organizations, constituted into groups of 20 to 30 each purportedly to discuss and examine an array of relevant interpersonal and organizational topics and problems. Over the course of their research effort, Blake and Mouton established 150 such groups, but at any given time at least two and often more groups were functioning—and their members were aware of this. As each group entered into its problem discussions, a degree of in-group cohesiveness began to develop. Along with this rise in attraction and solidarity within each group, the awareness of other, similar groups appeared to elicit rumblings of a desire for competition. The investigators, in the study's next phase, posed an identical problem to pairs of groups, instructing each group to find the best solution. Although explicit competitiveness had still not been instituted at this point by the researchers, group member comments repeatedly revealed it to be alive and running in their own minds. When in fact problem solution reports were duplicated and exchanged for study and analysis on a cross-group basis, both in-group favoritism in the form of overvaluation of their own group's solution and out-group discrimination in the form of pejorative evaluation of out-group solutions regularly emerged. In company with such biases, the competitiveness flowered and with it came frequent displays of out-group hostility. In fact, Blake and Mouton (1986) reported that "Sometimes intergroup antagonism grew so intense that the experiments had to be discontinued" (p. 72). Various strategies were implemented and evaluated as possible moderators of intergroup hostility—isolating groups, forcing combinations, adjudicating differences, mediation, and conciliation—but each appeared to have little positive impact. What did seem to function to reduce antagonisms was, again, positive interdependency in the form of intergroup collaboration and cooperation vis-à-vis superordinate goals. Other investigators, working in diverse settings, with diverse types of groups, and in diverse cultures, have similarly reported the in-group favoritism and out-group discrimination consequences of perceived or actual intergroup competition, as well as the ameliorative impact on such biases of the imposition of superordinate goals (Bass & Dunteman, 1963; Diab, 1970; Ryen & Kahn, 1975; Turner, 1981; Worchel, 1979; Worchel, Andreoli, & Folger, 1977).

Turner (1981) succinctly summarizes the combined results of these several investigations:

> Where two groups come into contact under conditions that embody a series of incompatible goals—where both groups urgently desire some objective which can be attained only at the expense of the other—competitive activity towards

the goal changes over time into hostility between the groups; also: a. unfavorable attitudes and images (stereotypes) of the outgroup come into use and become standardized, placing the outgroup at a definite social distance from the ingroup; b. intergroup conflict produces an increase in solidarity within the groups; and c. increased solidarity and pride in one's own group lead to ingroup biases which overevaluate the characteristics and performances of ingroup members and underevaluate those of outgroup members. Where conflicting groups come into contact under conditions that embody a series of superordinate goals, cooperative activity towards the goal has a cumulative impact in improving intergroup relations; in reducing social distance, dissipating hostile outgroup attitudes and stereotypes, and making future intergroup conflicts less likely. (p. 68)

Some investigators, however, reacted to this series of findings by wondering whether, for the biases to occur, competition might be sufficient but not necessary. Recall that in the Sherif et al. (1961) and Blake and Mouton (1961) series, as well as in some of the subsequent research, in-group favoritism, out-group discrimination, and even the gathering of the clouds of intergroup conflict began *before* formal intergroup competition or even its announcement. Further, both Ferguson and Kelly (1964) and Rabbie and Wilkins (1971) found evidence for intergroup favoritism in clearly noncompetitive conditions. Doise, Csepeli, Dann, Gouge, Larsen, and Ostell (1972), in an early contribution to what came to be known as *social categorization theory* and, later, as *social identity theory*, reported that simply being divided into groups, without social interaction, face-to-face contact, or anticipated intergroup behavior, can create in-group bias. Billig (1973), responding to these early findings and impressions, proposed that

the social categorization involved in group formation, and the development of ingroup consciousness and identity in relation to other groups initiates the process of intergroup attitude development: overt intergroup competition is not a necessary condition for intergroup attitudes. (p. 320)

Thus, the groundwork was prepared for the next phase of experimentation on in-group–out-group relations, the era of social identity theory.

SOCIAL IDENTITY THEORY

To test the proposition that the mere division of individuals into what they believe to be two or more groups is by itself sufficient to elicit both in-group favoritism and out-group bias, Tajfel and his research team conducted what appropriately came to be known as the *minimal group studies* (Tajfel, 1970; Tajfel, Flament, Billig, & Bundy, 1971). In part, their research hypotheses and design grew from investigations in what appears to be quite another field, object perception. Bruner (1957) had earlier explored the role of categorization in human perception. Campbell (1958)

broadly proposed that the diverse principles guiding such object perception might well apply with equal relevance in the domain of person
perception. Similarly, Doise and Weinberger (1973), and Doise,
Deschamps, and Meyer (1978), with direct applicability to the evolution of
social identity theory, found that perceptual categorization accentuated the
perceived similarity of items within a category and the perceived differences between items differentially categorized, a finding they suggested
might also hold at the social level for the perception of persons categorized
into different groups.

In the minimal group research, participating subjects were divided
into two "groups" ostensibly on the basis of some trivial criteria, for
example, their preference for the works of one or another of two painters
they had never heard of before. In reality, assignment to a "group" was
made randomly. The subjects did not interact during the experiment, either
within or between the "groups." Each subject was told to which "group"
he belonged, but the membership of all other participants, whether in his
own "group" or the other, remained anonymous to him. Each subject,
working alone, was asked to make a series of decisions regarding the
allocation of money to two other subjects, designated only by their "group"
membership and individual code number. Three types of designated recipient–subject pairs were used: (1) one from each "group," (2) both from
own "group," and (3) both from the "out-group." Across a series of such
investigations, including one (Billig & Tajfel, 1973) in which subjects were
assigned to "groups" not on the basis of purported aesthetic preferences,
but based on a random toss of a coin conducted in front of the subject, most
subjects consistently allocated monies in the direction of favoring in their
decisions anonymous members of their own "groups" at the expense of
anonymous members of the "out-groups." Thus, in the absence of social
interaction between or within groups, contact, conflict of interest, previous
hostility, any links between self-interest and group membership, or any
other form of functional interdependence within or between groups, the
mere perception or cognition that one belonged to a particular group
appeared to be sufficient to elicit discrimination in favor of purported
in-group members, and against those perceived to belong to the out-group.
The discriminatory potency of this minimal group effect is highlighted by
the fact that in a number of the relevant investigations, not only did subjects
give more money to in-group than out-group members when this was
unrelated to their personal gain, but they also gave less in an absolute sense
to in-group members in order to give them relatively more than out-group
members.

The original minimal group studies, given their explicit challenge to
the earlier realistic-group-conflict theory, generated a considerable amount

of subsequent research. Time and again these follow-up minimal group investigations replicated the basic findings of in-group favoritism and out-group discrimination, even though such research often varied the purported basis for categorization, or measured discrimination differently, or was conducted in a different culture (Brewer, 1979; Doise, 1971; Turner, 1975, 1980; Vaughan, 1978; Wetherell, 1982; Wetherell & Vaughan, 1979). It is worth noting that such successful replication even included two further studies in which assignment to "group" was done by flipping a coin while the subject watched (Locksley, Ortiz, & Hepburn, 1980; Turner, 1983). To further underscore the potency of the social categorization process, beyond its central discrimination consequences, it also produces more positive attitudes toward and more reported liking of in-group than out-group members; ethnocentric biases in perception, evaluation, and memory; and an altruistic bias toward in-group members (Howard & Rothbart, 1978; Turner, 1978). Given the breadth and depth of the perceptual, affective, and cognitive consequences of categorization, it is understandable that Tajfel (1978) paradoxically wondered whether they ought to be called maximal groups instead!

Tajfel's (1970) early explanation for these findings, generic norm theory, proposed that the regularity across cultures of discrimination against out-groups implied the broad existence of discriminatory norms which were taught, internalized, and regularly applied in "us" versus "them" contexts. However, both the circularity of such reasoning, as well as the existence of individuals and groups which are not highly ethnocentric, led to the generic norm explanation being short-lived. Why might social categorization reliably produce such a broad array of substantial, psychosocial effects? Gerard and Hoyt (1974) invoked an experimenter bias explanation. Experimental instructions and tasks, they held, led subjects to believe biased behavior was expected of them, and they conformed to such expectations.

A third explanation raised the possibility that the core explanatory mechanism was perceived similarity; that is, perhaps the discriminatory behavior was a result of the subject's perception—due to the purported basis on which the categories were constructed (e.g., shared aesthetic preference)—that he or she was, on this criterion, similar to in-group members and different from out-group subjects. Yet factorial studies in which the separate and combined effects of similarity and "pure" (random) categorization devoid of any basis in similarity were examined clearly demonstrated that categorization and not similarity was the potent condition (Billig & Tajfel, 1973; Billig, 1973; Rabbie & Huygen, 1974; Wilder & Allen, 1978).

Following these early explanatory efforts, social identity theory began to emerge as a comprehensive and, to date, satisfactory basis for categorization effect phenomena. The theory rests on the sequential unfolding of three processes—social categorization, social identity, and social comparison—employed by the individual or group in an effort to create positive group distinctiveness.

> The knowledge of our membership in various social categories, or groups of people, and the value attached to it is defined as our "social identity." Social identity, however, only acquires meaning by comparison with other groups. We interpret the social environment and act in a manner enabling us to make our own group favorably distinctive from other groups with which we may compare it. Such positive distinctiveness from relevant outgroups affords a satisfactory or adequate social identity. (Williams & Giles, 1978, p. 434)

To return to the minimal group studies which provided the initial impetus for the social identity perspective, it is argued (Turner, 1975) that it is not the division into groups per se which causes the reliable discrimination effects, but rather a more basic motivation to seek and find positive self-evaluation. Thus, to restate the core of this perspective, it is held that social categorizations are internalized to define the self in social situations, and such identity-shaping categorizations engender a self-evaluative social comparisons process. One's self-esteem as a group member, it is held, depends on the evaluative outcomes of such social comparisons between in-group and out-group. Since individuals desire positive self-esteem, the social comparisons search is for positive distinctiveness for the in-group as compared to the out-group. Hence the reliable in-group favoritism and out-group discrimination biases.

The manner in which this sequence unfolds, and its yield of positive distinctiveness self-esteem, is held by the theory to be a function of a number of factors, some of which are absolute or relative qualities of the groups being compared, and others of which concern the availability and perceived desirability of alternative routes to positive distinctiveness. One important moderating consideration is described in the theory by the concept of *insecurity*. Social relationships between groups, as Brown and Ross (1982) observe, are seldom static, and since any significant changes in intergroup power or status relations will influence the outcome of intergroup comparisons, the nature of the social identity dependent on such comparisons will also change. It is such changes which the theory describes as *manifestations of insecurity*. Insecurity is more likely to occur, the theory posits, when the power or status of one of the groups is seen as being illegitimately acquired. Further, the consequences of insecure social identity are a renewed search for positive distinctiveness—perhaps through direct competition, but also possibly by other means. The group member may engage in individual mobility: He or she may leave the group and even attempt to assume the positively valued qualities of the out-group, i.e., engage in a process of assimiliation. Or the person may seek positive distinctiveness by engaging in what the theory describes as *social creativity*, essentially an attempt to alter or redefine the elements of the intergroup comparative situation. One can seek to compare one's in-group with the out-group on a new dimension, a comparison more likely to yield positive distinctiveness. Alternatively, one may seek a different (lower status, less powerful) out-group against whom to compare one's in-group. Finally, group members may attempt to change their own values, transforming from negative to positive the valence of those qualities which define one's own identity, the oft-cited example of such a transformation being the "Black is beautiful" slogan.

The overview we have presented of social identity theory highlights the especially significant role of social categorization, as moderated by a number of intra- and intergroup characteristics, in the consequent search for identity-enhancing positive distinctiveness. Social categorization and the consequent promotion of in-group favoritism and out-group discrimination, it may further be noted, may be accentuated by external labeling, the use of intragroup symbols (name, flag, territory), and other sources of increased salience of group membership; by intergroup competition, as in the studies underpinning realistic-group-conflict theory; the more important is the attribute upon which the categorization is based to the social identity of ingroup members; and the more comparable the out-group is to the in-group. A number of factors have also been shown to reduce categorization-based in-group favoritism and out-group discrimination: common fate; value, attitude, or belief similarity; proximity; interdependence; anticipated and actual between-group interaction; and perception of a common enemy. Once in-group favoritism and out-group discrimination are set in motion, whether as a result of categorization or on other bases, an array of information-processing sequences often combines to maintain their existence and potency.

INFORMATION PROCESSING

In an article aptly titled "On the Self-Perpetuating Nature of Social Stereotypes," Snyder (1981) sought to apply information-processing research on memory to the domain of stereotyping. In this view, memory is construed to be not a replaying of some fixed memory traces but, instead, an active, reconstructive process. Exploring such notions as *retrospective reinterpretation, preferential remembering,* and *reconstructing the past by cognitive bolstering,* Snyder argues:

> Stereotypes influence and guide the remembering and interpretations of the past in ways that support and bolster current stereotyped interpretations of other people....How might such reconstruction processes operate? First of all, the individual may search preferentially for stereotype-confirming factual evidence. Second, when the individual is in doubt about specific events in the target's past, these same stereotypes may provide convenient sources of clues for augmenting or filling in the gaps in his or her knowledge with evidence that further bolsters and supports current stereotyped beliefs. Third, stereotypes...may provide guidelines for interpreting remembered events in ways that enhance their congruence with current stereotyped beliefs about the target. From this perspective, stereotypes function as "theories" that not only contain within them anticipation of what facts ought to be found in one's memory, but also initiate and guide the process of remembering and interpretation in ways that provide the individual with stereotype confirming evidence. (p. 191)

Such stereotype-driven cognitive bolstering may, in this view, be prospective, influencing the interpretation of later learned knowledge about the target person or group, and/or retrospective, acting upon the remembering and interpretation of previously learned information. A self-fulfilling prophecy may be the resultant of these processes, as they generate behaviors on the part of the target that confirm the stereotype.

Rothbart (1981) points to similar categorization-associated information-processing influences which may operate during the encoding, retrieval, and interpretation of information. For example, he suggests:

> ...activation of a category label...structures both encoding and retrieval....The widespread perception of ingroup superiority may be attributable to the fact that ingroup-outgroup categorizations implicitly activate the expectancy that "we" are better than "they," and subjects selectively learn to remember ingroup and outgroup behaviors consistent with that expectancy. (p. 161)

Such differential processing of in-group-relevant and out-group-relevant information permits one to conclude, suggest Hamilton and Trollier (1986), that the social categories we each construct and employ are more than just means to simplify and comprehend a complex interpersonal environment: "They are also categories that can bias the way we process information, organize and store it in memory, and make judgments about members of those social categories" (p. 133). The power of social categorizations to shape what we seek, we see, we remember, and we believe is by now well established—not only by earlier work on person perception and on social identity theory, and not only by the just-cited information-processing research on memory encoding, retrieval, and interpretation, but also by quite recent social cognition theory and investigation of what have been termed *social schemata.* A schema, according to Taylor and Fiske

(1981), is a cognitive structure that guides how people take in, remember, and make inferences about raw data. Stereotypes are held to be a particular type of schema, one that organizes both one's knowledge and one's expectancies about people who fall into certain socially defined categories. Such schemata influence perceptions of variability, complexity, and valence. Specifically, out-groups are stereotypically seen to be less variable, simpler, and more negative than one's in-group. Schemata are often robust and perseverant. Taylor and Fiske note that people often not only ignore many exceptions to the schemata, but they may even interpret the exception as proving the schemata! Thus it is clear that just as categorization and the consequent search for positive distinctiveness can powerfully initiate in-group–out-group biases, information-processing sequences may both accentuate and perpetuate such biases and their consequences.

From all these perspectives—realistic-group-conflict theory, social identity theory, and information-processing theory—the group is a social ecological force of great power and consequence. Membership, even in minimal groups, may substantially potentiate intergroup conflict and aggression. Relevant research has been examined to highlight the in-group–out-group circumstances which serve to either enhance or inhibit such potentiation.

CHAPTER 7

MACROLEVEL: THE MOB

Blending with, but often numerically and emotionally different from, *groups* is the macrolevel, social ecological collective, *mobs*. Chaplin (1985) defines a mob as a crowd acting under strong emotional conditions that often lead to violence or illegal acts. Milgram and Toch (1969) describe the actions of such a collective as "group behavior which originates spontaneously, is relatively unorganized, fairly unpredictable and planless in its course of development, and which depends on interstimulation among participants" (p. 507). Momboisse (1970) speaks of four types of mobs: escape, acquisitive, expressive, and aggressive. Thus a mob may be a panicked collective seeking safety by fleeing from some real or imagined threat. Or mob formation and expression may take such concrete benign forms as a congregation at an emotional religious meeting or an aroused audience at an athletic event or a rock concert. Far less benign mobs may emerge in the form of a collective urging a potential jumper suicide; a loosely affiliated, ganglike group of adolescent males engaged in wilding,[*] swarming,[**] or other violent behavior; or a full-scale riot destructive of property and persons in a community, prison, or other setting. As noted earlier (pp. 73–75), the United States has a long history of mob violence in the form of draft riots; vigilante or regulator groups; lynch mobs; landholder rebellions; maritime riots; agrarian strife; collective violence in

---

[*] A marauding series of group-initiated assaultive attacks on passersby in a street, park, or other community setting.

[**] A group invasion of a residence for purposes of committing theft, vandalism, and assault.

the mining, railroad, and auto industries; race riots; antiwar disturbances; and more. What does mob formation "feel" like?

Momboisse (1970) provides a process-oriented sense of mob development and coalescence:

> Mobs are the product of a process of evolution....The first step in the transformation of a preconditional and responsive group of individuals into a mob is some climactic event...This is the period when the mob "mutters."...It [the event] causes a crowd to gather at the scene. Its members mill about like a herd of cattle. The gathering of a crowd automatically causes more onlookers to gather. These persons usually have little if any direct knowledge of the incident which gave rise to the mob....Rumors are numerous and spread rapidly....As an incident proceeds to attract numbers of individuals, they are pressed together....They initiate conversation with strangers....Through the milling process, the crowd excites itself more and more. Individuals will break off to warn friends, enlist recruits, pass on rumors...and generate excitement. As the crowd grows, so do the rumors, and through social facilitation, increasingly dangerous behavior is encouraged...by circular influences, stimulation and restimulation of each other, a high state of collective tension and excitement is built up.
>
> As tension mounts, individuals become less and less responsive to stimulation arising outside the group and respond only to influences from within the crowd itself. This process creates among members of the crowd an internal rapport, a kind of collective hypnosis, in which the individual loses his self-control and responds only to the dictates of the crowd as a whole. The individual loses critical self-consciousness...for mob anonymity absolves him of individual responsibility...As group wrath generates, symbolic behavior becomes incapable of providing a satisfactory outlet for the feeling-states of the individuals involved. Some form of overt, nonsymbolic behavior is imperative. Such overt behavior is, of course, always violent and destructive. (pp. 16–17)

Over the past century, a number of both person-oriented and context-oriented theories have been offered in an effort to better understand such collective behavior. As we examine these formulations, we wish to stress the same person–environment view that has dominated the rest of this book, namely, that aggression—be it individual or collective—will be best understood and moderated when *both* person and contextual forces are jointly taken into account.

THEORIES OF MOB BEHAVIOR

CONTAGION THEORY

In 1895, Gustave Le Bon published his field-observation-based study *The Crowd* (1903), in which he proposed that the central mechanism governing mob formation and behavior was a process of contagion. Speaking of the "mental unity of crowds" and the "crowd mind," Le Bon (who, relevantly, was a physician) noted that specific behaviors and levels of arousal frequently began with a few individuals in the larger collective and spread throughout the crowd, in a manner he saw as analogous to the transmission of an infectious disease. Germ theory was relatively new and of growing popularity in the physical medicine of Le Bon's era, and it was the central theme of his mob-behavior-contagion theory. Interestingly, and equally a reflection of the predominant views of his times, the great interest in the late 19th century in hypnosis and mesmerism was captured in Le Bon's reliance on suggestibility as the primary mechanism underlying mob contagion.

Via a suggestibility-driven contagious process

> in the mass, the individual is radically transformed, loses his or her conscious personality, and it is in the grip of the "law of mental unity of crowds," that primitive, irrational elements emerge....What emerges is a collective mind that makes people feel, think, and act in a uniform or homogeneous way. (Kruse, 1986, p. 127)

Though group mind and related disembodied notions about collective behavior have largely passed from the contemporary scene, to Le Bon the credit remains for largely initiating and most certainly accelerating this area of inquiry.

CONVERGENCE THEORY

A second perspective on mob behavior, convergence theory, holds that rather than a more-or-less random group of individuals becoming a collective through a contagious spread of emotion, people sharing particular predispositions are drawn together to express shared conscious or unconscious needs. Forsyth (1983) describes this viewpoint as one suggesting that

> aggregates are not merely haphazard gatherings of dissimilar strangers, but rather represent the convergence of people with compatible needs, desires, motivations, and emotions. By joining in the group the individual makes possible the satisfaction of these needs, and the crowd situation serves as a trigger for the spontaneous release of previously controlled behaviors. (p. 311)

The convergers may share neighborhood grievances, athletic fandom, religious affiliation, or other "surface" concordances, but the theory speaks more to latent rather than to manifest similarities. For example, in one concrete expression of the convergence perspective on collective behavior, Freud (1922) proposed that people join and remain in collectives to satisfy shared repressed unconscious desires—sexual, aggressive, or otherwise.

EMERGENT-NORM THEORY

Turner and Killian (1972) have proposed a third perspective on mob behavior, responsive to their beliefs about the weaknesses of both the contagion and convergence approaches. Regarding contagion, a comprehensive theory needs also to explain the substantial portion of crowd members and bystanders who do not "catch the germ" of intensified emotion. As far as convergence is concerned, Turner and Killian (1972) hold that for most crowds the degree of attitudinal, emotional, or motivational homogeneity is appreciably lower than convergence theory proposes. Instead, in emergent-norm theory, newly developing guides to belief and behavior come into effect and are enacted by members of the emerging collective. Again quoting Forsyth (1983):

> Crowds, mobs, and other collectives only seem to be unanimous in emotions and actions, since the members all adhere to norms that are relevant in the given situation. Granted, these norms may be unique and sharply contrary to more general societal standards, but as they emerge in the group situation they exert a powerful influence on behavior. (p. 314)

A variant of this perspective, Rabbie's (1982) norm-enhancement theory, proposes that rather than the development of new norms in a group context, there is an increase in the perceived legitimacy and salience of normative beliefs and attitudes previously held by the individuals constituting the collective and brought with them to the collective's assemblage.

Mob aggression, as individual aggression, is complexly determined behavior. The three initial theories we have briefly sketched should be viewed as complementary perspectives, all of which may be operating concurrently in any given mob-aggression event:

> The three perspectives on collective behavior—convergence, contagion, and emergent-norm theory—are in no sense incompatible with one another....For example, consider the behavior of baiting crowds—groups of people who urge on a person threatening to jump from a building, bridge, or tower....Applying the three theories, the convergence approach suggests that only a certain type of person would be likely to bait the victim to leap to his or her death. Those shouts could then spread to other bystanders through a process of contagion until the onlookers were infected by a norm of callousness and cynicism. (Forsyth, 1983, p. 315)

Other psychological perspectives on mob behavior have emerged, and they too should be viewed as additive, not conflicting, in the difficult task of seeking to understand such complex collective behavior. Allport (1924), for example, was particularly interested in debunking such notions as group mind or other like constructs which suggested that the group, mob, or crowd was somehow greater than the sum of its individual members. For him, mob action was straightforwardly a process of the interstimulation, intensification, and social facilitation of the actions of individuals through the presence and actions of the others in the collective: "The individual in the crowd behaves just as he would behave alone, only more so" (Allport, 1924, p. 295).

DEINDIVIDUATION THEORY

Extending these several theoretical stances yet further, deindividuation theory has more recently emerged as a comprehensive perspective on the collective behavior of concern here. Festinger, Pepitone, and Newcombe (1952) introduced the deindividuation construct, defining it as a situation in which individuals behave as if they were "submerged" in the group, experiencing a reduction in inner restraint and a heightened freedom to engage in aggressive and other deviant behaviors. Zimbardo (1969) studied the deindividuation process in depth and identified its primary antecedents and manifestations (Table 1).

Submergence in a group or other collective, and the concomitant sense of loss of individuality, is promoted by a series of conditions, all of which are likely to occur in the case of mob aggression. Anonymity is one such condition, a condition itself facilitated when the individual group members believe they cannot be identified because of darkness, disguise, masks, or uniforms or because of the sheer size of the assemblage. Deindividuation is abetted when the collective situation's characteristics give a sense of absolving the individual of responsibility for the collective's actions. As Forsyth (1983) notes, such can be the circumstance when a leader emerges who demands

TABLE 1. The Process of Deindividuation

Conditions of deindividuation	State of deindividuation	Deindividuated behaviors
1. Anonymity	Loss of self-awareness	Behavior is emotional,
2. Responsibility	Loss of self-regulation:	impulsive, irrational,
3. Group membership		regressive, with high
4. Arousal	1. Low self-monitoring	intensity:
5. Others (sensory overload,	2. Failure to consider	
novel situations, drug	relevant norms	1. Not under stimulus
usage, altered states of	3. Little use of	control
consciousness, and so	self-generated behaviors	2. Counternormative
on)	4. Failure to formulate	3. Pleasurable
	long-range plans	

Note. From "The Human Choice" by P. G. Zimbardo. In 1969 *Nebraska Symposium on Motivation* (p. 293), edited by W. J. Arnold and D. Levine. Copyright ©1970 by the University of Nebraska Press. Adapted by permission.

individual compliance with the mob's behavior. Because of the sheer numbers of persons constituting the collective, personal responsibility may also be minimized, and deindividuation is also promoted via the sense that responsibility for actions taken is thus widely diffused.

In addition to anonymity and diminished responsibility, group membership itself is a facilitator of deindividuation. It can augment contagion, modeling, and a sense of power and can raise the level of individual arousal, in much the same way as Allport (1924) spoke earlier of a spiral of interstimulation and social facilitation. It is largely via such heightened emotional arousal that the anonymity, diffused responsibility, and group membership are transformed into the high-intensity behaviors often characteristic of the deindividuated state.

Given the facilitative conditions described, a collective of deindividuated individuals is likely to display diminished self-awareness and self-regulation. Diener (1980) has examined this latter process in depth. Its consequences appear to be poor monitoring of one's own behavior, less monitoring of relevant behavioral norms, a failure to make long-range plans, and heightened attention to the immediate situation only. Forsyth (1983) notes that these several consequences of diminished self-awareness and self-regulation may cause a group to "not even consider the moral implications of its actions and . . . lose its ability to understand fully the violent actions it performs" (p. 321). In a state of deindividuation, as Table 1 suggests, the collective may behave emotionally, impulsively, irrationally, regressively, and with high intensity:

> Although the appearance of legal authorities—police cars, officers, attack dogs—is sufficient to warn a group of bystanders that riotous actions will be punished, when a mob becomes deindividuated these symbols of authority lose their power to control action. As a result of deindividuation, completely blameless individuals may be attacked, perceptions of the environment may be massively distorted...and violent actions intensify as feedback–control mechanisms break down. (Forsyth, 1983, pp. 322–323)

Deindividuation theory is the most recent, and most comprehensive, approach to identifying and unraveling the complexities of mob behavior. It stands on a firm foundation of empirical support and well deserves the prominence it is assuming in this group dynamics domain (Diener, 1976; Prentice-Dunn & Rogers, 1980; Singer, Brush, & Lublin, 1965; Zillman et al., 1975; Zimbardo, 1969).

SOCIOCULTURAL THEORIES

Mobs are constituted of individuals, each of whom has his or her own (even if shared) histories, perceptions, emotions, and motivations. To the degree that these individual characteristics are brought to bear in a collective context, and both shape and are shaped in that context, the mob is a *person* phenomenon, and the four psychological theories we have examined are both relevant and useful. However, as concepts such as contagion, convergence, emergent norms, and deindividuation make clear, these person phenomena unfold in a social and cultural context, a context constituted of forces both within and outside the group. Yes, mob behavior is a psychological phenomenon, but it is also and simultaneously very much a sociocultural phenomenon. Stated otherwise, as we have commented often throughout this book, aggression—in this instance, mob aggression—is very much a person–environment event. Thus, it is necessary that an accurate and comprehensive view of such behavior fully incorporate an ecological perspective.

The work of Erwin Staub is most useful in this regard. In Staub's (1993) view, the ecological context for mob violence consists of three types of instigating circumstances.

Nonspecific instigators, providing broad background facilitation, as it were, include such phenomena as crowding (see pp. 48–53) and high ambient temperatures (see pp. 79–82). Indeed, the United States Riot Commission (1968) pointed to the consistent presence of large proximate populations, in a real sense a pool of potential rioters, located at the eventual riot scene prior to the riots it studied. It also noted that for 9 of the 18 riots examined, the ambient temperature the day the riot began was 90° F or higher, and in the high 80s for the remainder. Both crowding and high ambient temperature have also been implicated as nonspecific instigators in prison rioting (Barak-Glantz, 1985).

Specific instigators, in Staub's (1993) view, include especially such background features of the environmental context as its sociocultural climate and its relative economic vitality. He cites the urban riots of the 1960s as but one of many possible examples of a sociocultural context whose characteristics were conducive to generating riotous behavior:

> The urban riots of the 1960s occurred in a social climate created by the desegregation decisions of the Supreme Court and the civil rights movement. There was an increased awareness of discrimination and injustice, and increased expectation by Black people of improvement in their social and economic conditions. There was also a less punitive climate for intense expressions of Black frustration. (p. 12)

Similar observations regarding the facilitativeness for riot, rebellion, and other forms of mob violence of diverse social, cultural, and political climates have been made by many other social commentators and investigators (Berkowitz, 1972; Milgram & Toch, 1969; Perry & Pugh, 1978; Smelser, 1962; Zimbardo, 1978).

Economic considerations are especially salient background facilitators of subsequent mob violence, but most investigators agree that it is relative, rather than absolute, economic deprivation which is particularly significant (Davies, 1969; Gurr, 1970; Runciman, 1966; Stouffer, Suchman, DeVinney, Star, & Williams, 1949). While straightforward frustration–aggression thinking would predict collective violence from slum living, high unemployment, and similar privation, a variety of evidence suggests that, rather than such direct effects, riots much more frequently grow from a sense of *relative* deprivation. Relative deprivation is the belief that others are climbing up the economic ladder while oneself is not, or the belief that one's own earlier economic gains are being lost. This sense of blocked opportunity and unjust exclusion from economic gain has been an especially potent specific instigator of riot and rebellion in American history (Goldstein & Segall, 1983; Gurr, 1989). It is a perspective formalized by Davies (1969) and elaborated on by Perry and Pugh (1978), who observe:

> The J-curve of rising expectations...is an attempt to explain why riots and revolutions occur *not* when social deprivation is extreme, but rather in periods of improving social conditions. When social conditions are generally improving, people supposedly expect further improvements in the future. A rising standard of living promotes a sense of optimism and the belief that "tomorrow will bring better things than today." Unfortunately, the rising expectations of many deprived groups may outstrip their capacity for achievement just when some ultimate goal appears to be close at hand. Desired improvements can rarely be achieved quickly enough to avoid an "intolerable gap" between what people want and what they can actually get. According to Davies [1969], the development of an intolerable gap is a direct cause of collective violence. (p. 151)

Given an ecological context in which nonspecific and/or specific background conditions instigative of collective violence exist, a number of *immediate instigators* have been suggested by Staub (1993) as events which actually light the fuse. In recent United States history, such flashpoints or precipitating events have included the assassination of a respected leader (e.g., Martin Luther King); a judicial decision deemed to be unjust by one or more groups (e.g., the verdict in the criminal trial of the police officers who arrested Rodney King); alleged violations of important community mores (e.g., the purported rapes of white women by black males resulting in lynch mobs); local, state, or federal government decisions or policy enactments (e.g., the commitment to armed-forces expansion in Vietnam and the consequent antiwar riots); the taking away of a previously granted privilege (e.g., as Colvin, 1982, notes has occurred preceding a number of prison riots); and the defeat of one's team, or provocation by opposing fans, at an athletic contest (e.g., as Buford, 1991, has described as preceding several European soccer riots).

Staub's (1993) summary view of the contribution of these several ecological characteristics as preconditions to and instigators of mob violence is of interest:

> Difficult life conditions can affect a whole society, or a specific group of people. They can take the form of economic problems or decline, political upheaval, or great social changes that create the experience of disorganization and chaos with loss of guiding values and a sense of community. Relative deprivation, the perception of unfair treatment and injustice, and powerlessness in improving one's fate or affecting change also function as background instigators. The easing of repression, discrimination or economic problems can give rise to mob violence by decreasing fear, empowering people and increasing hope which remains essentially unfulfilled. The changes involved in such improvements can themselves contribute to social disorganization. Devaluation or antagonism between groups can create persistent cultural potential for mob violence.
>
> The motivations that arise can vary as a function of instigating conditions and cultural characteristics. The reasons for participation in mob violence can include frustration, hostility, exploding anger and the desire to hurt; the desire for institutional and social change motivated partly by self interest and partly by response to perceived injustice; feelings of connection to and unity with others; feelings of control, power and even intense excitement and peak experience that arise from group processes; or the desire for personal gain. (pp. 17–18)

The several person and environment features we have examined in this chapter, in reciprocal interaction with one another, can and not infrequently do eventuate in mob violence. A graphic sense of such violence has been described well by Buford in his *Among the Thugs* (1991), a text best described as a "violent ethnographic adventure" examining English soccer fan violence, an excerpt from which serves as a fitting means to conclude the present chapter.

> he was repeating the phrase, It's going off, it's going off. Everyone around him was excited. It was an excitement that verged on being something greater, an emotion more transcendent—joy at the very least, but more like ecstasy. There was an intense energy about it; it was impossible not to feel some of the thrill....There was more going on than I could assimilate: there were violent noises constantly—something breaking or crashing—and I could never tell where they were coming from. In every direction something was happening. I have no sense of sequence.
>
> The group crossed a street, a major intersection. It had long abandoned the pretense of invisibility and had reverted to the arrogant identity of the violent crowd, walking, without hesitation, straight into the congested traffic, across the hoods of the cars, knowing they would stop. At the head of the traffic was a bus, and one of the supporters stepped up to the front of it, and from about six feet, hurled something with great force—it wasn't a stone, it was big and made of metal, like the manifold of a car engine—straight into the driver's windshield....The sound of the shattering windshield...was a powerful stimulant, physical and intrusive, and it had been the range of sounds, of things

breaking and crashing, coming from somewhere in the darkness, unidentifiable, that was increasing steadily the strength of feeling of everyone around me.

...Someone came rushing at the bus with a pole...and smashed a passenger window. A second crashing sound. Others came running over and started throwing stones and bottles with great ferocity. They were, again, in a frenzy....A window shattered, and another shattered, and there was screaming inside....All around me people were throwing stones and bottles, and I felt afraid for my own eyes.

I looked behind me and I saw that a large vehicle had been overturned, and that further down the street flames were issuing from a building....There was now the sound of sirens, many sirens, different kinds, coming from several directions. The city is ours, Sammy said, and he repeated the possessive each time with greater intensity: It is ours, ours, ours. (pp. 89–92)

PART IV

INTERVENTION

CHAPTER 8

PHYSICAL ECOLOGICAL INTERVENTION: ENVIRONMENTAL DESIGN

Earlier chapters have presented and examined site, neighborhood, and regional characteristics which, in interaction with person qualities, function as antecedents or correlates of crime and aggression. In seeking to reduce the occurrence of such antisocial behavior, criminology, sociology, and psychology have traditionally focused primarily on the person component of the person–environment duet. Crimes, such disciplines hold, grew from those person characteristics collectively finding expression in criminal motivation. Reducing crime, therefore, required preventive and rehabilitative actions directed toward potential and existing perpetrators—counseling, behavior modification, probationary or parole stipulations, diversion programming, and so forth. In major contrast to this broadly held and widely implemented dispositional perspective on crime and aggression control, there has emerged in recent decades a series of philosophies which concern themselves with environmental, rather than perpetrator, intervention. These are each primarily criminal-opportunity-altering, rather than criminal-motivation-altering approaches. Each places its targeting emphasis much more heavily on the prevention of crime or aggression yet to occur than on the rehabilitation of already-existing criminals. Their names clearly reflect this focus: crime prevention through environmental design (CPTED; Angel, 1968; Jacobs, 1961; Wood, 1991), situational crime prevention (Clarke, 1992; Jeffery, 1977), and environmental criminology

121

(Brantingham & Brantingham, 1991). Their ecological targeting flavor is communicated well by Clarke (1992):

> Situational Crime Prevention comprises opportunity-reducing measures that are (1) directed at highly specific forms of crime, (2) that involve the management, design or manipulation of the immediate environment in as systematic and permanent a way as possible, (3) so as to increase the effort and risks of crime and reduce the rewards as perceived by a wide range of offenders. (p. 4)

In a similar spirit, Jeffery (1977) notes regarding CPTED:

> Crime can focus either on the environment or the criminal. When we deal with the environment, we consider the object stolen or the person assaulted or murdered. When we deal with criminals, we deal with the individual who commits the crime. We can also deal with crime before it occurs, or after it occurs. If we deal with crime before it occurs, we are structuring the environment so as to prevent crimes; if we deal with crime after it occurs, we are treating or rehabilitating criminals....In addition...crime control techniques may be viewed in terms of direct or indirect controls over human behavior....Direct controls of crime include only those which reduce environmental opportunities for crime. Indirect controls include all other measures, such as job training, remedial education....Placing a man on probation or giving him remedial education will not prevent him from breaking the window and stealing jewelry; placing a steel bar over the window will prevent the theft of jewelry from that window. Our current method of controlling crime is predominantly through indirect measures after the offense has been committed. (p. 20)

Although these perspectives may differ in some degree in terms of the scope of their focus (e.g., macro vs. micro) or in their primary implementation techniques (social control, surveillance promotion, design change), each seeks to reduce criminal opportunity and increase the likelihood that potential perpetrators will perceive the cost of doing crime as more expensive, more effortful, and more risky. The remainder of this chapter will concretize these approaches by comprehensively cataloging the wide and diverse array of specific techniques and tactics which have been suggested as means for their effective implementation. To do so, we will employ the category system developed for such taxonomic purposes by Clarke (1992). The specific techniques assigned to each category derive from the works of a number of ecologically oriented theorists and investigators, namely Brantingham and Brantingham (1991), Clarke (1992), Cromwell et al. (1991), Geason and Wilson (1989), Jacobs (1961), Jeffery (1977), Newman (1976), Poyner and Webb (1991), and Wallis and Ford (1980).

SITUATIONAL CRIME PREVENTION TECHNIQUES

The first subset of situational crime prevention techniques we wish to define and illustrate (I through IV) employs environmental design tactics aimed at increasing the effort or difficulty for the perpetrator associated with crime initiation and completion:

I. *Target hardening.* This situational crime prevention approach involves the use of devices or materials designed to obstruct the vandal or the thief by physical barriers:

1. Bandit or security screens
2. Deadbolt, vertical-bolt, and steering-column locks
3. Metal doors and door jambs
4. Slug rejector device
5. Toughened glass
6. Tamper-proof seals
7. Locked safes or money boxes
8. Slash-proof transit vehicle seating

II. *Access control.* These are architectural features, mechanical and electronic devices, and related means for maintaining prerogatives over the ability to gain entry:

1. Locked gates, doors, windows
2. Fenced yards
3. Reception desk
4. Entry phones
5. ID badges
6. Electronic personal ID numbers
7. Blocked-off streets or neighborhoods
8. Turnstiles
9. Electronic garage door openers
10. Reduced number of building entrances

III. *Deflecting offenders.* This is the channeling of potentially criminal or aggressive behavior in more prosocial directions by means of architectural, equipment, and related alterations:

1. Graffiti boards
2. Street detours
3. Litter bins
4. Next-step posters on broken equipment
5. Activity decoys in empty houses:
   - Automatic (timed) on/off of lights, radio, TV
   - Newspaper, mail taken in by neighbors
   - Blinds, shades open and closed daily by neighbors
   - Car in driveway
   - Lawn mowed

6. Differential pricing at crowd events

IV. *Controlling facilitators.* This is the alteration of the means to criminal and aggressive behavior by making such means less accessible and/or less potentially injurious:

1. Use of plastic rather than glass containers at crowd events
2. Spray-can sales control
3. Gun control
4. Telephone caller ID
5. Breathalyzer built into auto ignition system
6. Public phone placement
7. Bus stop placement

The second subset of situational crime prevention techniques (V through VIII), suggested by Clarke (1992) and elaborated on here, is designed to increase the real and/or perceived risks of apprehension to the potential perpetrator:

V. *Entry–exit screening.* Rather than seek to exclude potential perpetrators, as in access control, this set of tactics seeks to increase the likelihood of detecting persons not in conformity with entry requirements (entry screening) or detecting objects that should not be removed from protected areas (exit screening):

1. Baggage screening
2. Border searches
3. Intercoms, entry phones
4. Automatic ticket gates
5. Infrared entry beams
6. Closed-circuit TV
7. Buzzer-required entry
8. Merchandise tags
9. Library tags
10. Metal detectors

VI. *Formal surveillance.* This is surveillance by police, guards, store detectives, and similar paid or volunteer security personnel:

1. Use of real and dummy TV cameras in stores, at intersections
2. Burglar alarms
3. Informant hotlines
4. Use of guard kiosks
5. Provision of on-site living quarters for security personnel
6. Neighborhood watch, block watch, and block parent programs

7. Tenant patrols, senior citizen patrols
8. House-sitting programs
9. Location of police precincts and substations in visible neighborhood areas

VII. *Surveillance by employees.* This is surveillance by nonsecurity personnel, such as train conductors, parking-lot attendants, salespersons, building doormen, and so forth:

1. Increased number of employees
2. Aisle mirrors, cameras
3. Low counters
4. Alteration of store layout (e.g., removal of view-blocking columns)
5. Clustering of commercial establishments with similar operating hours
6. Reduction of bus and train station waiting area with movable barriers as passenger density varies
7. Reduction in school size to lower personnel–student ratio

VIII. *Natural surveillance.* This is surveillance provided by home owners, apartment dwellers, pedestrians, and others going about their daily activities:

1. Improvement in exterior and interior lighting
2. Pruning of hedges and shrubbery
3. Lowering or removal of privacy fencing
4. Addition of windows, stoops, lobby sitting areas
5. Building of low-rise (three to five stories) rather than high-rise housing
6. Creation of shared open spaces and communal facilities (e.g., laundries) for tenants
7. Clearing of store windows of ads and merchandise
8. Design of parks and parking lots in long strips to increase visibility by passers-by
9. Clustering and orienton of houses for mutual surveillance

The final subset of situational crime prevention categories (IX through XII) seeks to reduce the rewards to potential perpetrators for engaging in criminal or aggressive behavior:

IX. *Target removal.* The physical removal of potential crime targets:

1. Exact-change fares
2. Removable car radios
3. Use of phonecards
4. Encouragement of payment by check
5. Posted notices of limited cash-on-hand

6. Staggering of the departure of fans from crowd events by having postgame or postconcert events
7. Use of graffiti dissuaders
   • Teflon covering
   • Plastic laminate covering
   • Fiberglas and Melamine covering
   • Rock cement surface
   • Slanted-cedar siding surface
   • Deeply grooved surface

X. *Identifying property.* This is the physical identification marking of potential crime targets:

1. Vehicle-parts-identification marking
2. Vehicle licensing
3. Cattle branding
4. Use of logos
5. Property marking with social security numbers
6. Numbering of houses or apartments with uniformly placed numbers

XI. *Removing inducements.* This is the physical alteration of potential crime targets:

1. Rapid graffiti cleaning
2. Rapid repair of damaged property
3. Automatic teller machines
4. Gender-neutral phone lists
5. Use of small windowpanes
6. Use of plywood road signs
7. Use of enclosed garages

XII. *Rule setting.* This is the making of clear prior statements of acceptable and unacceptable behaviors:

1. Drug-free school zones
2. Limitations on alcohol purchase and use
3. Building security codes
4. Building design specifications
5. Increase in the use of fines, suspensions, and other sanctions for sports violence

Perhaps because of its relative newness on the criminological scene, and also because so much of criminology remains oriented in its intervention efforts toward altering criminal motivation rather than criminal opportunity, the sheer amount of research evaluating the efficacy of environmental design strategies and tactics is rather modest. However, a not insubstantial portion of what does exist is largely positive in outcome. Many of the initial studies in this area were stimulated by Newman's (1975, 1976) writings on defensible space and were conducted in public-housing contexts. In Newman's view, defensible space results from three characteristics of design:

> One, the space outside the individual apartment units should be designed in ways that cause tenants and outsiders to perceive that the public spaces comprising the project are part of the tenants' personal territory. For example, locate the apartment buildings in ways that define and break up the grounds they occupy; limit the project to 1,000 units or less; and use low walls, hedges, stoops, changes in the texture of walking surfaces, and entry portals to create symbolic barriers between the public street and the semipublic grounds of the project. Two, the grounds of the project and the building interiors should be designed in ways that provide residents and formal authorities with natural opportunities to observe all public and semiprivate spaces and paths. For example, divide housing projects into small, recognizable enclaves; locate building entrances close to the street and facing the street; illuminate paths and entrances; make lobbies and elevator entrances visible to passersby; build windows into firestair walls; and have kitchen windows face building entrances, play areas, and parking lots. Three, projects should be designed in ways that minimize residents' and outsiders' perception of the project as unique, isolated, and stigmatized. For example, build two to three, rather than ten to twenty high rise buildings; avoid materials that create an institutional atmosphere, such as glazed tiles and mercury-vapor type exterior lighting; and provide automobiles with access to streets within the project. (Newman, 1976, pp. 148–149)

In a major test of this design perspective, Newman (1975) compared two New York City housing projects: Van Dyke and Brownsville. The two projects, which were located across the street from one another, contained very similar residents—in number, racial composition, average family size, income, proportion of minors, percentage on welfare, and percentage of broken homes. However, in layout and design, they were dramatically different. Van Dyke consisted mostly of fourteen-story, rectangular buildings, each one of which had its main entrance 60 feet from the street, out of range of street surveillance, and used by about 125 families. Its interior stairwells were enclosed. Brownsville comprised three- to six-story cross-shaped buildings, their entrances but a few feet from the street, to be used by 9 to 13 families. Its stairwells were open and viewable. While crime rates were substantial in both venues, Van Dyke reported twice as many robberies and 60 per cent more felonies during the study period. Hand (1977) similarly compared public housing sites in Cincinnati which either were or were not explicitly designed to improve natural surveillance and found a predicted crime-reduction difference favoring the defensible space housing. Ley and Cybriwsky (1974), in an investigation also primarily concerned with the surveillance component of defensible space, studied the distribution of stripped cars in Philadelphia's inner city. The locations of such vehicles were closely related to the physical features of the sites at which they were found. Most frequently, they were located at places of industrial land use, next to vacant buildings, or near the windowless or doorless sides of residential sites, and only rarely in locations readily surveilled. Chenoweth (1977) and Kohn, Franck, and Fox (1975) examined the crime reduction potency of such design features as fences, paths, speed bumps, and other demarcators and failed to find evidence supportive of a defensible space position. Yet Fowler and Mangione (1979) report that such environmental design changes in their research as narrowing streets, changing their direction, building cul-de-sacs, and creating territorial markers impacted favorably on both crime rate and residents' fear of crime. Some added, and especially interesting, evidence supportive of a defensible space perspective is provided by Merry (1981) in an interview study not of victims or potential victims, but of crime perpetrators:

> These robbers are very conscious of architectural features which constitute defensible space. They try to commit crimes where they will not be observed. Favorite places are the narrow and enclosed pathways where visibility is poor and witnesses nonexistent. The open courtyards are considered poor robbery locations since there are "so many eyes there."...Ideal locations are those which provide multiple routes [for escape] with several turns and corners. (p. 409)

Mawbry (1977) has been critical of this line of research, and in particular of Newman's own studies, for their experimental design inadequacy. Stoks (1982) is justly critical of the absence of adequate theory and speculation regarding the psychological processes which intervene between design characteristics and overt criminal or noncriminal behavior. Further, in a critique especially relevant to the person–environment theme of the present book, Brower, Dockett, and Taylor (1983) assert that defensible space thinking is too deterministic, too environmental, and not sufficiently responsive to person–environment transactionalism. With due appreciation of the pioneering nature of Newman's work, we concur with Brower, Dockett, and Taylor (1983). Defense of space is *both* an environmental quality *and* a person quality, in interaction. As Merry (1981) concludes from his own work in this domain:

> ...Much of the defensible space is undefended, half the households I interviewed have been victimized, and many residents live in fear. A series of subtle design features undermine the overall defensible space features of the project, while the pervasive anonymity, distrust, and fear among the residents inhibits [sic] their formation of defended territories. (p. 415)

Beyond defensible space research, other studies of the impact on crime and aggression of environmental design changes have been conducted. These investigations have affirmed the crime- and aggression-reduction value of locks (Rengert & Wasilchick, 1985; Riley & Mayhew, 1980; Murray, Motoyama, & Rouse, 1980), alarms (Murray et al., 1980), increased pedestrian traffic (Duffalo, 1976; Letkemann, 1973; Pablant & Baxter, 1975), street-facing windows (Poyner & Webb, 1991), increased number of store clerks (Walsh, 1978), bandit screens (Ekblom, 1988), next-step posters (Moser & Levy-Leboyer, 1985), slug rejector devices (Barry, 1969), cashbox hardening (Clarke, 1992), and, for fear of crime but not crime rate itself, increased lighting (Tien, O'Donnell, Barnett, & Mirchandani, 1979) and a reduction in the crime-enhancing potency of surveillance-diminishing trees, shrubs, and walls (Molumby, 1976); low vehicular or pedestrian traffic (Luedtke, 1970); or house or store placement on the corners of blocks or the outer fringe of neighborhoods rather than in their interior (Stoks, 1982).

Though certainly an encouraging, if not unmixed, research pattern emerges from these several investigations, there remains the problem of displacement. This is the belief "that blocking opportunities for crime will simply result in its being displaced elsewhere or to some other time, being committed in another way, or even being transformed into some other kind of offense" (Clarke, 1989). In an entirely different domain, the field of psychodynamic psychotherapy, it was long held that clients possessed underlying neurotic motivations which manifested themselves in one or more maladaptive behaviors. Such behaviors were viewed as symptoms of the underlying neurosis, and if treatment or other circumstances led to the alteration of or reduction of a given maladaptive behavior, the neurosis would—via a process termed *symptom substitution*—manifest itself anew in a different maladaptive behavior. Those in criminology and related disciplines who emphasize the causative role of criminal motivation claim similar substitutive consequences in their assertions about crime displacement. Yet, as has frequently been true of fears of purported symptom substitution, crime displacement is far from a reliable phenomenon. True, early studies seemed supportive of displacement predictions. Press (1971) reported that augmenting the size of the police force in one New York City precinct succeeded in reducing crime there, but also apparently resulted in increased crime levels in adjacent precincts. Chaiken, Lawless, and Stevenson (1974) found a reduction in robberies on New York City buses when an exact-fare system was installed, but a corresponding increase in subway robberies. Mayhew, Clark, Sturman, and Hough (1976) reported an increase in thefts of older motor vehicles when newer ones were fitted with steering-column locks. Yet other studies, however, have reported no such crime displacement (Barr & Pease, 1990; Ekblom, 1988; Gabor, 1990), and some have even found a "diffusion of benefits":

As evidence accumulates of the limits to displacement, it seems likely that much
of the skepticism about the value of situational prevention will diminish.
Indeed, the debate about effectiveness may take an altogether different turn
with the newly growing realization that situational prevention can sometimes
produce the "complete reverse" of displacement, a reduction in crimes not
directly addressed by the preventive measures. (Clarke, 1989, p. 25)

Here again there appears to be operating an analogue of the purported symptom-substitution phenomenon noted above. Not only does
such a substitutive process fail to take place in many (probably most)
clients, it is far from uncommon that what does occur is an experience in
which one positively changed behavior appears to potentiate the likelihood that other, still untreated, maladaptive behaviors will also change for
the better. As Clarke (1989) notes, with regard to criminal behavior, such
diffusion of benefit is apparently sufficiently common so that it has been
observed by, and named by, several different investigators: the multiplier
effect (Chaiken et al., 1974), free-rider effects (Miethe, 1991), the drip-feed
effect (Pease, 1991), the halo effect (Scherdin, 1986), and spillover benefits
(Clarke, 1989).

Intervention by environmental design is a physical ecological strategy concretized in a viable array of diverse and demonstrably useful tactics
and procedures. While far from the entire answer to the challenge of crime
and aggression reduction, it is a strong partner to those more traditional
dispositional interventions which seek to reshape the criminal motivations
of potential and actual perpetrators.

CHAPTER 9

SOCIAL ECOLOGICAL INTERVENTION: INTERPERSONAL CONTACT

INTRODUCTION

Groups in conflict typically interact with one another in a manner characterized by suspicion, mistrust, tension, competition, stereotyped perceptions, and perhaps overt aggression, or they interact not at all. Such destructive contact, or absence of contact, perpetuates and even exacerbates the conflict that gave root to such behaviors and attitudes. Early thinking held that individual prejudice was the primary source of intergroup conflict. Such prejudice, it was believed, grew from ignorance about one another, and thus its remediation ought to be largely a matter of education—particularly education provided by interaction and contact which exposed the protagonists to the realities of one another. As Pettigrew (1981) observed:

> ...The human relations movement constructed a sanguine theory of intergroup contact. Since it viewed individual prejudice as largely the result of ignorance, it believed that contact between groups could only be advantageous. Once together, all but the most extreme fringe would surely see the common humanity shared by the groups and prejudice would necessarily dissipate. (p. 173)

Such optimistic, information-providing intergroup exposure was concretized in the 1940s by interracial dinners, brotherhood meetings, intergroup summer camps, and similar events and experiences. The early 1950s in America saw this same antiprejudice spirit reflected in a series of contact-promoting public policy initiatives, especially with regard to employment and housing. These initiatives provided a substantial series of opportunities for social and behavioral scientists to evaluate the real-world consequences of intergroup and interracial contact in such work (Harding & Hogrefe, 1952; Saenger & Gilbert, 1950) and daily-living contexts (Deutsch & Collins, 1951; Festinger, Schacter, & Back, 1950; Jahoda & West, 1951). Their combined findings revealed the earlier human relations view of the role of contact to be too simplistic. In both the job and housing studies, as well as parallel field research appearing at this time regarding interracial contact in the armed forces (Saenger, 1953; Stouffer et al., 1949), it was clear that the contact–conflict-reduction relationship was a complex one. Exposure seemed necessary but not sufficient. A number of conditions in which the contact was embedded either facilitated or inhibited its constructive consequences. When the conditions were met, as in a portion of the research cited above, intergroup contact appeared to function to reduce intergroup conflict; when they were unmet—as was true, for example, when Sherif et al. (1961) brought their warring camp groups together in an unstructured manner—outgroup hostility actually increased. It fell to Allport (1954) to offer the initial statement of what has come to be known as the *contact hypothesis*, which incorporated his view at the time of its facilitative mediating conditions:

> Prejudice may be reduced by equal status contact between majority and minority groups in the pursuit of common goals. The effect is greatly enhanced if this contact is sanctioned by institutional supports (i.e., by law, custom, or local atmosphere), and provided it is of a sort that leads to the perception of common interests and common humanity between members of the two groups. (p. 281)

Thus, circa 1954, intergroup contact was held to reduce prejudice and intergroup conflict if the participants in said contact were of equal status, shared common goals, and believed their interaction was supported by relevant social or institutional groups. Enthusiasm for the value of contact grew. The early evaluative studies were a substantial part of the social science statement that accompanied the brief to the U.S. Supreme Court in *Brown v. Board of Education* (1954), the milestone decision against racial segregation. In both laboratory and field settings, research on the effects of contact and its facilitators and inhibitors proliferated. In the present chapter we will examine the conditions whose presence promotes and whose absence retards the positive effects of contact, and we will consider the circumstances which enable such positive consequences to generalize beyond the immediate parties involved in the contact experience to the larger groups of which they are a part.

FACILITATIVE AND INHIBITORY CONDITIONS OF CONTACT

Contact research since the mid-1950s has been both diverse and substantial. Those of the studies conducted in the social psychological laboratory have employed a considerable variety of groups, tasks, measures, and methods, thus adding to the credibility of their collective results. The field studies of intergroup contact, while continuing in employment and housing contexts, have in particular focused upon the effects of contact in America's schools, as the major social experiment of racial desegregation was instituted and implemented in thousands of elementary and secondary educational institutions. What has been learned?

EQUAL STATUS

One of the central processes which intergroup contact seeks to influence is individuation. As Wilder (1981) described it:

> If deindividuation of target persons lessens our regard for them, then individuation of those persons may enhance our favorability toward them....Individuation of outgroup members may mediate a reduction of bias for any of several reasons. First, individuation of the outgroup breaks down the simple perception of the outgroup as a homogeneous unit. Second, individuation of outgroup members focusses attention on these persons and may enable one to notice points of similarity between oneself and the individuated members of the outgroup. Third, if attention is focussed on the individuated outgroup members, one should be more prone to take their role and, perhaps, empathize with them. (p. 235)

Thus, Wilder (1981) proposed that contact-mediated individuation may enhance the perceived heterogeneity of the outgroup, perceived similarity between in-group and out-group members, and the level of expressed empathy. One of a number of purported means of advancing the process of contact-mediated individuation is for the interacting parties involved to be, or to be perceived to be, of equal status. When such perceptions hold, there apparently exists a diminished likelihood of categorical responding and an enhanced probability not only of individuated perception, but of positively valenced individuated perception. That is, equal status and purportedly *all* of the facilitative conditions considered in this chapter "reduced prejudice because they maximize the probability that shared values and beliefs will be demonstrated and perceived and will therefore provide the basis for interpersonal attraction between ingroup and outgroup members" (Hewstone & Brown, 1986, p. 6).

Contact research on the role of group member status has, however, questioned whether its positive effects follow from equality of status *within* or *outside* the contact situation itself. Is it that when they actually meet, equality of in-group and out-group members' ability and power are the significant contact effect mediators? Or is it their relative status levels in the groups they each, in effect, represent? Or even of the groups themselves? While debate regarding these alternative views has long continued (Kramer, 1950; Pettigrew, 1971; Norwell & Worchel, 1981), we are in accord with Riordan (1978), who sees merit in all of the interpretations of "equal status" and views them as interrelated, mutually influencing perceptions. In any event, while acknowledging that seeking to equalize status by reducing or reversing existing status differences may be difficult and may elicit resistance from members of the initially higher status group (Brewer & Miller, 1984), if it is successful, category distinctions may become less salient, and the persons involved in the contact situation may perceive one another more as individuals and less in dichotomous us-versus-them terms.

Casual versus Intimate Contact

Relevant research supports the conclusion that

> casual intergroup contact has little or no effect on basic attitude change. Intimate contact, on the other hand, tends to produce favorable changes. When intimate relations are established, the ingroup member no longer perceives the member of the outgroup in a stereotyped way but begins to consider him as an individual and thereby discovers many areas of similarity. (Amir, 1969, p. 334)

Miller, Brewer, and Edwards (1985) have similarly underscored the opportunity provided by intimate contact for individuating perception. Working in the context of desegregated school settings, they distinguish among three different levels of intergroup interactions: (1) category-based, (2) differentiated, and (3) personalized. Category-based contact, at one extreme, is marked by the depersonalization and deindividuation of out-group members by in-group members. As Miller et al. (1985) describe it, "Outgroup members are responded to as interchangeable representatives of their social category" (p. 64). Categorical identification and, hence, categorical responding are much less salient at the other extreme: personalization. Here, more personalized information regarding individual outgroup members, information not correlated with category membership, becomes focal. Such enhanced intimacy in intergroup relating, it appears, may not only increase the favorableness of the intergroup contact itself, it may also heighten the likelihood that the positiveness of perception and interaction thus engendered will generalize beyond the parties involved in the contact interaction itself to relations with other members of the out-group.

MULTIPLE CONTACTS

Toward the same decategorizing, individuating ends, multiple contacts are generally more effective than are single contacts. As Taylor (1981) aptly describes it:

> ...Increasing contact with any category of objects, be it tools, food items, or social groups, enables one to make finer and finer discriminations within the category. For example, although initial contact with a group (e.g., a football team) may lead to trait stereotyping (e.g., big, dumb), eventually contact with the group should facilitate the perception of subtypes (e.g., the playboy; the shy; the arrogant hero type). At some point the diversity and volume of contact with any social group should be substantial enough that abstract trait conceptions of the group would no longer have any descriptive value. (p. 102)

Much the same point is offered by Linville, Salovey, and Fischer (1986), in their emphasis on *familiarity* and *exposure* as prime sources of category differentiation. Both Ashmore (1970) and Wilder (1981) add that generalization of such positive consequences of multiple contacts follows from the fact that repeated instances of such experiences are more difficult than single occurrences to dismiss as oddities or exceptions to the rule. Rose (1981) also points out that novelty may function as an obstacle to positive contact effects, with multiple exposures functioning to decrease its influence.

Given the not-uncommon high levels of intergroup mistrust, hostility and discrimination which exist in real-world contexts, it is not surprising that for intergroup contact to have beneficial effects, multiple exposures appear necessary. It may well be, as Pettigrew (1981) suggests, that single exposures, at best, yield subtle, latent effects that are likely to accumulate and become manifest only after repeated contacts.

INSTITUTIONAL SUPPORT

As Allport (1954) concluded, subsequent research has affirmed the view that intergroup contact sanctioned by law, custom, community climate, outside authority, institutional norms favoring intergroup equality, or other significant social or institutional means is more likely to yield reductions in out-group bias and misperception than occurs when such support is weak or lacking. Institutional support, Slavin (1985) suggests, may function in this facilitative manner to the degree that it relieves the in-group members themselves from having to make intergroup contact a legitimate activity and thus may help overcome their reluctance to initiate such contact efforts. In addition to legitimization, such support has been shown in school desegregation contexts to lead to an array of procontact teacher activities. Epstein (1985), for example, examined teacher attitudes in 94 desegregating elementary schools and found:

> Results suggest that positive attitudes toward integration influence teachers' selection of grouping practices that promote student interaction, such as active learning and equal-status programs. Negative attitudes toward integration, or teachers' beliefs in separate education for Blacks and Whites, promote their use of less flexible, resegregative practices, such as tracking and within-class grouping. (p. 23)

A number of earlier studies, such as those by Johnson, Gerard, and Miller (1975) and the National Opinion Research Center (1973), report similar results, underscoring the central importance of broad, relevant support in order that intergroup contact experiences be instituted and yield positive effects.

COOPERATIVE CONTACT

Cooperative contact, in contrast to that characterized by competition or independence, appears to foster conflict-reducing, individuating consequences of intergroup contact. Such positive effects are more likely when (1) the cooperative endeavor results in success, rather than failure; (2) when there are multiple, rather than single cooperative contacts; and (3) when the individual personality characteristics of the parties to the interaction are characterized by trust, openmindedness, equalitarianism, and a high need for achievement, rather than dogmatism, authoritarianism, suspicion, and Machiavellianism. Factors which maintain group boundaries despite cooperative encounters will inhibit positive contact effects. According to Worchel (1979), such factors may include distinctive physical or visible differences between in-group and out-group members, the intensity of previous conflict between the groups, and disparities in their relative power.

Examples of desirable outcomes following from intergroup cooperative contact, in the form of joint striving to achieve superordinate goals, were examined in detail in Chapter 6, as we presented the Sherif et al. (1961) camp studies. Considerable additional research confirming this general finding has subsequently emerged, largely in the context of cooperative learning in educational settings. Both cross-ethnic interactions in desegregation research (DeVries, Edwards, & Slavin, 1978; Slavin, 1977; Slavin & Oickle, 1981) and cross-handicapped interactions in mainstreaming research (Johnson & Johnson, 1975; Martino & Johnson, 1979; Rynders, Johnson, Johnson, & Schmidt, 1980) are significantly enhanced by the shared experience of cooperative learning. Unfortunately, such research findings notwithstanding, most classroom intergroup interaction in the

United States fails to benefit from this facilitator of contact effects. As Slavin (1985) observes, with the exception of athletics, most school-based contact is anything but cooperative:

> Black, Anglo, Hispanic, and other groups compete for grades, for teacher approval, for places on the student council, or on the cheerleading squad. Interaction between students of different ethnic groups is usually of a superficial nature. In the classroom, the one setting in which students of different races or ethnicities are likely to be at least sitting side by side, traditional instructional methods permit little contact between students that is not superficial. Otherwise, Black, Anglo, and Hispanic students usually ride different buses to different neighborhoods, participate in different kinds of activities, and go to different social functions. Thus, opportunities for positive intergroup interaction are limited. One major exception is sports; sports teams create conditions of cooperation and nonsuperficial contact among team members. Correlational research by Slavin and Madden (1979) has shown that students who participate in sports in desegregated high schools are much more likely to have friends outside of their own race group and to have positive racial attitudes than students who do not participate in integrated sports teams. Sports teams fulfill the requirements of contact theory, in that interaction among teammates tends to be nonsuperficial, cooperative, and of equal status. (p. 47)

INDIVIDUAL CHARACTERISTICS

It is clearly not only qualities of the contact experience itself (cooperative versus competitive, single versus multiple, casual versus intimate, etc.) which determine its positive or negative consequences, but also qualities of the participants themselves. One such quality is obvious and perhaps needs little elaboration: the level of intensity of prejudicial belief held toward the out-group. But there are other, somewhat more subtle or less direct, individual member qualities which also apparently influence the degree to which intergroup contact ameliorates or worsens in-group favoritism, out-group bias, and the like. One is the group member's cognitive complexity, that is, his or her ability to integrate information complexly, and to make fine and even subtle discriminations:

> An individual with a relatively simple structure is likely to make simplistic black-white categorizations....The relatively complex person should be more tolerant of ambiguity, less rigid, and better able to handle exceptions to rules. (Wilder, 1986, pp. 58–59)

Cognitive complexity, in turn, is substantially influenced by the individual's arousal level. As Kahneman and Tversky (1973) have shown, as arousal increases, so, too, does the restriction of attention to fine discriminations (e.g., among out-group members) as more of the individual's effort is spent monitoring and coping with the arousal. In an intergroup contact situation, if the in-group member anticipates an unpleasant experience, his or her arousal (anxiety) may be particularly high. Stephan and Brigham (1985) suggest in this regard that

> high levels of intergroup anxiety lead to amplified behavioral responses, increased reliance on information-processing biases, intensified self-awareness, and augmented emotional reactions to outgroup members. [This] model helps explain why the absence of the conditions outlined in the contact hypothesis (i.e., unequal status, competition, and lack of support by authority figures) have [sic] negative effects on intergroup relations: their absence creates anxiety. A clear implication of the model is that contact situations should be designed to minimize anxiety. (p. 6)

The group member's level of self-esteem is apparently one further relevant individual characteristic. Wagner and Schonbach (1984) suggest that low self-esteem may increase the importance of group identification for the individual, as his or her means of establishing a positive social identity. Such persons may be particularly uninfluenced by intergroup contact experiences, as their strongly maintained group identification perpetuates their needed sense of separateness and differentiation.

In addition to cognitive complexity, arousal level, and self-esteem, the degree to which the group member utilizes biased information processing will impact upon the perception and sequelae of the intergroup contact. Wilder (1986) proposes that such biases can be minimized in a number of ways:

1. By making the positive actions of out-group member(s) as salient as possible, in order to minimize the in-group member's reliance on stereotypes and categorical expectations.
2. By making the behavior of the out-group member(s) consistently positive across a variety of settings, in order to minimize "exception-to-the-rule" discounting of the behavior as an unusual or chance event.
3. By tailoring the positive behaviors of the out-group member(s) so as to increase their appeal to the in-group members, in order to maximize the personalism of the contact experience.
4. By dissociating the positive behaviors of the out-group member(s) from any benefit or gain they could receive from such actions, in order to minimize suspicion of insincerity of attributions of manipulativeness.
5. By providing personal information about or otherwise individuating the out-group member(s) in order to enhance the possibility of an empathic response by members of the in-group.
6. By emphasizing the typicalness of the out-group member(s) contacted to the out-group as a whole, in order to maximize the generalization of perception and behavior by members of the in-group to the full out-group.

A CASE HISTORY: CONTACT PLUS FACILITATIVE
CONDITIONS

Much of what we have had to say regarding the conditions whose presence is facilitative of constructive consequences as a result of the contact experience is illustrated in the following brief case history, drawn from Fox (1970), of a "live-in" contact event between police and gang youth in Philadelphia. The apparent success of the experience, the research we have reviewed would suggest, may well be a result, in large part, of the structure of the contact involved, namely, equal status (within the experience), multiple exposures that were intimate rather than casual, and the cooperative nature of both its planning and its implementation.

The precontact intergroup attitudes of members of both groups, police and gang youth, were singularly negative. Fox (1970) comments:

> A common bond between all the aggressive teenage gang members in Philadelphia is their undisguised and unadulterated hatred of the police. Nowhere was this more pronounced than in the Tioga section of North Philadelphia, where three gangs defended their turf and corners against all comers, including the cops. To them, the policemen were pigs. To the police, the undisciplined and defiant kids were "fresh punks." And in between was a mutual disrespect, distrust and actual dislike. (p. 26)

Members of the business, home, and school community in which the youths resided and the police patrolled believed that an in-depth contact experience between the two groups would foster improved relationships and in-community behavior, and they proceeded to secure the funding and other arrangements necessary to carry it out. Contact began with a series of three planning meetings, to which the nine youth-gang planners and the nine "most hated" police officers they nominated were invited. With initial suspicion and intergroup hostility, a live-in weekend at a retreat estate 20 miles from Philadelphia was agreed upon. The 9 officers and 25 gang youths were invited to attend.

At the beginning of the three-day experience, considerable hostility, exchanges of accusations, and intergroup distance largely characterized the police–youth interactions. But slowly, over the course of a series of structured and unstructured combined-group activities, attitudes and behavior began to change. An attitudes-disclosing game was played, in which participants could share their views about drinking, violence, legalizing marijuana, the Black Panthers, abortion, and other salient matters. Police–youth relations were energetically discussed. Meals were shared. Informal football and basketball games emerged; informal rap sessions were held. Some of the youths were given rides on one of the officer's new motorcycles. Three police–youth work groups were formed, and each

proceeded to engage in a series of role reversal exercises in which hypothetical police–youth confrontations were structured and the participants
had to respond—police as gang youths, gang youths as police. Girlfriends
of the youths were bussed in for a Saturday evening dance. On Sunday,
further police–youth discussions were held, and an elaborate formal dinner took place. As part of the ceremony accompanying the dinner

> the oldest, biggest and most experienced policeman stood up. Marty Meredith
> had been hated and ridiculed when he arrived. Now you could sense a glow of
> respect and a tinge of liking from the boys at the adjoining tables. "All I got to
> say is this," Marty smiled. "It was better than I thought it would be. I got a chance
> to know you. You got a chance to know me." He paused and then continued,
> "I'm only one cop, but when I go back to the district I'll tell the others about this.
> You're only a part of all the kids in Tioga. I hope when you go back to the corner
> you'll talk to the others, especially the younger ones." With a sober expression,
> he ended, "There's been enough hate, fights and problems between us. Let's try
> to live together in peace." (Fox, 1970, p. 235)

GENERALIZATION OF CONTACT-INDUCED CHANGE

As noted earlier, largely as a function of the degree to which the
several conditions just considered are present or absent, intergroup contact
may be for better or worse. When absent, contact may increase, not decrease, intergroup tension. (Mis)perceptions may appear confirmed, dis-
like may intensify, trust may diminish, and conflict or even aggression may
result. Or with the wind of facilitative conditions in its sails, intergroup
contact may augment perceived similarity, demystify the unfamiliar or
seemingly strange, diminish tension, increase trust, and reduce the likelihood of conflict or aggression. Out of the laboratory, the real world of
intergroup contact is often *not* buttressed by these facilitative conditions,
and thus it is unfortunately the case that such contact very often is for
worse, and not a conflict-reducing or aggression-reducing force:

> ...Intergroup contact per se has only questionable value for reducing prejudice
> unless it is accompanied by an equal status between the participants—accom-
> panied, if possible, by cooperative relations and supported by institutional
> norms. The rub, however, is that prejudice itself is a major obstacle to creating
> opportunities for equal-status cooperative contact. It leads ingroup members to
> keep outgroup members down, to preserve not only distance but also inequal-
> ity. (Stephan & Brigham, 1985, p. 1)

> The classic prescription for reducing prejudice is intergroup contact, under
> conditions of equal status, common goals, cooperation, and moderate intimacy.
> Unfortunately, the in-group/out-group literature indicates that these very con-
> ditions are difficult to create as soon as people categorize each other into "us"
> and "them." Out-groups are perceived as inferior, as adversaries, as competi-
> tive, and as different from one's own group. (Taylor & Fiske, 1981, p. 166)

In the remainder of this chapter, we wish to consider those factors which augment or diminish the likelihood that the positive consequences following from intergroup contact will generalize to the out-group as a whole.

As noted above, a substantial amount of research supports the conclusion that the positive consequences of intergroup contact, when they do occur *within* the contact experience, often fail to generalize beyond that contact setting to the larger out-group (e.g., Amir, 1969; Wilder & Thompson, 1980; Wilder, 1984). The extent to which generalization occurs may be a function of the manner in which the contact experience is structured. Brewer and Miller (1984) urge that it be *interpersonally* oriented, that the category or group to which the other belongs should be deemphasized. In this manner, the in-group member will, they believe, be more able to perceptually decategorize the out-group member—as it were, see him or her more as an individual and less as one of "them." Brown and Turner (1981), in direct contrast, assert that the out-group member's category should be stressed in the contact situation, in order to decrease the likelihood that the in-group member will, as Allport (1954) put it, "re-fence the group" and perceive the other as "an exception to the rule," as a person whose positive qualities bear little implication for the perception of the out-group as an entity. Interestingly, both sets of investigators—Brewer and Miller, who wish to minimize the salience of the out-group member's group membership, and Brown and Turner, who wish to maximize it— take their respective positions as a means of promoting generalization of the new, positive contact-caused perceptions to the out-group as a whole. As Ben-Ari and Amir (1986), Pettigrew (1981), and others note, ample theoretical and research support exists for both positions, and it appears to us not unlikely that research may eventually demonstrate that a combination of personalizing and categorical structuring will prove optimal for the promotion of generalization.

Other facets of the structure of the intergroup contact experience have also been suggested as relevant to the generalization of its effects. Cook (1978) proposes:

> Attitude change will result from cooperative interracial contact only when such contact is accompanied by a supplementary influence that promotes the process of generalization from favorable contact with individuals to positive attitudes toward [their] group. (p. 103)

Such supplementary influence, Cook proposed, might in particular take the form of support of the new attitude toward the out-group by members of the perceivers' peer (in)-group. Peer support offered in this manner, Cook believed, might serve as a generalization-enhancing "cognitive booster." Other such boosters, according to Hewstone and Brown

(1986), may include (1) establishing superordinate goals, to potentiate the generalization of contact effects by, in effect, creating a new, combined in-group; (2) encouraging cross-cutting group memberships, making sure that such alternative categories do not correspond to the original in-group–out-group division; and (3) manipulating the generalizability expectancies of the parties to the contact.

Yet generalization of contact-induced gains is not only a function of aspects of the contact experience itself and is not only influenced by qualities of the out-group whose member(s) were contacted. The macro-context of the intergroup contact also looms large. The seed may be healthy and the rain generous, but the soil infertile. A wider society characterized by Balkanization, polarization, fractiousness, racist norms, and other mani-festations of and support for us-versus-them structuring, is not likely to be receptive to the growth and spread of contact-induced intergroup har-mony. Yet one ought not go too far in assigning potency for intergroup change too singularly to macrolevel alteration, as perhaps Racher (1986) does:

> racism will not be overcome through individual acts, which leave the racist structure of British society intact, but only through action to change the nature of that society. It will not change by contact, but by collective action. (p. 167)

We would hold, contrariwise, that a combination of individual action, such as provided by the contact experience, and collective structural change—in such domains as employment, housing, politics, the media, immigration—will be the most promotive of positive intergroup conse-quences. The outcomes of desegregation in the United States, reflecting both macro (school, school district) and individual (student contact) altera-tions are one major positive (if mixed) example (e.g., Higher Education Research Institute, 1980; National Center for Educational Statistics, 1981; Ohio State University Center for Human Resource Research, 1981; Scott & McPartland, 1982; Stephan & Rosenfeld, 1979). We are in accord with Hewstone and Brown (1986), who concluded their book *Contact and Conflict in Intergroup Encounters* by urging the combining of microlevel (contact) and macrolevel (societal) level change:

> The message of this book is that intergroup contact can play a role in improving intergroup relations in society, but that the contact hypothesis as traditionally conceived is too narrow and limited. To create the conditions for truly successful intergroup contact, more radical social changes are a prerequisite. For exam-ple...blacks and other oppressed groups must seek a share of power; members of majority groups secure in *their* identity must learn the value and integrity of *other* groups or cultures....These changes will not come easily and will have to be fought for on many fronts. (p. 42)

We have considered the role of intergroup contact in promoting intergroup harmony. Early overenthusiasm for its potency was tempered by research demonstrating that its positive consequences are facilitated or diminished by a number of conditions in which the contact may be embedded. These include the relative status equality of the participants; the intimacy, frequency, and cooperativeness of their meetings; relevant social or institutional norms; and a number of individual qualities of the contacting in-group and out-group members. Even when such conditions are present, and thus favorable for constructive outcomes, whether such outcomes will generalize beyond the parties involved in the contact experience itself to the larger groups they in effect represent is itself a function of several influences. These may be factors characterizing the contact event itself, such as its interpersonal versus intergroup focus. Or generalization may be encouraged or impeded by macrolevel forces, particularly the levels of prejudice, racism, polarization, and other broad manifestations of us-versus-them belief and behavior operative in the larger society.

Intergroup contact, in sum, is viewed by us not as a panacea, not as *the* cure-all for intergroup disharmony, but as one useful, demonstrably effective part of a broader, multifaceted strategy for the reduction of in-group–out-group conflict and aggression and the promotion of in-group–out-group harmony.

PART V

CONCLUSION

CHAPTER 10

FUTURE DIRECTIONS

The term *ecology* derives from the Greek *oikas* (household or living place) and in its original usage was employed in the natural sciences, especially biology, as a description of organism–environment interaction. An explicitly human ecology developed as a branch of sociology, largely through the work of Robert Park and his University of Chicago group starting in 1914. In the present book, we have been concerned with both usages: place and person. Thus, theory and research dealing with both the physical and the social environment have been explored, as they conjointly impact upon the behaviors of concern to this book: aggression and crime. We have considered sites, neighborhoods, and regions; victims, groups, and mobs; environmental design and interpersonal contact. There remain yet other crime-relevant and aggression-relevant constructs and concerns that have characteristically not been, but might profitably be, viewed through person–environment interactional glasses. In this final chapter, we wish to briefly highlight these additional avenues of potentially valuable exploration.

PREDICTION OF CRIME AND AGGRESSION

An enduring problem in criminology, forensic psychology, penology, and other disciplines seeking to predict dangerousness, violence, recidivism, or, more generally, crime and aggression is the persistent difficulty in doing so accurately. Success rates are quite modest; false-positive rates are substantial (American Psychiatric Association, 1974; Cooke, 1986; Kozol, Boucher, & Garofalo, 1972; Megargee, 1982; Monahan, 1981). Inspection of the predictors employed has, with very rare exceptions, revealed the almost singular use of person (perpetrator) qualities (Loeber & Stouthamer-Loeber, 1987; Steadman, 1982). The question, "Will he do it again?" is addressed by examining *perpetrator* demographic, historical, and institutional behavior and psychological test data (Clarke, 1989; Clum, 1975; Dietz, 1985; Farrington, 1985; Gottfredson & Gottfredson, 1985; Hill, 1985; Wilbanks, 1985). In spite of calls to conceptualize and implement such predictions in a person–environment manner, in a manner responsive to *both* who the perpetrator is and where, with whom, and under what external conditions he or she will function (Cohen, Groth, & Siegel, 1978; Gabor, 1986; Loeber & Stouthamer-Loeber, 1987; Monahan & Klassen, 1982; Moos, 1975; Norton, 1988), such calls have rarely been heeded. It is a difficult task, for, among other prerequisites, we are still lacking in utilitarian taxonomies for classifying ecological characteristics in a functionally useful manner—though some excellent beginnings have been made in this regard (Argyle, Furnham, & Graham, 1981; Frederickson, 1972; Moos, 1974; Schoggen, 1989).

To reiterate and concretize this call and its necessity, we note that the prediction of aggressive and criminal behavior has proven accurate in approximately one prediction out of three on average (Megargee, 1982; Monahan, 1981), and about 40 per cent of the time at best (Kozol, Boucher, & Garofalo, 1972), at least in large part, we believe, because the predictors employed have almost exclusively been *person* characteristics such as time in prison, felony convictions, past probation/parole violations, employment/marital history, and prison punishments (Wilbanks, 1985); days lost for disciplinary infractions, California Personality Inventory scale scores, increase in academic achievement during confinement, custody-level reductions during confinement, and efforts to secure employment during parole period (Hill, 1985); age at admission, age at discharge, previous convictions, type of offense, education, previous occupation, Wechsler Adult Intelligence scores, and MMPI scores (Black & Spinks, 1985); commitment offense, dollar value of offense, age at first arrest, longest time free since first commitment, number of prior convictions, number of prior probation/parole revocations, marital/employment status at admission, and escape history (Gottfredson & Gottfredson, 1985); and teacher/peer ratings of troublesomeness, teacher/peer ratings of daring, teacher/parent ratings of conduct disorder, family background (income, housing, size), Maudsley Inventory scores (extroversion, neuroticism, lying), and nonverbal IQ (Farrington, 1985). Needed are classification systems of a variously labeled ecological (Schoggen, 1989), situational (Clarke, 1989), contextual (Steadman, 1982), environmental (Gabor, 1986), and circumstantial (Loeber & Stouthamer-Loeber, 1987) nature which combine such person data with both such microlevel information as the standing patterns of behavior expected in and characteristic of the diverse sites the individual is likely to frequent (Frederickson, 1972; Schoggen, 1989) and macrolevel classification of broader, more encompassing environments (Argyle et al., 1981; Moos, 1974). A useful operationalization of this proposal has been provided by Monahan and Klassen (1982), who urge the predictive use of data reflecting the perpetrator's, or potential perpetrator's, family, peer, and job environments and the availability of victims, weapons, and alcohol. A small but significant beginning in acting upon this operationalizaiton has been made by Gottfredson and Gottfredson (1985), who found that the likelihood of recidivism posed by parolees released back into 90 neighborhoods in Baltimore was in part explainable by the level of each neighborhood's incivilities and deterioration.

Our person–environment interactional perspective on the prediction of crime and aggression is well summarized by Gabor (1986), who notes:

> A major factor undermining prediction is the situational element in all human behavior—the effects on behavior of such things as the physical environment, provocations, and the presence of drugs, alcohol, and weapons. Studies dealing with this element have merely attempted to determine the independent effects of situational factors on behavior. Because an individual's personality will affect his or her choice of situations, as well as his or her reaction to these, situational and personality variables must be viewed in concert. Thus, the likely outcomes of the exposure of varying persons to varying situations must be determined. More difficult, still, is the anticipation of the situations a person will actually encounter. (p. 79)

> The effect of the environment and specific situations on behavior may vary from one offender to the next. While hard-core or pathological offenders might commit crimes regardless of the conditions in which they live, most offenders are probably responsive to changes in their circumstances. As Walker (1980) has said, there are opportunity-makers and opportunity-takers. The more offenders there are in the latter category, the more relevant is the situational factor in criminological prediction. (p. 88)

AUDIENCE EFFECTS

In addition to the facilitation of more reliable prediction, what else is available in the relevant literature that at least hints at other potentially viable avenues for understanding and moderating crime and aggression via person–environment interactional means? Audience effects are likely to be one such avenue, in this instance of concern in the social ecology of both individual and collective antisocial behavior. Zajonc (1976) and Fisher (1976) provided evidence demonstrating such social facilitation consequences in individual behavior from the presence of others. Cottrell, Sekerak, Wack, and Rittle (1968) proposed, and Klinger (1969) confirmed in his study of audience impact, that it was not the mere presence of others that appeared to influence performance, but instead the performer's perception that the audience was a potential source of positive or negative evaluation of his or her performance. When others were present but could not evaluate the performer's responses, no effects on quality of performance were found. Consistent with such a finding, Toch (1980) comments with regard to one common manifestation of aggression:

> Public violence is violence that makes a point for consumption, or seeks to do so. The point is something like, "Look how tough I am," or "You can see, nobody fools with me," or "Guess who is in charge around here?" Where violence is the medium for such messages, spectators are a requisite; where there is no audience the show closes. (p. 32)

Borden (1975) and Cratty (1981) have replicated this finding of a facilitative influence of the presence of an audience on aggressive behavior. It is also quite relevant to the ecological theme of this book to note in parallel with this finding that the presence of an audience—through processes of social influence, inhibition, and diffusion of responsibility—has generally been shown to decrease the likelihood that an individual will engage in helping behavior in emergency situations (Bickman, 1971; Clark & Word, 1972; Latane & Dabbs, 1975; Latane & Darley, 1970).

OTHER ECOLOGICAL ANTECEDENTS

Other features of the physical and social context may, in interaction with person characteristics, serve to influence the likelihood of aggressive behaviors and thus well deserve further investigative scrutiny. The presence of weapons is clearly one such characteristic, as suggested by the "weapons effect" notion that under certain cuing circumstances, the "trigger pulls the finger," i.e., the stimulus pull of the sheer presence of a gun, via its regular association with aggressive responding, may yield arousal consequences which are aggression-promoting (Berkowitz, 1993; Berkowitz & LePage, 1970; Carlson, Marcus-Newhall, & Miller, 1990; Turner, Simons, Berkowitz, & Frodi, 1977). The clothing worn by potential perpetrators (Frank & Gilovich, 1988) and by potential victims (Lavender, 1987) may, respectively, encourage or discourage aggressive behavior. Other ecological influences are undoubtedly operative, are probably impactful in their consequences, but are yet to be fully identified and evaluated.

In 1981, Argyle et al. wrote:

> Perhaps one of the most confused, ambiguous and least researched branches of modern psychology is the social and physical context in which behavior occurs, and its effects on behavior. (p. 12)

We hope the present book can serve as a useful addition toward reducing such confusion and ambiguity, and also as a bridge to the next tasks in this domain. Andrews (1985) has sought to explore the linkages between and among microlevel, mesolevel, and macrolevel ecological variables. His fine beginning strongly encourages continued efforts. Craik and McKechnie (1974) have proposed a merging of concepts from personality theory and environmental psychology toward what they label "environmental dispositions"; Cohen and Land (1987) have sought to concretize this challenge by offering a merger of person-oriented control theory and environment-oriented criminal opportunity theory; and both Clarke and Felson (1993) and Kennedy and Baron (1993), in the same person–environment interactional spirit, have presented a beginning blending of rational-choice and routine-activity theories. A fine start has been made. There remains much person–environment work to be done.

REFERENCES

Abadinsky, H. (1979). *Social service in criminal justice*. Englewood Cliffs, NJ: Prentice-Hall.

Abbott, E. (1927). The Civil War and the crime wave of 1865–1870. *Social Service Review, 1*, 212–234.

Akers, R. L. (1985). *Deviant behavior*. Belmont, CA: Wadsworth.

Albrecht, T. L., & Adelman, M. B. (1987). *Communication and social support*. Newbury Park, CA: Sage.

Alexander, F., & Healy, W. (1935). *Roots of crime*. New York: Knopf.

Allen, N. H. (1980). *Homicide: Perspectives on prevention*. New York: Human Sciences Press.

Allport, F. H. (1924). *Social psychology*. Boston: Houghton Mifflin.

Allport, G. W. (1954). *The nature of prejudice*. Cambridge/Reading, MA: Addison-Wesley.

Altman, I., & Chemers, M. (1980a). *Culture and environment*. Monterey, CA: Brooks/Cole.

Altman, I., & Chemers, M. (1980b). Personal space. In I. Altman & M. Chemers (eds.), *Culture and environment* (pp. 101–119). New York: Cambridge University Press.

Altman, J., & Zube, E. (1987). *Neighborhood and community environments*. New York: Plenum.

Altman, I., Brown, B. B., Staples, B., & Werner, C. M. (1992). A transactional approach to close relationships: Courtship, weddings, and placemaking. In W. B. Walsh, K. H. Craik, & R. H. Price (Eds.), *Person–environment psychology: Models and perspectives*. Hillsdale, NJ: Erlbaum.

American Humane Society. (1986). *The national study on child neglect and abuse reporting*. Denver: Author.

American Psychiatric Association. (1974). *Clinical aspects of the violent individual*. Washington, DC: Author.

American School Health Association. (1989). *National adolescent student health survey*. Denver: Author.

Amir, M. (1971). *Patterns of forcible rape*. Chicago: University of Chicago Press.

Amir, Y. (1969). Contact hypothesis in ethnic relations. *Psychological Bulletin, 71*, 319–342.

Ammerman, R. T., Cassisi, J. E., Hersen, M., & Van Hasselt, V. B. (1986). Consequences of physical abuse and neglect in children. *Clinical Psychology Review, 6*, 291–310.

153

Anderson, C. A. (1987). Temperature and aggression: Effects on quarterly, yearly, and city rates of violent and nonviolent crime. *Journal of Personality and Social Psychology, 52,* 1161–1173.

Anderson, C. A. (1989). Temperature and aggression: Ubiquitous effects of heat on occurrence of human violence. *Psychological Bulletin, 106,* 74–96.

Andrews, H. F. (1985). The ecology of risk and the geography of intervention: From research to practice for the health and well-being of urban children. *Annals of the Association of American Geographers, 75,* 370–382.

Angel, S. (1968). *Discouraging crime through city planning.* Berkeley: University of California Press.

Angyal, A. (1959). *Foundations for a science of personality.* Cambridge, MA: Harvard University Press.

Appleton, J. (1975). *The experience of place.* London: Wiley.

Arbuthnot, J., & Gordon, D. A. (1987). Personality. In H. C. Quay (Ed.), *Handbook of juvenile delinquency.* New York: Wiley.

Archer, D., & Gartner, R. (1984). *Violence and crime in cross-national perspective.* New Haven, CT: Yale University Press.

Ardrey, R. (1966). *The territorial imperative.* New York: Atheneum.

Argyle, M., Furnham, A. & Graham, J. A. (1981). The analysis of social situations. In M. Argyle, A. Furnham, & J. A. Graham (Eds.), *Social situations.* New York: Cambridge University Press.

Ashmore, R. D. (1970). Solving the problem of prejudice. In B. E. Collins (Ed.), *Social psychology.* Reading, MA: Addison-Wesley.

Atlas, R. I. (1982). *Violence in prison: Architectural determinism.* Dissertation. Florida State University.

Aultman, M. G., & Wilford, C. F. (1978). Towards an integrated model of delinquency causation: An empirical analysis. *Sociology and Social Research, 63,* 316–327.

Bailey, W. C. (1976). Some further evidence on homicide and a regional culture of violence. *Omega, 2,* 145–170.

Baker, R. K., & Ball, S. J. (Eds.) (1969). *Violence and the media.* Washington, DC: U.S. Government Printing Office.

Baldassare, M. (1979). *Residential crowding in urban America.* Berkeley: University of California Press.

Baldwin, J., & Bottoms, A. E. (1976). *The urban criminal: A study in Sheffield.* London: Tavistock.

Ban, J. R., & Ciminillo, L. M. (1977). *Violence and vandalism in public education.* Danville, IL: Interstate Printers & Publishers.

Bandura, A. (1973). *Aggression: A social learning analysis.* Englewood Cliffs, NJ: Prentice-Hall.

Barak-Glantz, I. L. (1985). The anatomy of another prison riot. In M. Braswell, S. Dillingham, & R. Montgomery, Jr. (Eds.), *Prison violence in America* (pp. 47–71). Cincinnati, OH: Anderson.

Barker, R. G., & Gump, P. (1964). *Big school, small school.* Stanford, CA: Stanford University Press.

Barker, R. G., & Wright, H. F. (1954). *Midwest and its children.* New York: Harper & Row.

Baron, R. A. (1977). *Human aggression.* New York: Plenum.

Baron, R. A., & Bell, P. A. (1975). Aggression and heat: Mediating effects of prior provocation and exposure to an aggressive model. *Journal of Personality and Social Psychology, 31,* 825–832.

Barr, R., & Pease, K. (1990). Crime placement, displacement and deflection. In M. Tonry & N. Morris (Eds.), *Crime and justice: A review of research,* Vol. 12. Chicago: University of Chicago Press.

Barrera, M. (1986). Distinctions between social support concepts, measures, and models. *American Journal of Community Psychology, 14,* 413–445.

Barry, R. (1969). To slug a meter: A study of coin frauds. *Criminologica, 6,* 4–9.

Bass, B. M. & Dunteman, G. (1963). Biases in the evaluation of one's own group, its allies and opponents. *Journal of Conflict Resolution, 7,* 16–20.

Baum, A., & Valins, S. (1979). *Architecture and social behavior: Psychological studies of social density.* Hillsdale, NJ: Erlbaum.

Baumgartner, M. P. (1993). Violent networks: The origins and management of domestic conflict. In R. B. Felson & J. T. Tedeschi (Eds.), *Aggression and violence: Social interactionist perspectives.* Washington, DC: American Psychological Association.

Bayh, B. (1975, April). *Our nation's school—A report card: "A" in school violence and vandalism.* Washington, DC: Preliminary Report of the Subcommittee to Investigate Juvenile Delinquency, U.S. Senate.

Beasley, R. W., & Antunes, C. (1974). The etiology of urban crime: An ecological analysis. *Criminology, 11,* 439–461.

Becker, H. S. (1963). *Outsiders: Studies in the sociology of deviance.* Glencoe, IL: Free Press.

Bell, P. A. (1992). In defense of the negative affect escape model of heat and aggression. *Psychological Bulletin, 111,* 342–346.

Bell, R. G., & Harper, L. V. (Eds.). (1977). *Child effects on adults.* Hillsdale, NJ: Erlbaum.

Belle, D. (1989). *Children's social networks and social supports.* New York: Wiley.

Belsky, J. (1978). A theoretical analysis of child abuse remediation strategies. *Journal of Clinical Child Psychology, 7,* 117–121.

Ben-Ari, R., & Amir, Y. (1986). Contact between Arab and Jewish youth in Israel: Reality and potential. In M. Hewstone & R. Brown (Eds.), *Contact and conflict in intergroup encounters* (pp. 45–58). London: Basil Blackwell.

Bensing, R. S., & Schroeder, O. (1960). *Homicide in an urban community.* Springfield, IL: Charles C Thomas.

Berkowitz, L. (1962). *Aggression: A social psychological analysis.* New York: McGraw-Hill.

Berkowitz, L. (1972). Frustrations, comparisons, and other sources of emotion arousal as contributors to social unrest. *Journal of Social Issues, 28,* 77–91.

Berkowitz, L. (1983). Aversively stimulated aggression: Some parallels and differences in research with animals and humans. *American Psychologist, 38,* 1135–1144.

Berkowitz, L. (1989). The frustration-aggression hypothesis: An examination and reformulation. *Psychological Bulletin, 106,* 59–73.

Berkowitz, L. (1993). Guns and youth. In American Psychological Association, *Report of the American Psychological Association Commission on Youth Violence.* Washington, DC: American Psychological Association.

Berkowitz, L., & LePage, A. (1967). Weapons as aggression-eliciting stimuli. *Journal of Personality and Social Psychology, 7,* 202–207.

Berkowitz, L., & LePage, A. (1970). Weapons as aggression-eliciting stimuli. In E. I. Megargee & J. E. Hokanson (Eds.), *The dynamics of aggression*. New York: Harper & Row.

Berndt, T. J. (1989). Obtaining support from friends during childhood and adolescence. In D. Belle (Ed.), *Children's social networks and social supports*. New York: Wiley.

Bernstein, H. A. (1981). Survey of threats and assaults directed toward psychotherapists. *American Journal of Psychotherapy, 35,* 542–549.

Bickman, L. (1971). The effect of another bystander's ability to help on bystander intervention in an emergency. *Journal of Experimental Social Psychology, 7,* 367–379.

Billig, M. G. (1973). *Social psychology and intergroup relations*. London: Academic Press.

Billig, M. G., & Tajfel, H. (1973). Social categorization and similarity in intergroup behaviour. *European Journal of Social Psychology, 3,* 27–52.

Black, T., & Spinks, P. (1985). Predicting outcomes of mentally disordered and dangerous offenders. In D. P. Farington & R. Tarling (Eds.), *Prediction in criminology*. Albany: State University of New York Press.

Blake, R. R., & Mouton, J. S. (1961). Reactions to intergroup competition under win-lose conditions. *Management Scence, 7,* 420–435.

Blake, R. R., & Mouton, J. S. (1986). From theory to practice in intergroup problem solving. In S. Worchel & W. G. Austin (Eds.), *Psychology of intergroup relations*. Chicago: Nelson-Hall.

Blau, J., & Blau, P. (1982). The cost of inequality: Metropolitan structure and violent crime. *American Sociological Review, 47,* 114–129.

Block, A. (1977). The battered teacher. *Today's Education, 66,* 58–62.

Block, R. (1977). *Violent crime, environment, interaction and death*. Lexington, MA: Lexington Books.

Block, R. (1981). Victim-offender dynamics in violent crime. *Journal of Criminal Law and Criminology, 72,* 743–761.

Bluth, B. J. (1980). *Social and psychological problems of extended space mission*. Presented at American Institute of Aeronautics and Astronautics, Baltimore.

Boissevain, J., & Mitchell, J. C. (1973). *Network analysis: Studies in human interaction*. The Hague, Netherlands: Mouton.

Booth, A., & Edwards, P. (1976). *Urban crowding and its consequences*. New York: Praeger.

Borden, R. J. (1975). Witnessed aggression: Influence of an observer's sex and values on aggressive responding. *Journal of Personality and Social Psychology, 31,* 567–573.

Bowlby, J. (1949). *Why delinquency?* (Report of the Conference on the Scientific Study of Juvenile Delinquency). London: National Association for Mental Health.

Boyanowsky, E. O., Calvert, J., Young, J., & Brideau, L. (1981–1982). Toward a thermoregulatory model of violence. *Journal of Environmental Systems, 1,* 81–87.

Brantingham, P. J., & Brantingham, P. L. (1991). *Environmental criminology*. Newbury Park, CA: Sage.

Brantingham, P. L., Brantingham, P. J., & Wong, P. (1990). Malls and crime: A first look. *Security Journal, 1,* 175–181.

Brearly, H. C. (1932). *Homicide in the United States*. Montclair, NJ: Patterson-Smith.

Brenner, H. (1976). *Effects of the economy on criminal behavior and the administration of criminal justice in the United States, Canada, England, Wales and Scotland*. Rome: United Nations Social Defense Research Institute.

Brewer, M. B. (1979). Ingroup bias in the minimal intergroup situation: A cognitive-motivational analysis. *Psychological Bulletin, 86,* 307–324.

Brewer, M. B., & Miller, N. (1984). Beyond the contact hypothesis: Theoretical perspectives on desegregation. In N. Miller & M. B. Brewer (Eds.), *Groups in contact: The psychology of desegregation.* New York: Academic Press.

Brill, W. (1977). *Controlling access in highrise buildings: Approaches and guidelines.* Washington, DC: U.S. Government Printing Office.

Brim, J. A. (1974). Social network correlates of avowed happiness. *Journal of Nervous and Mental Disorders, 158,* 432–439.

Bronfenbrenner, U. (1977). Toward an experimental ecology of human development. *American Psychologist, 32,* 513–531.

Brower, R., Dockett, K., & Taylor, R. B. (1983). Residents' perceptions of territorial features and perceived local threat. *Environment and Behavior, 15,* 419–437.

Brown, B. B., & Altman, I. (1981). Territoriality and residential crime: A conceptual framework. In P. J. Brantingham & P. L. Brantingham (Eds.), *Environmental criminology.* Newbury Park, CA: Sage.

Brown, E., Flanagan, T., & McLeod, M. (Eds.). (1984). *Sourcebook of criminal justice statistics—1983.* Washington, DC: U.S. Government Printing Office.

Brown, R. J. & Ross, G. F. (1982). The battle for acceptance: An investigation into the dynamics of intergroup behaviour. In H. Tajfel (Ed.), *Social identity and intergroup relations.* New York: Cambridge University Press.

Brown, R., & Turner, J. C. (1981). Interpersonal and intergroup behaviour. In J. Turner & H. Giles (Eds.), *Intergroup behaviour.* Oxford: Basil Blackwell.

Brownell, A., & Shumaker, S. A. (1985). Where do we go from here? The policy implications of social support. *Journal of Social Issues, 41,* 111–121.

Bruner, J. S. (1957). On perceptual readiness. *Psychological Review, 64,* 123–151.

Buford, B. (1991). *Among the thugs: The experience, and the seduction of crowd violence.* New York: W. W. Norton.

Bullock, H. A. (1955). Urban homicide in theory and fact. *Journal of Criminal Law, Criminology and Police Science, 45,* 567–575.

Bureau of Justice Statistics. (1992). *Criminal victimization in the United States, 1991.* Washington, DC: U.S. Government Printing Office.

Buret, E. (1842). *De la misère des classes laborieuses en Angleterre et en France.* Cited in R. D. Hunter. (1988). *The relationship of selected environmental characteristics to the incidence of convenience store robbery within the State of Florida.* Unpublished doctoral dissertation, Florida State University.

Burgess, R. L., & Conger, R. D. (1978). Family interactions in abusive, neglectful, and normal families. *Child Development, 49,* 1163–1173.

Bursik, R. J., Jr. (1986). Delinquency rates as sources of ecological change. In J. M. Byrne & R. J. Sampson (Eds.), *The social ecology of crime* (pp. 63–74). New York: Springer-Verlag.

Burton, R. (1963). The generality of honesty reconsidered. *Psychological Review, 70,* 481–499.

Bushman, B. J., & Cooper, H. M. (1990). Effects of alcohol on human aggression: An integrative research review. *Psychological Bulletin, 107,* 341–354.

Buss, A. H. (1961). *The psychology of aggression.* New York: Wiley.

Byrne, J. M. (1986). Cities, citizens, and crime: The ecological/non-ecological debate reconsidered. In J. M. Byrne & R. J. Sampson (Eds.), *The social ecology of crime* (pp. 77–101). New York: Springer-Verlag.

Calhoun, L. G., Selby, J. W., Cann, A., & Keller, G. T. (1978). The effects of victim physical attractiveness and sex of respondent on social reactions to victims of rape. *British Journal of Social and Clinical Psychology, 17,* 191–192.

Campbell, A. (1986). The streets and violence. In A. Campbell & J. J. Gibbs (Eds.), *Violent transactions: The limits of personality* (pp. 115–132). Oxford: Basil Blackwell.

Campbell, D. E. (1982). Lunar-lunacy research: When enough is enough. *Environment and Behavior, 14,* 418–424.

Campbell, D. T. (1958). Common fate, similarity and other indices of the status of aggregates of persons as social entities. *Behavioural Science, 3,* 14–25.

Caplan, G. (1974). *Support systems and community mental health: Lectures on concept development.* New York: Behavioral Publications.

Capone, D. L., & Nichols, W. W., Jr. (1976). Urban structure and criminal mobility. *American Behavioral Scientist, 20,* 199–214.

Carlson, M., Marcus-Newhall, A., & Miller, N. (1990). Effects of situational aggression cues: A quantitative review. *Journal of Personality and Social Psychology, 58,* 622–633.

Carroll, L., & Jackson, P. I. (1983). Inequality, opportunity, and crime rates in central cities. *Criminology, 21,* 178–194.

Carter, R. L., & Hill, K. Q. (1980). Area-images and behavior: An alternative perspective for understanding urban crime. In D. E. Georges-Abeyie & K. D. Harries (Eds.), *Crime: A spatial perspective* (pp. 193–204). New York: Columbia University Press.

Cash, W. (1941). *The mind of the South.* New York: Knopf.

Casserly, M. D., Bass, S. A., & Garrett, J. R. (1980). *School vandalism: Strategies for prevention.* Lexington, MA: Lexington Books.

Center to Prevent Handgun Violence. (1990). *Caught in the crossfire: A report on gun violence in our nation's schools.* Washington, DC: Center to Prevent Handgun Violence.

Cerbus, G. (1970). Seasonal variation in some mental health statistics: Suicides, homicides, psychiatric admissions, and institutional placement of the retarded. *Journal of Clinical Psychology, 26,* 60–63.

Chaiken, J., Lawless, M., & Stevenson, K. (1974). *The impact of police activity on crime: Robberies on the New York City subway system.* Report No. R-1424–N.Y.C. Santa Monica, CA: Rand Corporation.

Chaplin, J. P. (1985). *Dictionary of psychology* (2nd ed.). New York: Bantam Doubleday Dell.

Chase, L. J., & Mills, N. H. (1973). Status of frustration as a facilitator of aggression: A brief note. *Journal of Psychology, 84,* 225–226.

Cheatwood, D. (1988). Is there a season for homicide? *Criminology, 26,* 287–306.

Check, J. V. P., & Malamuth, N. M. (1983). Sex role stereotyping and reactions to depictions of stranger versus acquaintance rape. *Journal of Personality and Social Psychology, 45,* 344–356.

Chenoweth, R. E. (1977). *The effects of territorial markings on residents of two multifamily housing developments: A partial test of Newman's theory of defensible space.* Unpublished doctoral dissertation. University of Illinois.

Choldin, H., & Roncek, D. (1975). Density, population potential and pathology: A block-level analysis. *Public Data Use, 4,* 19–30.

Clark, R., & Word, L. (1972). Why don't bystanders help? Because of ambiguity? *Journal of Personality and Social Psychology, 24,* 392–400.

Clarke, R. V. (1989). Theoretical background to crime prevention through environmental design (CPTED) and situational prevention. In S. Geason & P. Wilson (Eds.), *Designing out crime.* Canberra: Australian Institute of Criminology.

Clarke, R. V. (1992). *Situational crime prevention: Successful case studies.* New York: Harrow & Heston.

Clarke, R. V., & Felson, M. (Eds.). (1993). *Routine activity and rational choice.* New Brunswick, NJ: Transaction.

Clifford, F. (1989). Traffic or no, we love our autos. *Los Angeles Times* (Oct. 4), pp. 1–3.

Clifton, W., Jr., & Callahan, P. T. (1987). *Convenience store robberies in Gainesville, Florida: An intervention strategy by the Gainesville Police Department.* Gainesville, FL: Gainesville Police Department.

Clum, G. A. (1975). Intrapsychic variables and the patient's environment as factors in prognosis. *Psychological Bulletin, 82,* 413–431.

Cobb, S. (1976). Social support as a moderator of life stress. *Psychosomatic Medicine, 38,* 300–314.

Cohen, J. (1941). The geography of crime. *Annals of the American Academy of Political and Social Science, 217,* 29–37.

Cohen, J. (1983). The relationship between friendship selection and peer influence. In J. L. Epstein & N. Karweit (Eds.) *Friends in school.* New York: Academic Press.

Cohen, L. E., & Felson, M. (1979). Social change and crime rate trends: A routine activity approach. *American Sociological Review, 44,* 588–608.

Cohen, L. E., & Land, K. C. (1987). Sociological positivism and the explanation of criminality. In M. R. Gottfredson & T. Hirschi (Eds.), *Positive criminology.* Newbury Park, CA: Sage.

Cohen, L. E., Kleugel, J., & Land, K. (1981). Social inequality and predatory crime victimization: An exposition and test of a formal theory. *American Sociological Review, 46,* 505–524.

Cohen, M. L., Groth, A. N., & Siegel, R. (1978). The clinical prediction of dangerousness. *Crime and Delinquency, 24,* 28–39.

Cohen, R., Poag, C. K., & Goodnight, J. A. (1982). The impact of physical setting on the adolescent. In S. W. Henggeler (Ed.), *Delinquency and adolescent psychopathology* (pp. 163–183). Boston: John Wright.

Cohen, S. (1971). Direction for research on adolescent school violence and vandalism. *British Journal of Criminology, 9,* 319–340.

Coleman, A. (1985). *Utopia on trial: Vision and reality in planned housing.* London: Hilary Shipman.

Colvin, M. (1982). The 1980 New Mexico prison riot. *Social Problems, 29,* 119–153.

Comstock, G. (1983). Media influences on aggression. In Center for Research on Aggression (Ed.), *Prevention and control of aggression.* New York: Pergamon.

Cook, S. W. (1978). Interpersonal and attitudinal outcomes in cooperating interracial groups. *Journal of Research and Development in Education, 12,* 97–113.

Cooke, M. (1986). *Social isolation and violent behavior.* Philadelphia: Temple University.

Cordilia, A. T. (1986). Robbery arising out of a group drinking context. In A. Campbell & J. J. Gibbs (Eds.), *Violent transaction: The limits of personality.* Oxford: Basil Blackwell.

Cortes, J. B., & Gatti, F. M. (1972). *Delinquency and crime.* New York: Seminar.

Cotton, J. L. (1986). Ambient temperature and violent crime. *Journal of Applied Social Psychology, 16,* 786–801.

Cottrell, N. B., Sekerak, A. J., Wack, D. L., & Rittle, R. H. (1968). Social facilitation of dominant responses by the presence of an audience and the mere presence of others. *Journal of Personality and Social Psychology, 9,* 245–250.

Craik, K. H., & McKechnie, G. E. (1974). *Perception of environmental quality: Preferential judgments versus comparative appraisals.* Unpublished manuscript, University of California, Berkeley.

Cratty, B. J. (1981). *Social psychology in athletics.* Englewood Cliffs, NJ: Prentice-Hall.

Cromwell, P. F., Olson, J. N., & Avary, D. W. (1991). *Breaking and entering: An ethnographic analysis of burglary.* Newbury Park, CA: Sage.

Crow, W. J., & Bull, J. L. (1975). *Robbery deterrence: An applied behavioral science demonstration.* La Jolla, CA: Western Behavioral Sciences Institute.

Culbertson, J. L., & Schellenbach, C. J. (1992). Prevention of maltreatment in infants and young children. In D. J. Willis, E. W. Holden, & M. Rosenberg (Eds.), *Prevention of child maltreatment.* New York: Wiley.

Curtis, L. A. (1974). *Criminal violence.* Lexington, MA: Lexington.

D'Alessio, S., & Stolzenberg, L. (1990). A crime of convenience. *Environment and Behavior, 22,* 255–271.

Davidson, R. N. (1981). *Crime and environment.* New York: St. Martin's Press.

Davies, J. L. (1969). The J-curve of rising and declining satisfactions as a cause of some great revolutions and a contained rebellion. In H. D. Graham & T. R. Gurr (Eds.), *Violence in America.* New York: Bantam Books.

Deaux, K. K. (1971). Honking at the intersection: A replication and extension. *Journal of Social Psychology, 84,* 159–160.

DeFronzo, J. (1984). Climate and crime. *Environment and Behavior, 16,* 185–210.

Depp, F. C. (1976). Violent behavior patterns on psychiatric wards. *Aggressive Behavior, 2,* 295–306.

Deutsch, M., & Collins, M. (1951). *Interracial housing: A psychological evaluation of a social experiment.* Minneapolis: University of Minnesota Press.

DeVries, D. L., Edwards, K. J., & Slavin, R. E. (1978). Biracial learning teams and race relations in the classroom: Four field experiments using Teams-Games-Tournament. *Journal of Educational Psychology, 70,* 356–362.

Dexter, E. G. (1904). *Weather influences: An empirical study of the mental and physiological effects of definite meteorological conditions.* New York: Macmillan.

Diab, L. (1970). A study of intragroup and intergroup relations among experimentally produced small groups. *Genetic Psychology Monographs, 82,* 49–82.

Diener, E. (1976). Effects of prior destructive behavior, anonymity, and group presence on deindividuation and aggression. *Journal of Personality and Social Psychology, 33,* 497–507.

Diener, E. (1980). Deindividuation: The absence of self-awareness and self-regulation in group members. In P. P. Paulus (Ed.), *Psychology of group influence.* Hillsdale, NJ: Erlbaum.

Dietz, P. E. (1985). Hypothetical criteria for the prediction of individual criminality. *Dangerousness, probability, & prediction in psychiatry and public policy.* New York: Cambridge University Press.

Doerner, W. G. (1975). A regional analysis of homicide rates in the United States. *Criminology, 13,* 90–101.

Doise, W. (1971). An apparent exception to the extremitization of collective judgements. *European Journal of Social Psychology, 1,* 511–518.

Doise, W., & Weinberger, M. (1973). Représentations masculines dans différentes situations de rencontres mixtes. *Bulletin de Psychologie, 26,* 649–657.

Doise, W., Csepeli, G., Dann, H. D., Gouge, C., Larsen, K., & Ostell, A. (1972). An experimental investigation into the formation of intergroup representations. *European Journal of Social Psychology, 2,* 202–204.

Doise, W., Deschamps, J. C., & Meyer, G. (1978). The accentuation of intra-category similarities. In H. Tajfel (Ed.), *Differentiation between social group.* London: Academic Press.

Dollard, J., Doob, L. W., Miller, N. E., Mowrer, O., & Sears, R. (1939). *Frustration and aggression.* New Haven, CT: Yale University Press.

Doob, A., & Gross, A. E. (1968). Status of frustrator as an inhibitor of horn-honking responses. *Journal of Social Psychology, 76,* 213–218.

Dovey, K. (1985). Home and homelessness. In I. Altman & C. M. Werner (Eds.), *Home environments.* New York: Plenum Press.

Downing, L., & Bothwell, K. (1979). Open space schools: Anticipation of peer interaction and development of cooperative independence. *Journal of Educational Psychology, 71,* 478–484.

Doyle, D. P. (1984). *Community control and crime: An ecological analysis.* Unpublished doctoral dissertation. University of Washington.

Duffalo, D. C. (1976). Convenience stores, armed robbery and physical environmental features. *American Behavioral Scientist, 20,* 227–246.

Dunn, C. J. (1980). The social area structure of suburban crime. In D. E. Georges-Abeyie & K. D. Harries (Eds.), *Crime: A spatial perspective.* New York: Columbia University Press.

Dunn, C. S. (1974). *The analysis of environmental attribute/crime incident characteristic interrelationships.* Unpublished doctoral dissertation, State University of New York at Albany.

Durkheim, E. (1933). *The division of labor in society.* New York: Free Press.

Edwards, J. G., & Reid, W. H. (1983). Violence in psychiatric facilities in Europe and the United States. In J. R. Lon & W. H. Reid (Eds.), *Assaults within psychiatric facilities.* New York: Grune & Stratton.

Eichelman, B. (1991). Violence toward clinicians. In R. Baenninger (Ed.), *Targets of violence and aggression* (pp. 327–347). North Holland: Elsevier Science.

Ekblom, P. (1988). Preventing post office robberies in London: Effects and side effects. *Journal of Security Administration, 11,* 36–43.

Elliott, D. S., Ageton, S. S., & Canter, R. J. (1979). An integrated theoretical perspective on juvenile delinquency. *Journal of Research in Crime and Delinquency, 16,* 3727.

Elmer, E., & Gregory, G. S. (1967). Developmental characteristics of abused children. *Journal of Pediatrics, 40,* 596–602.

Emde, R. N. (1980). Emotional availability: A reciprocal reward system for infants and parents with implications for prevention of psycho-social disorders. In P. M. Taylor (Ed.), *Parent-infant relationships.* New York: Grune & Stratton.

Endler, N. S. & Magnusson, D. (1976). Toward an interactional psychology of personality. *Psychological Bulletin, 83,* 956–974.

Epps, P., & Parnell, R. W. (1952). Physique and temperament of women delinquents compared with women undergraduates. *British Journal of Medical Psychology, 25,* 249–255.

Epstein, J. L. (1985). After the bus arrives: Resegregation in desegregated schools. *Journal of Social Issues, 41,* 23–43.

Epstein, Y. M. (1981). Crowding stress and human behavior. *Journal of Social Issues, 37,* 126–144.

Epstein, Y. M., & Karlin, R. A. (1975). Effects of acute experimental crowding. *Journal of Applied Social Psychology, 4,* 34–53.

Erlanger, H. S. (1975). Is there a "subculture of violence" in the South? *Journal of Criminal Law and Criminology, 66,* 483–490.

Evans, G. W. (1978). Crowding and the developmental process. In A. Baum & Y. Epstein (Eds.), *Human response to crowding.* Hillsdale, NJ: Erlbaum.

Exner, F. (1927). *Krieg und Kriminalitat in Oesterreich.* Vienna: Holder-Pickler-Tempsky.

Eysenck, H. J. (1977). *Crime and personality.* London: Routledge & Kegan Paul.

Fagot, B. I. (1977). Variations in density: Effects on task and social behaviors of pre-school children. *Developmental Psychology, 13,* 166–167.

Farrington, D. P. (1985). Predicting self-report and official delinquency. In D. P. Farrington & R. Tarling (Eds.), *Prediction in criminology.* New York: State University of New York Press.

Fattah, E. A. (1967). Toward a criminologic classification of victims. *International Criminal Police Review, 22,* 163–169.

Federal Bureau of Investigation. (1990). *Uniform Crime Report, 1989.* Washington, DC: U.S. Government Printing Office.

Federal Bureau of Investigation. (1991). *Uniform Crime Report, 1990.* Washington, DC: U.S. Government Printing Office.

Federation of Child Abuse and Neglect. (1990). *Fact Sheet.* New York: National Committee for Prevention of Child Abuse.

Feild, H. S. (1978). Attitudes toward rape: A comparative analysis of police, rapists, crisis counsellors and citizens. *Journal of Personality and Social Psychology, 36,* 156–179.

Feirling, C., & Lewis, M. (1989). The social networks of girls and boys from early through middle childhood. In D. Belle (Ed.), *Children's social networks and social supports.* New York: Wiley.

Feldhausen, J. (1978). Behavior problems in secondary schools. *Journal of Research and Development in Education, 11,* 17–28.

Feldman, M. P. (1977). *Criminal behavior: A psychological analysis.* London: Wiley.

Feldman, H. S., & Jarman, R. G. (1979). Factors influencing criminal behavior in Newark: A local study in forensic psychiatry. *Journal of Forensic Sciences, 24,* 234–239.

Felson, M. (1987). Routine activities and crime prevention in the developing metropolis. *Criminology, 25,* 911–931.

Felson, M., & Cohen, L. E. (1980). Human ecology and crime: A routine activity approach. *Human Ecology, 8,* 389–406.

Felson, R. B., & Steadman, H. J. (1983). Situational factors in disputes leading to criminal violence. *Criminology, 21,* 59–74.

Felson, R. B., Baccaglini, W., & Gmelch, G. (1986). Bar-room brawls: Aggression and violence in Irish and American bars. In A. Campbell & J. J. Gibbs (Eds.), *Violent transactions: The limits of personality.* Oxford: Basil Blackwell.

Ferguson, C. K., & Kelly, H. H. (1964). Significant factors in overevaluation of our group's product. *Journal of Abnormal and Social Psychology, 69,* 223–228.

Feshbach, S. (1970). Aggression. In P. H. Mussen (Ed.), *Carmichael's manual of child psychology* (Vol. 2). New York: Wiley.

Feshbach, S., & Singer, R. D. (1971). *Television and aggression: An experimental field study.* San Francisco: Jossey-Bass.

Festinger, L., Schacter, S., & Back, K. (1950). *Social pressures in informal groups.* New York: Harper.

Festinger, L., Pepitone, A., & Newcombe, T. (1952). Some consequences of deindividuation in a group. *Journal of Abnormal and Social Psychology, 47,* 382–389.

Fine, B. J. (1963). Introversion-extroversion and motor vehicle driver behavior. *Perceptual and Motor Skills, 16,* 95–100.

Fingerhut, L. A., & Kleinman, J. C. (1990). International and interstate comparisons of homicide among young males. *Journal of the American Medical Association, 263,* 3292–3295.

Fischer, C. S. (1977). *Networks and places.* London: Free Press.

Fischer, C. S. (1982). *To dwell among friends.* Chicago: University of Chicago Press.

Fischer, L. S. (1981). The public and private worlds of city life. *American Sociological Review, 46,* 306–316.

Fisher, A. C. (1976). *The psychology of sport: Issues and insight.* Palo Alto, CA: Mayfield.

Fisher, B. S., & Nasar, J. L. (1992). Fear of crime in relation to the exterior site features: Prospect, refuge, and escape. *Environment and Behavior, 24,* 35–65.

Fletcher, J. (1849). *Moral and educational statistics of England and Wales.* London.

Fletcher, J. (1850). *Summary of moral statistics of England and Wales.* London.

Forgas, J. P. (1986). Cognitive representations of aggression. In A. Campbell & J. J. Gibbs (Eds.), *Violent transactions: The limits of personality.* Oxford: Basil Blackwell.

Forsyth, D. R. (1983). *An introduction to group dynamics.* San Francisco: Brooks/Cole.

Fowler, F., & Mangione, T. W. (1979). *Reducing residential crime and fear: The Hartford Neighborhood Prevention Program.* Boston: University of Massachusetts.

Fox, H. G. (1970). Gang youth and police: Live-in. *The Police Chief, 37,* 233–235.

Fragier, H. A. (1840). *Des classes dangereuses de la population dan les grandes villes.* Cited in R. D. Hunter. (1988). *The relationship of selected environmental characteristics to the incidence of convenience store robbery within the State of Florida.* Unpublished doctoral dissertation, Florida State University.

Frank, M. G., & Gilovich, T. (1988). The dark side of self and social perception: Black uniforms and aggression in professional sports. *Journal of Personality and Social Psychology, 54,* 74–85.

Franklin, S. (1956). *The militant south: 1800–1861.* New York: Belknap.

Frederickson, N. (1972). Toward a taxonomy of situations. *American Psychologist, 27,* 114–123.

Freedman, J. L., Levy, A. S., Buchanan, R. W., & Price, J. (1972). Crowding and human aggressiveness. *Journal of Experimental Social Psychology, 8,* 528–548.

Freud, S. (1922). *Group psychology and the analysis of the ego.* London: Hogarth Press.

Freud, S. (1961). *The complete works of Sigmund Freud.* London: Hogarth Press.

Furman, W. (1989). The development of children's social networks. In D. Belle (Ed.), *Children's social networks and social supports.* New York: Wiley.

Gabor, T. (1986). *The prediction of criminal behavior: Statistical approaches.* Toronto: University of Toronto Press.

Gabor, T. (1990). Crime displacement and situational prevention: Toward the development of some principles. *Canadian Journal of Criminology, 32,* 41–74.

Gaes, G. G., & McGuire, W. J. (1985). Prison violence: The contribution of crowding versus other determinants of prison assault rates. *Journal of Research in Crime and Delinquency, 22,* 41–65.

Galle, O. R., Gove, W. R., Miller, T., & McPherson, J. M. (1972). Population density and social pathology. *Science, 176*, 23–30.

Garbarino, J. (1973). High school size and adolescent social development. *Human Ecology Forum, 4*, 26–29.

Garbarino, J. (1977). The human ecology of child maltreatment: A conceptual model for research. *Journal of Marriage and the Family, 39*, 721–735.

Garbarino, J., & Sherman, D. (1980). Identifying high-risk neighborhoods. In J. Garbarino & S. H. Stocking (Eds.), *Protecting children from abuse and neglect*. San Francisco: Jossey-Bass.

Garbarino, J., & Stocking, S. J. (1980). *Protecting children from abuse and neglect*. San Francisco: Jossey-Bass.

Garbarino, J., Brookhouser, P. E., & Authier, K. J. (1987). *Special children–special risks: The maltreatment of children with disabilities*. New York: Aldine de Gruyter.

Gardner, C. B. (1990). Safe conduct: Women, crime, and self in public places. *Social Problems, 37*, 311–328.

Gastil, R. D. (1971). Homicide and a regional culture of violence. *American Sociological Review, 36*, 412–427.

Gates, L., & Rohe, W. (1987). Fear and reaction to crime. *Urban Affairs, 22*, 425–453.

Gayford, J. J. (1975). Wife battering: A preliminary survey of 100 cases. *British Medical Journal, 1*, 194–197.

Geason, S., & Wilson, P. R. (1989). *Designing out crime*. Canberra: Australian Institute of Criminology.

Gelles, R. J. (1972). *The violent home: A study of physical aggression between husbands and wives*. Newbury Park, CA: Sage.

Gelles, R. J. (1972). "It takes two": The roles of victim and offender. In R. J. Gelles (Ed.), *The violent home: A study of physical aggression between husband and wives*. Newbury Park, CA: Sage.

Gelles, R. J., & Straus, M. A. (1979). Determinants of violence in the family: Toward a theoretical integration. In W. R. Burr, R. Hill, I. Nye, & I. L. Reiss (Eds.), *Contemporary theories about the family*. New York: Free Press.

George, C., & Main, M. (1979). Social interactions of young abused children: Approach, avoidance and aggression. *Child Development, 50*, 306–318.

Gerard, H. B., & Hoyt, M. F. (1974). Distinctiveness of social categorization and attitude toward in-group members. *Journal of Personality and Social Psychology, 29*, 836–849.

Gibbens, T. C. (1963). *Psychiatric studies of Borstal lads*. London: Oxford University Press.

Gibbs, J. J. (1986). Alcohol consumption, cognition and context: Examining tavern violence. In A. Campbell & J. J. Gibbs (Eds.), *Violent transactions: The limits of personality*. Oxford: Basil Blackwell.

Gil, D. G. (1970). *Violence against children: Physical child abuse in the United States*. Cambridge, MA: Harvard University Press.

Gillis, A. R. (1974). Population density and social pathology: The case of building type, social allowance and juvenile delinquency. *Social Forces, 53*, 306–315.

Glass, D. C., & Singer, J. E. (1972). Behavioral aftereffects of unpredictable and uncontrollable aversive events. *American Scientist, 60*, 457–465.

Glueck, S., & Glueck, E. T. (1950). *Unraveling juvenile delinquency*. Cambridge, MA: Harvard University Press.

Goffman, E. (1971). *Relations in public places*. New York: Basic Books.

Goldman, N. (1961). A socio-psychological study of school vandalism. *Crime and Delinquency, 7,* 221–230.

Goldstein, A. P. (1988). New directions in aggression reduction. *International Journal of Group Tensions, 18,* 286–313.

Goldstein, A. P. (1990). *Delinquents on delinquency.* Champaign, IL: Research Press.

Goldstein, A. P. (1992a). *Delinquent gangs: A psychological perspective.* Champaign, IL: Research Press.

Goldstein, A. P. (1992b). *School violence: Its community context and potential solutions.* Testimony presented to Subcommittee on Elementary, Secondary and Vocational Education, Committee on Education and Labor, U.S. House of Representatives, May 4, 1992.

Goldstein, A. P., & Segall, M. (1983). *Aggression in global perspective.* New York: Pergamon.

Goldstein, A. P., Harootunian, B., & Conoley, J. C. (1994). *Student aggression: Prevention, control, replacement.* New York: Guilford.

Goodchild, J. D., & Zellman, G. L. (1984). Sexual signaling and sexual aggression in adolescent relationships. In N. M. Malamuth & E. Donnerstein (Eds.), *Pornography and sexual aggression.* Orlando: Academic Press.

Goranson, R. E., & King, D. (1970). *Rioting and daily temperature: Analysis of the U.S. riots in 1967.* Unpublished manuscript, York University.

Gordon, R. A. (1967). Issues in the ecological study of delinquency. *American Sociological Review, 32,* 927–944.

Gottfredson, G. D. (1989). The experience of violent and serious victimization. In N. A. Weiner & M. E. Wolfgang (Eds.), *Pathways to criminal violence.* Newbury Park, CA: Sage.

Gottfredson, S. D. & Gottfredson, D. M. (1985). Screening for risk among parolees: Policy, practice, and method. In D. P. Farrington & R. Tarling (Eds.), *Prediction in criminology.* New York: State University of New York Press.

Graham, K., LaRocque, L., Yetman, R., Ross, T. V., & Guistra, Y. (1980). Aggression and barroom environment. *Journal of Studies on Alcohol, 41,* 277–292.

Green, R. G. (1976). The study of aggression. *Perspectives on aggression.* New York: Academic Press.

Greenberg, B. (1969). *School vandalism: A national dilemma.* Menlo Park, CA: Stanford Research Institute.

Greenberg, M. R., Carey, G. W., & Popper, F. J. (1987). Violent death, violent states and American youth. *The Public Interest, 87,* 38–48.

Greenberg, S. W., Rohe, W., & Williams, J. (1982). Safety in urban neighborhoods. *Population and Environment, 5,* 141–165.

Greenberg, S. W. (1986). Fear and its relationship to crime, neighborhood deterioration, and informal social control. In J. M. Byrne & R. J. Sampson (Eds.), *The social ecology of crime.* New York: Springer-Verlag.

Guerry, A. M. (1833). Essai sur la statistique morale de la France. *Westminster Review, 18,* 357.

Gurr, T. R. (1970). *Why men rebel.* Princeton: Princeton University Press.

Gurr, T. R. (1981). Historical trends in violent crimes: A critical review of evidence. In N. Morris & M. Tonry (Eds.), *Crime and justice: An annual review* (Vol. 3). Chicago: University of Chicago Press.

Gurr, T. R. (1989). The history of protest, rebellion, and reform in America: An overview. In T. R. Gurr (Ed.), *Violence in America: Vol. 2. Protest, rebellion, reform.* Newbury Park, CA: Sage.

Hackney, S. (1969). Southern violence. *American Historical Review, 74*, 906–925.

Hall, E. T. (1966). *The hidden dimension.* New York: Doubleday.

Hamilton, D. L. & Trollier, T. K. (1986). Stereotypes and stereotyping: An overview of the cognitive approach. In J. F. Davidio & S. T. Gaertner (Eds.), *Prejudice, discrimination and racism.* New York: Academic Press.

Hammer, M., Gutwirth, L., & Phillips, S. L. (1981). Parenthood and social networks: A preliminiary view. *Social Science and Medicine, 16*, 2091–2100.

Hand, L. (1971, March). Cincinnati housing authority builds safety into projects. *HUD Challenge.*

Hansen, C. M. (1977). *Failure-to-thrive: A manual prepared for social workers.* Piscataway, NJ: Rutgers Medical School.

Harding, J., & Hogrefe, R. (1952). Attitudes of white department store employees towards negro co-workers. *Journal of Social Issues, 8*, 18–28.

Harries, K. D. (1976). Cities and crime: A geographic model. *Criminology, 14*, 369–386.

Harries, K. D. (1990). *Serious violence patterns of homicide and assault in America.* Springfield, IL: Charles C Thomas.

Harries, K. D., & Stadler, S. J. (1983). Determinism revisited: Assault and heat stress in Dallas, 1980. *Environment and Behavior, 15*, 235–256.

Harris, J. D., Gray, B. A., Rees-McGee, S. R., Carroll, J. L., & Zaremba, E. T. (1987). Referrals to school psychologists: A national survey. *Journal of School Psychology, 25*, 343–354.

Hartshorne, H., & May, M. (1928). *Studies in the nature of character: Studies in deceit.* New York: Macmillan.

Hauber, A. R. (1980). The social psychology of driving behaviour and the traffic environment: Research on aggressive behavior in traffic. *International Review of Applied Psychology, 29*, 461–474.

Hawkey, E. W. (1983). *Southern political cutlure: A North-South comparison of localism, conservatism, racism and violence 1952–1976.* Unpublished doctoral dissertation. University of Missouri–Columbia.

Hawkins, J. D., & Weiss, J. G. (1985). The social development model: An integrated approach to delinquency prevention. *Journal of Primary Prevention, 6*, 73–97.

Hawkins, R., & Tiedemann, G. (1975). *The creation of deviance: Interpersonal and organizational determinants.* Columbus, OH: Merrill.

Helfer, R. E., & Kempe, C. H. (Eds.). (1976). *The battered child.* Chicago: University of Chicago Press.

Heller, K., Swindle, R. W., & Dusenbury, L. (1986). Component social support processes: Comments and integration. *Journal of Consulting and Clinical Psychology, 54*, 466–470.

Hewstone, M., & Brown, R. (1986). *Contact and conflict in intergroup encounters.* London: Basil Blackwell.

Higher Education Research Institute (1980). *Longitudinal follow-up of ACE 1971 college freshmen.* Los Angeles: University of California at Los Angeles.

Hill, G. (1985). Predicting recidivism using institutional measures. In D. P. Farrington & R. Tarling (Eds.), *Prediction in criminology.* New York: State University of New York Press.

Hindlelang, M. J., & Davis, B. L. (1977). Forcible rape in the United States: A statistical profile. In D. Chappell & S. Geis (Eds.), *Forcible rape: The crime, the victim, the offender.* New York: Columbia University Press.

Hindelang, M. J., Gottfredson, M. R., & Garofalo, J. (1978). *Victims of personal crime.* Cambridge: Ballinger.

Hirsch, B. J. (1980). Natural support systems and coping with major life changes. *American Journal of Community Psychology, 8,* 159–172.

Hirschi, T. (1969). *Causes of delinquency.* Berkeley: University of California Press.

Hoch, I. (1974). Factors in urban crime. *Journal of Urban Economics, 1,* 184–229.

Hoffman, F. (1925). *The homicide problem.* Newark, NJ: Prudential Press.

Hogan, R., & Jones, W. H. (1985). A role-theoretical model of criminal conduct. In W. S. Laufer & J. M. Day (Eds.), *Personality theory, moral development, and criminal behavior.* Lexington, MA: Lexington Books.

Holahan, C. J. (1982a). Environmental cognition. In C. J. Holahan (Ed.), *Environmental psychology.* New York: Random House.

Holahan, C. J. (Ed.). (1982b). *Environmental Psychology.* New York: Random House.

Holcomb, W. R., & Anderson, W. P. (1982). Alcohol and drug abuse in accused murderers. *Psychological Reports, 52,* 159–164.

House, J. S. (1981). *Work stress and social support.* Reading, MA: Addison-Wesley.

House, J. S., Umberson, D., & Landis, K. R. (1988). Structures and processes of social support. *Annual Review of Sociology, 14,* 293–318.

Howard, J. L. (1978). Factors in school vandalism. *Journal of Research and Development in Education, 11,* 13–18.

Howard, J., & Rothbart, M. (1978). Social categorization and memory for ingroup and outgroup behaviour. *Journal of Personality and Social Psychology, 38,* 301–310.

Howitt, D., & Cumberbatch, G. (1975). *Violence and the mass media.* London: Paul Elek.

Huff-Corzine, L., Corzine, J., & Moore, D. C. (1986). Southern exposure: Deciphering the south's influence on homicide rates. *Social Forces, 64,* 906–924.

Huggins, M. D., & Strauss, M. A. (1975). Violence and the social structure as reflected in children's books from 1850 to 1970. Presented at Eastern Sociological Society, New York.

Humphries, D., & Wallace, D. (1980). Capitalist accumulation and urban crime, 1950–1971. *Social Problems, 28,* 179–193.

Hunt, D. E. (1972). Matching models for teacher training. In B. R. Joyce & M. Weil (Eds.), *Perspectives for reform in teacher education.* Englewood Cliffs, NJ: Prentice-Hall.

Hunter, J. (1978). Defensible space in practice. *The Architect's Journal* (October), 675–677.

Hutt, C., & Vaizey, M. J. (1966). Differential effects of group density on social behavior. *Nature, 209,* 1371–1372.

Hutton, J. B. (1985). What reasons are given by teachers who refer problem behavior students. *Psychology in the Schools, 22,* 79–92.

Ianni, F. A. J. (1978). The social organization of the high school: School-specific aspects of school crime. In E. Wenk & N. Harlow (Eds.), School crime and disruption. Davis, CA: Responsible Action.

Inciardi, J. A., & Pottieger, A. E. (Eds.). (1978). *Violent crime: Historical and contemporary issues.* Beverly Hills, CA: Sage.

Jacobs, J. (1961). *The death and life of great American cities.* New York: Vintage.

Jacobson, A. L. (1975). Crime trends in Southern and Nonsouthern cities: A twenty-year perspective. *Social Forces, 54,* 226–242.

Jahoda, M., & West, P. (1951). Race relations in public housing. *Journal of Social Issues, 7,* 132–139.

Jain, U. (1987). *The psychological consequences of crowding*. Newbury Park, CA: Sage.

Janowitz, M. (1975). Sociological theory and social control. *American Journal of Sociology, 81,* 82–108.

Jason, J., & Andereck, N. D. (1983). Fatal child abuse in Georgia: The epidemiology of severe physical child abuse. *Child Abuse and Neglect, 7,* 1–9.

Jeffery, C. R. (1977). *Crime prevention through environmental design*. Newbury Park, CA: Sage.

Jeffery, C. R., Hunter, R. D., & Griswold, J. (1987). Crime prevention and computer analysis of convenience store robberies in Tallahassee, Florida. *Security Systems* (August), 33–40.

Jersild, A. T., & Markey, F. V. (1935). Conflicts between pre-school children. *Child Development Monograph, 21.*

Johnson, A. M. (1949). Sanctions for super-ego lacunae. In K. R. Eissler (Ed.), *Searchlights on delinquency*. New York: International Universities Press.

Johnson, A. M. (1959). Juvenile delinquency. In S. Arieti (Ed.), *American handbook of psychiatry*. New York: Basic Books.

Johnson, A. M., & Szurek, S. A. (1952). The genesis of antsocial acting out in children and adults. *Psychoanalytic Quarterly, 21,* 323–343.

Johnson, D. W., & Johnson, R. (1975). *Learning together and alone: Cooperation, competition and individualization*. Englewood Cliffs, NJ: Prentice-Hall.

Johnson, E. B., Gerard, H. G., & Miller, N. (1975). Teacher influence in the desegregated classroom. In H. B. Gerard & N. Miller (Eds.), *School desegregation: A long-term study*. New York: Plenum.

Johnson, R. (1986). Institutions and the promotion of violence. In A. Campbell & J. J. Gibbs (Eds.), *Violent transactions: The limits of personality*. Oxford: Basil Blackwell.

Johnson, S. D., Gibson, L., & Linden, R. (1978). Alcohol and rape in Winnepeg, 1966–1975. *Journal of Studies on Alcohol, 39,* 1887–1894.

Jones, C., & Aronson, E. (1973). Attribution of fault to a rape victim as a function of respectability of the victim. *Journal of Personality and Social Psychology, 26,* 415–419.

Kadushin, A., & Martin, J. A. (1981). *Child abuse: An interactionist event*. New York: Columbia University Press.

Kahn, R., & Antonucci, T. (1980). Attachment, role, and social support. In P. Baltes & O. Brim (Eds.), *Life-span development and behavior*. New York: Academic Press.

Kahneman, D., & Tversky, A. (1973). On the psychology of prediction. *Psychological Review, 80,* 237–251.

Kalt, N. C., & Zalkind, S. S. (1976). Effects of the urban environment. In N. C. Kalt & S. S. Zalkind (Eds.), *Urban problems: Psychological inquiries readings and text* (pp. 475–482). New York: Oxford University Press.

Kaufman, J., & Cicchetti, D. (1989). Effects of maltreatment on school-age children's socioemotional development: Assessments in a day-camp setting. *Developmental Psychology, 25,* 516–524.

Keller, S. I. (1968). *The urban neighborhood: A sociological perspective*. New York: Random House.

Kempe, C. H., Silverman, F. N., Steele, B. F., Droegemueller, W., & Silver, H. K. (1962). The battered child syndrome. *Journal of the American Medical Association, 181,* 17–24.

Kennedy, L. W., & Baron, S. W. (1993). Routine activities and a subculture of violence. *Journal of Research in Crime and Delinquency, 30,* 88–112.

Kennedy, L. W., & Forde, D. R. (1990). Routine activities and crime: An analysis of victimization in Canada. *Criminology, 28,* 137–152.

Kenrick, D. T., & MacFarlane, S. W. (1986). Ambient temperature and horn-honking: A field study of the heat/aggression relationship. *Environment and Behavior, 18*, 179–191.

King, J. W. (1992). *Situational factors and the dynamics of criminal violence.* Dissertation, State University of New York at Albany.

Klinger, E. (1969). Feedback effects and social facilitation of the vigilance performance: Mere coaction versus potential evaluation. *Psychonomic Science, 14*, 161–162.

Knutson, J. F., Schartz, H. A., & Zaidi, L. Y. (1992). Victim risk factors in the physical abuse of children. In R. Baenniger (Ed.), *Targets of violence and aggression.* Amsterdam: Elsevier.

Kohn, L., Franck, K., & Fox, A. (1975). *Defensible space modifications in row housing communities.* New York: Institute for Community Design Analysis.

Koller, A. J. (1937). *The Abbé du Bos—His advocacy of the theory of climate.* Champaign, IL: Garrad Press.

Kornhauser, R. (1978). *Social sources of delinquency.* Chicago: University of Chicago Press.

Kowalski, C., Dittman, D. E., & Bung, S. (1980). Spatial distribution of criminal offenses by states: 1970–1976. *Delinquency, 17*, 4–25.

Kozol, H., Boucher, R., & Garofalo, R. (1972). The diagnosis and treatment of dangerousness. *Crime and Delinquency, 18*, 371–392.

Kramer, B. (1950). *Residential contact as a determinant of attitudes towards Negroes.* Unpublished Ph.D. dissertation, Harvard University.

Krause, D. R. (1976). *Violence: A territorial analysis.* Dissertation, University of Illinois, Chicago Circle.

Krupat, E. (1985). *People in cities: The urban environment and its effects.* New York: Cambridge University Press.

Kruse, L. (1986). Conceptions of crowds and crowding. In C. F. Graumann & S. Moscovici (Eds.), *Changing conceptions of crowd mind and behavior* (pp. 117–142). New York: Springer-Verlag.

LaGrange, R. L., Ferraro, K. R., & Supanic, M. (1992). Perceived risk and fear of crime: Role of social and physical incivilities. *Journal of Research in Crime and Delinquency, 29*, 311–334.

Lamb, S. (1986). Treating sexually abused children: Issues of blame and responsibility. *American Journal of Orthopsychiatry, 56*, 303–307.

Latané, B. & Darley, J. (1970). *The unresponsive bystander: Why doesn't he help?* New York: Appleton.

Laufer, W. S., & Day, J. M. (Eds.). (1983). *Personality theory, moral development, and criminal behavior.* Lexington, MA: Lexington Books.

Lavender, A. (1987). The effects of nurses changing from uniforms to everyday clothes on a psychiatric rehabilitation ward. *British Journal of Medical Psychology, 60*, 189–199.

Lebeau, J. L. (1978). *The spatial dynamics of rape: The San Diego example.* Unpublished doctoral dissertation, Michigan State University.

Le Bon, G. (1903). *The crowd.* London: Unwin (originally published in 1895).

Lefkowitz, M. M., Eron, L. D., Walder, L. O., & Huesmann, L. R. (1977). Television violence and child aggression: A followup study. In G. A. Comstock, E. A. Rubinstein, & J. P. Murray (Eds.), *Television and social behavior.* Washington, DC: U.S. Government Printing Office.

Leftwich, D. (1977). *A study of vandalism in selected public schools in Alabama.* Unpublished doctoral dissertation, University of Alabama.

Lemert, E. M. (1967). *Human deviance, social problems, and social control.* Englewood Cliffs, NJ: Prentice-Hall.

Leming, J. (1978). Interpersonal variations in stage of mental reasoning among adolescents as a function of situational context. *Journal of Youth and Adolescence, 1,* 405–416.

Lester, D. (1979). Temporal variation in suicide and homicide. *American Journal of Epidemiology, 109,* 517–520.

Letkemann, P. (1973). *Crime as work.* Englewood Cliffs, NJ: Prentice-Hall.

Levy, L., & Herzog, A. N. (1974). Effects of population density and crowding on health and social adaptation in the Netherlands. *Journal of Health and Social Behavior, 15,* 228–240.

Lewin, K. (1935). *A dynamic theory of personality.* New York: McGraw-Hill.

Lewin, K. (1936). *Principles of topological psychology.* New York: McGraw-Hill.

Lewis, D. A., & Salem, G. (1986). Community crime prevention: An analysis of a developing perspective. *Crime and Delinquency, 27,* 405–421.

Lewis, L. T., & Alford, J. J. (1975). The influence of season on assault. *The Professional Geographer, 27,* 214–217.

Ley, D., & Cybriwsky, R. (1974). The spatial ecology of stripped cars. *Environment and Behavior, 6,* 53–68.

Libbey, P., & Bybee, R. (1979). Physical abuse of adolescents. *Journal of Social Issues, 35,* 101–125.

Liebert, R. M., Neale, J. M., & Davidson, E. S. (1973). *The early window: Effects of television on children and youth.* New York: Pergamon.

Lin, N. (1986). Conceptualizing social support. In N. Lin, A. Dean, & W. Ensel (Eds.), *Social support, life events and depression.* Orlando, FL: Academic.

Linville, P. W., Salovey, P., & Fischer, G. W. (1986). Stereotyping and perceived distributions of social characteristics: An application to ingroup-outgroup perception. In J. F. Dovidio & S. L. Gaertner (Eds.), *Prejudice, discrimination and racism.* New York: Academic.

Little, B. R. (1987). Personality and the environment. In D. Stokols & I. Altman (Eds.), *Handbook of environmental psychology.* Malabar, FL: Krieger.

Locksley, A., Ortiz, V., & Hepburn, C. (1980). Social categorization and discriminatory behaviour: Extinguishing the minimal intergroup discrimination effect. *Journal of Personality and Social Psychology, 39,* 773–783.

Loeber, R., & Stouthamer-Loeber, M. (1987). Prediction. In H. C. Quay (Ed.), *Handbook of juvenile delinquency.* New York: Wiley.

Lofland, L. (1973). *A world of strangers.* New York: Basic Books.

Loftin, C., & Hill, R. H. (1974). Regional subculture and homicide: An examination of the Gastil-Hackney thesis. *American Sociological Review, 39,* 714–724.

Lombrosco, C. (1911). *Crime, its causes and remedies.* Boston: Little, Brown.

London, B., & Robinson, T. D. (1989). The effect of international dependence on income inequality and political violence. *American Sociological Review, 54,* 305–308.

Loo, C. (1972). The effects of spatial density on the social behavior of children. *Journal of Applied Social Psychology, 2,* 372–381.

Lorenz, K. (1963). *On aggression.* New York: Harcourt, Brace & World.

Los Angeles County Office of Education. (1988a). *1988 Pupil Services Digest* (Publication 88–9–04R). Downey, CA: Author.

Los Angeles County Office of Education. (1988b). *Vandalism in Los Angeles County Schools.* Los Angeles: Author.

Lottier, S. (1938). Distribution of criminal offenses in sectional regions. *Journal of Criminal Law and Criminology, 29,* 239–344.

Luckenbill, D. F. (1977). Criminal homicide as a situated transaction. *Social Problems, 25,* 176–186.

Luedtke, G. (1970). *Crime and the physical city: Neighborhood design techniques for crime reduction.* Springfield, VA: National Technical Information Service.

Lukianowicz, N. (1971). Battered children. *Psychiatrica Clinica, 4,* 257–280.

Lundberg-Love, P., & Geffner, R. (1989). Date rape: Prevalence, risk factors, and a proposed model. In M. A. Perog-Good & J. E. Stets (Eds.), *Violence in dating relationships.* New York: Praeger.

Lunde, D. T. (1975). Murder in other countries. *Murder and madness* (pp. 39–45). Stanford, CA: Stanford Alumni Association.

Lunden, W. A. (1963). *War and delinquency.* Ames, IA: Art Press.

Lyman S. M., & Scott, M. B. (1967). Territoriality: A neglected sociological dimension. *Social Problems, 15,* 236–249.

Lynch, M. A. (1975). Ill-health and child abuse. *The Lancet, 2,* 317–319.

MacAndrew, C., & Edgerton, R. (1969). *Drunken comportment: A social explanation.* Chicago: Aldine.

MacDonald, J. M. (1961). *The murderer and his victim.* Springfield, IL: Charles C Thomas.

MacDonald, W. S., & Oden, C. W., Jr. (1973). Effects of extreme crowding on the performance of five married couples during twelve weeks of intensive training. *The American Psychological Association, 8,* 209–290.

Macmillan, J. (1975). *Deviant drivers.* Westmead, UK: Saxon House, D. C. Heath Ltd.

Maden, M. F., & Wrench, D. F. (1977). Significant findings in child abuse research. *Victimology, 2,* 196–224.

Marin, R. S., & Marycz, R. K. (1990). Victims of elder abuse. In R. T. Ammerman & M. Hersen (Eds.), *Treatment of family violence.* New York: Wiley.

Martin, H. P., & Beezley, P. (1974). Prevention and the consequences of child abuse. *Journal of Operational Psychiatry, 6,* 68–77.

Martin, J. M. (1961). *Juvenile vandalism: A study of its nature and prevention.* Springfield, IL: Charles C Thomas.

Martino, L., & Johnson, D. W. (1979). The effects of cooperative versus individualistic instruction on interaction between normal-progress and learning-disabled students. *Journal of Social Psychology, 107,* 177–183.

Marx, C., & Engels, F. (1947). *The German ideology.* New York: International Publishers.

Mawbry, R. I. (1977). Kiosk vandalism: A Sheffield study. *British Journal of Criminology, 17,* 30–46.

Mayer, G. R., & Sulzer-Azaroff, B. (1991). Interventions for vandalism. In G. Stoner, M. R. Shinn, & H. M. Walker (Eds.), *Interventions for achievement and behavior problems.* Silver Spring, MD: National Association of School Psychologists.

Mayhew, H. (1861). *London labour and the London poor.* London: Griffin-Bohn.

Mayhew, H. (1862). *The criminal prisons of London.* London: Griffin-Bohn.

Mayhew, P., Clarke, R. V., Sturman, A., & Hough, J. M. (1976). *Crime as opportunity.* London: HMSO.

McAlhany, D. A. (1984). *Highway abuse and violence: Motorists' experiences as victims.* Unpublished master's thesis, North Texas State University.

McCain, G., Paulus, P. B., & Cox, V. C. (1980). *The effect of prison crowding on inmate behavior.* Final report, Law Enforcement Assistance Authority. Arlington: University of Texas.

McClelland, D. C., Davis, R., Kalin, B., & Wanner, E. (Eds.). (1972). *The drinking man.* New York: Free Press.

McCord, W., & McCord, J. (1964). *The psychopath: An essay on the criminal mind.* Princeton, NJ: Van Nostrand Reinhold.

McDermott, M. J. (1979). *Rape victimization in 26 American cities.* New York: Criminal Justice Research Center.

McDonald, S. C. (1986). Does gentrification affect crime rates? In A. J. Reiss & M. Tonry (Eds.), *Communities and crime* (pp. 163–201). Chicago: University of Chicago Press.

McGahey, R. M. (1986). Economic conditions, neighborhood organization, and urban crime. In A. J. Reiss, Jr. & M. Tonry (Eds.), *Communities and crime* (pp. 231–270). Chicago: University of Chicago Press.

McGrew, W. S. (1972). Interpersonal spacing of preschool children. In J. S. Bruner & K. J. Connolly (Eds.), *The development of competence in early childhood.* London: Academic.

McKinney, J. C., & Bourque, L. B. (1971). The changing South: National incorporation to a region. *American Sociological Review, 36,* 399–412.

Megargee, E. (1977). The association of population density, reduced space, and uncomfortable temperatures with misconduct in a prison community. *American Journal of Community Psychology, 5,* 289–298.

Megargee, E. I. (1982). Psychological determinants and correlates of criminal violence. In M. E. Wolfgang & N. A. Weiner (Eds.), *Criminal violence* (pp. 81–170). Newbury Park, CA: Sage.

Meier, R. (1976). The new criminology: Continuity in criminological theory. *Journal of Criminal Law and Criminology, 67,* 461–469.

Mendelsohn, B. (1963). The origin of the doctrine of victimology. *Excerptia Criminologica, 3,* 239–244.

Merry, S. E. (1981). Defensible space undefended. *Urban Affairs Quarterly, 16,* 397–422.

Messner, S. F., & Tardiff, K. (1985). The social ecology of urban homicide: An application of the "routine activities" approach. *Criminology, 23,* 241–267.

Metfessel, M., & Lovell, C. (1942). Recent literature on individual correlates of crime. *Psychological Bulletin, 39,* 133–142.

Michael, R. P., & Zumpe, D. (1986). Annual rhythms in human violence and sexual aggression in the United States and the role of temperature. *Social Biology, 30,* 263–278.

Michalowski, R. J. (1975). Violence in the road: The crime of vehicular homicide. *Journal of Research in Crime and Delinquency, 12,* 30–43.

Michelson, W. (1970). *Man and his urban environment.* Reading, MA: Addison-Wesley.

Miethe, T. D. (1991). Citizen-based crime control activity and victimization risks: An examination of displacement and free-rider effects. *Criminology, 29,* 429–440.

Miethe, T. D., Stafford, M. C., & Long, J. S. (1987). Social differentiation in criminal victimization: A test of routine activities lifestyle theories. *American Sociological Review, 52,* 184–194.

Milgram, S. (1970). The experience of living in cities. *Science* (March), 1461–1468.

Milgram, S., & Toch, H. (1969). Collective behavior: Crowds and social movements. In G. Lindzey & E. Aronson (Eds.), *The handbook of social psychology* (Vol. 4, 2nd ed.). Reading, MA: Addison-Wesley.

Miller, G., & Prinz, R. J. (1991). Designing interventions for stealing. In G. Stoner, M. R. Shinn, & H. M. Walker (Eds.), *Interventions for achievement and behavior problems*. Silver Spring, MD: National Association of School Psychologists.

Miller, N., Brewer, M. B., & Edwards, K. (1985). Cooperative interaction in desegregated settings: A laboratory analogue. *Journal of Social Issues, 41,* 63–79.

Miller, W. B. (1958). Lower class culture as a generating milieu of gang delinquency. *Journal of Social Issues, 14,* 5–19.

Mills, C. A. (1942). *Climate makes the man.* New York: Harper.

Milner, J. S., & Wimberley, R. C. (1980). Prediction and explanation of child abuse. *Journal of Clinical Psychology, 36,* 875–884.

Mischel, W. (1968). *Personality and assessment.* New York: Wiley.

Mitchel, R. E. (1971). Some social implications of high density housing. *American Sociological Review, 36,* 18–28.

Molumby, T. (1976). Patterns of crime in a university housing project. *American Behavioral Scientist, 20,* 247–259.

Momboisse, R. M. (1970). *Riots, revolts and insurrections.* Springfield, IL: Charles C Thomas.

Monahan, J. (1981). *Predicting violent behavior: An assessment of clinical techniques.* Newbury Park, CA: Sage.

Monahan, J., & Klassen, D. (1982). Situational approaches to understanding and predicting individual violent behavior. In M. E. Wolfgang & N. A. Weiner (Eds.), *Criminal violence.* Newbury Park, CA: Sage.

Moos, R. H. (1968). Situational analysis of a therapeutic community milieu. *Journal of Abnormal Psychology, 73,* 49–61.

Moos, R. (1973). Conceptualization of human environments. *American Psychologist, 28,* 652–665.

Moos, R. (1974). *Evaluating treatment environments: A social ecological approach.* New York: Wiley.

Moos, R. (1975). *Evaluating correctional and community settings.* New York: Wiley.

Moos, R., & Houts, P. (1968). The assessment of the social atmospheres of psychiatric wards. *Journal of Abnormal Psychology, 73,* 595–604.

Moran, E. F. (1979). *Human adaptability: An introduction to ecological anthropology.* North Scituate, MA: Duxbury.

Morokoff, P. J. (1983). Toward the elimination of rape: A conceptualization of sexual aggression against women. In Center for Research on Aggression (Ed.), *Prevention and control of aggression.* New York: Pergamon.

Morris, D. (1967). *The naked ape.* New York: McGraw-Hill.

Morris, D. E., & Hess, K. (1975). *Neighborhood power: The new localism.* Boston: Beacon Press.

Moser, G., & Levy-Leboyer, C. (1985). Inadequate environment and situation control: Is a malfunctioning phone always an occasion for aggression? *Environment and Behavior, 17,* 520–533.

Muehlenhard, C. L. (1989). Misinterpreted dating behaviors and the risk of date rape. In M. A. Pirog-Good & J. E. Stets (Eds.), *Violence in dating relationships: Emerging social issues.* New York: Praeger.

Muehlenhard, C. L., Friedman, D. E., & Thomas, C. M. (1985). Is date rape justifiable? The effects of dating activity, who initiated, who paid, and men's attitudes toward women. *Psychology of Women Quarterly, 9,* 297–309.

Mulvihill, D. J., Tumin, M. M., & Curtis, S. A. (1969). *Crimes of violence.* Washington, DC: National Commission on the Causes and Prevention of Violence.

Murphy, G. (1947). *Personality: A biosocial approach to origins and structure.* New York: Harper.

Murray, C., Motoyama, T., & Rouse, W. V. (1980). *The link between crime and the built environment: The current state of knowledge.* Washington, DC: U.S. Government Printing Office.

Murray, H. (1938). *Explorations in personality.* New York: Oxford University Press.

Myers, H. P. (1980). *An ecological study of Southern homicide.* Unpublished doctoral dissertation. Florida State University.

Myers, T. (1982). Alcohol and violent crime re-examined: Self-reports from two subgroups of Scottish male prisoners. *British Journal of Addiction, 77,* 399–413.

Nacci, P. L., Teitelbaum, H. E., & Prather, J. (1977). Population density and inmate misconduct rates in the federal prison system. *Federal Probation, 41,* 26–31.

National Association of School Security Directors. (1975). *Crime in schools: 1974.* Washington, DC: Author.

National Center for Educational Statistics. (1981). *National longitudinal study of the high school class of 1972.* Washington, DC: Author.

National Coalition on Television Violence. (1990, July–September). *NCTV News* (Vol. 2). Champaign, IL: Author.

National Education Association. (1977). *Danger—school ahead: Violence in the public schools.* Washington, DC: Author.

National Opinion Research Center. (1973). *Southern schools: An evaluation of the effects of the Emergency School Assistance Program and school desegregation.* Chicago: Author.

Nelson, E., Grinder, R., & Mutter, M. (1969). Sources of variance in behavioral measure of honesty in temptation situations: Methodological analyses. *Developmental Psychology, 1,* 265–279.

Nevins, A. (1924). *The American states during and after the revolution.* New York: Macmillan.

New Jersey Commissioner's Report to the Education Committee. (1988). Trenton.

Newman, O. (1972). *Defensible space—crime prevention through urban design.* New York: Collier.

Newman, O. (1975). *Design guidelines for creating defensible space.* Washington, DC: U.S. Government Printing Office.

Newman, O. (1976). Defensible space: Crime prevention through urban design. In N. C. Kalt & S. S. Zalkind (Eds.), *Urban problems: Psychological inquiries, readings and text.* New York: Oxford University Press.

Newman, O. (1979). *Community of interest.* New York: Doubleday.

Newman, O. (1980). *Community of interest.* New York: Anchor.

Newman, O., & French, K. A. (1980). *Factors influencing crime and instability in urban housing developments.* Washington, DC: U.S. Government Printing Office.

New York Times. (1991, Nov. 25). Youth violence rates increase nationwide.

New York Times. (1992, Jan. 13). Handgun ownership increases over 2 million in 1990.

Nichols, W. W., Jr. (1980). Mental maps, social characteristics, and criminal mobility. In D. E. Georges-Abeyie & K. D. Harries (Eds.), *Crime: A spatial perspective* (pp. 156–166). New York: Columbia University Press.

Nietzel, M. T. (1979). *Crime and its modification.* New York: Pergamon.

Nietzel, M. T., Guthrie, P. R., & Susman, D. T. (1990). Utilization of community and social support resources. In F. H. Kanfer & A. P. Goldstein (Eds.), *Helping people change.* Elmsford, NY: Pergamon.

Nisbett, R. E. (1993). Violence and U.S. regional culture. *American Psychologist, 48,* 441–449.

Norton, S. C. (1988). Predictor variables of violent behavior. *American Journal of Forensic Psychology, 6,* 53–66.

Norwell, N., & Worchel, S. (1981). A re-examination of the relation between equal status contact and intergroup attraction. *Journal of Personality and Social Psychology, 41,* 902–908.

Novaco, R. W. (1986). Anger as a clinical and social problem. In R. Blanchard & C. Blanchard (Eds.), *Advances in the study of aggression* (Vol. 2). New York: Academic Press.

Novaco, R. W. (1991). Aggression on roadways. In R. Baenniger (Ed.), *Targets of violence and aggression.* Amsterdam: Elsevier Science.

Novaco, R. W., Kliewer, W., & Broquet, A. (1991). Home environmental consequences of commute travel impedance. *American Journal of Community Psychology, 19,* 881–909.

Ochitill, H. N., & Krieger, M. (1982). Violent behavior among hospitalized medical and surgical patients. *Southern Medical Journal, 75,* 151–155.

O'Donnell, C. R., & Lydgate, T. (1980). The relationship to crimes of physical resources. *Environment and Behavior, 12,* 207–230.

Odum, H. (1936). *Southern regions of the United States.* Chapel Hill: University of North Carolina Press.

Ogburn, W. F. (1935). Factors in the variation of crime among cities. *Journal of the American Statistical Society, 30,* 12.

Ohio State University Center for Human Resource Research. (1981). *The national longitudinal surveys handbook.* Columbus, OH: College of Administrative Science, Ohio State University.

O'Leary, K. D., & Murphy, C. (1992). Clinical issues in the assessment of spouse abuse. In R. T. Ammerman & M. Hersen (Eds.), *Assessment of family violence.* New York: Wiley.

Oliver, J. E. (1973). *Climate and man's environment.* New York: Wiley.

Olweus, D. (1991). Victimization among school children. In R. Baenninger (Ed.), *Targets of violence and aggression.* North Holland: Elsevier Science.

O'Neal, E. C., & McDonald, P. J. (1976). The environmental psychology of aggression. In R. G. Green & E. C. O'Neal (Eds.), *Perspectives on aggression.* New York: Academic Press.

Pablant, P., & Baxter, J. C. (1975). Environmental correlates of school vandalism. *Journal of the American Institute of Planners, 41,* 270–279.

Page, R. A. (1977). Noise and helping behavior. *Environment and Behavior, 9,* 311–334.

Page, R. A., & Moss, M. K. (1976). Environmental influences on aggression: The effects of darkness and proximity of victim. *Journal of Applied Social Psychology, 6,* 126–133.

Pallanick, J. (1968). Fighting frowned on. *Peace Corps Volunteer, 6,* 28–29.

Pancoast, D. L. (1980). Finding and enlisting neighbors to support families. In J. Garbarino & S. Stocking (Eds.), *Protecting children from abuse and neglect.* San Francisco: Jossey-Bass.

Parent-Duchatelet, L. (1837). *La prostitution dans la ville de Paris.* Paris. Cited in R. D. Hunter (1988). *The relationship of selected environmental characteristics to the incidence of convenience store robbery within the State of Florida.* Unpublished doctoral dissertation, Florida State University.

Park, R. E., & Burgess, E. W. (1916). *The city.* Chicago: University of Chicago Press.

Parry, M. H. (1968). *Aggression on the road.* London: Tavistock.

Patchen, M. (1993). Reciprocity of coercion and cooperation between individuals and nations. In R. B. Felson & J. T. Tedeschi (Eds.), *Aggression and violence: Social interactionist perspectives.* Washington, DC: American Psychological Association.

Patterson, G. R. (1982). *Coercive family process.* Eugene, OR: Castalia.

Pease, K. (1991). The Kirkholt project: Preventing burglarly on a British public housing estate. *Security Journal, 2,* 73–77.

Pelton, L. H. (1978). Child abuse and neglect: The myth of classlessness. *American Journal of Orthopsychiatry, 48,* 608–617.

Pernanen, K. (1976). Alcohol and crimes of violence. In B. K. Kissin & H. Begleiter (Eds.), *The biology of alcoholism: Social aspects of alcoholism.* New York: Plenum.

Perry, J. B., & Pugh, M. D. (1978). *Collective behavior: Response to Social Stress.* New York: West Publishing.

Perry, J. D., & Simpson, M. E. (1987). Violent crimes in a city: Environmental determinants. *Environment and Behavior, 19,* 77–90.

Pervin, L. (1986). Persons, situations, interactions: Perspectives on a recurrent issue. In A. Campbell & J. J. Gibbs (Eds.), *Violent transactions: The limits of personality.* Oxford: Basil Blackwell.

Petersilia, J. (1987). Other technical research: Architectural design for crime prevention. In Rand Corporation (Ed.), *The influence of product-oriented research.* Santa Monica, CA: Author.

Pettigrew, T. F. (1971). *Racially separate or together?* New York: McGraw-Hill.

Pettigrew, T. F. (1981). Extending the stereotype concept. In D. L. Hamilton (Ed.), *Cognitive processes in stereotyping and intergroup behavior.* Hillsdale, NJ: Erlbaum.

Pettigrew, T. F., & Spier, R. B. (1962). The ecological structure of negro homicide. *American Journal of Sociology, 67,* 621–629.

Phillips, P. D. (1980). Characteristics and typology of the journey to crime. In D. E. Georges-Abeyie & K. D. Harries (Eds.), *Crime: A spatial perspective.* New York: Columbia University Press.

Pittman, D. J., & Handy, W. (1964). Patterns in criminal aggravated assault. *Journal of Law, Criminal and Police Science, 55,* 17–28.

Pokorny, A. D. (1965). Human violence: A comparison of homicide, aggravated assault, suicide and attempted suicide. *Journal of Criminal Law, Criminology and Police Science, 56,* 488–497.

Pope, C. E. (1978). *Victimization rates and neighborhood characteristics.* Presented at American Society of Criminology, Dallas.

Porterfield, A. L. (1949). Personality, crime and the cultural patterns. In A. L. Porterfield (Ed.), *Current approaches to delinquency.* New York: National Parole Board Association.

Powers, R. J. (1986). Aggression and violence in the family. In A. Campbell & J. J. Gibbs (Eds.), *Violent transactions: The limits of personality.* Oxford: Basil Blackwell.

Poyner, B., & Webb, B. (1991). *Crime free housing.* Oxford: Butterworth Architecture.

Prentice-Dunn, S., & Rogers, R. W. (1980). Effects of deindividuating situation cues and aggressive models on subjective deindividuation and aggression. *Journal of Personality and Social Psychology, 39,* 104–113.

Press, S. J. (1971). *Some effects of an increase in police manpower in the 20th precinct of New York City.* New York: Rand Institute.

Price, J. M. (1971). The effects of crowding on social behavior of children. *Dissertation Abstracts International, 33,* 471B.

Price, R. H., & Bouffard, D. L. (1974). Behavioral appropriateness and situational constraint as dimensions of social behavior. *Journal of Personality and Social Psychology, 30,* 579–596.

Proshansky, H. M., Ittleson, W. H., & Rivlin, L. G. (1970). Introduction. In H. M. Proshansky, W. H. Ittleson, & L. G. Rivlin (Eds.), *Environmental psychology: Man and his physical setting.* New York: Holt, Rinehart & Winston.

Proshansky, H. M., Fabian, A. K., & Kaminoff, R. (1983). Place-identity: Physical world socialization of the self. *Journal of Environmental Psychology, 3,* 57–83.

Quay, H. C. (1965). Psychopathic personality as pathological stimulation-seeking. *American Journal of Psychiatry, 122,* 180–183.

Quetelet, A. (1833). *A treatise on man.* Edinburgh: William and Robert Chambers.

Quinsey, V. L., & Varney, G. W. (1977). Characteristics of assaults and assaulters in a maximum security psychiatric unit. *Crime and Justice, 5,* 212–220.

Rabbie, J. M. (1982). *Are groups more aggressive than individuals?* Presented at British Psychological Society, Oxford.

Rabbie, J. M., & Huygen, K. (1974). Internal disagreements and their effects on attitudes toward in- and outgroups. *International Journal of Group Tensions, 4,* 222–246.

Rabbie, J. M., & Wilkins, G. (1971). Intergroup competition and its effects on intragroup and intergroup relations. *European Journal of Social Psychology, 1,* 215–234.

Racher, S. (1986). Contact, action and racialization: Some British evidence. In M. Hewstone & R. Brown (Eds.), *Contact and conflict in intergroup encounters.* Oxford: Basil Blackwell.

Radloff, R. W. & Helmreich, R. (1968). *Groups under stress: Psychological research in SEALAB II.* New York: Appleton-Century-Crofts.

Rainwater, L. (1966). *Behind ghetto walls: Black families in a federal slum.* Chicago: Aldine.

Rand, A. (1984). *Patterns in juvenile delinquency: A spatial perspective.* Dissertation, University of Pennsylvania.

Raush, H. L. (1965). Interaction sequences. *Journal of Personality and Social Psychology, 2,* 487–499.

Raush, H. L. (1972). Process and change. *Family Processes, 11,* 275–298.

Rawson, R. W. (1839). An inquiry into the statistics of crime in England and Wales. *Journal of the Statistical Society, 2,* 316–344.

Redfield, H. V. (1880). *Homicide, north and south.* Philadelphia: Lippincott.

Reed, J. S. (1971). To live—and die—in Dixie: A contribution to the study of Southern violence. *Political Science Quarterly, 86,* 429–443.

Reiss, A. J. (1985). Policing a city's central district: The Oakland story. Washington, DC: U.S. Department of Justice.

Reiss, A. J., & Roth, J. A. (Eds.). (1993). Panel on the Understanding and Control of Violent Behavior, Committee on Law and Justice, Commission on Behavioral and Social Sciences and Education, National Research Council, Patterns of Violence in American Society. *Understanding and preventing violence.* Washington, DC: National Academy Press.

Reiss, A. J., & Tonry, M. (1986). *Communities and crime.* Chicago: University of Chicago Press.

Rengert, G., & Wasilchick, J. (1985). *Suburban burglary: A time and a place for everything.* Springfield, IL: Charles C Thomas.

Reppetto, T. A. (1974). *Residential crime.* Cambridge, MA: Ballinger.

Rice, M. E., Harris, G. T., Varney, G. W., & Quinsey, V. L. (1989). *Violence in institutions: Understanding, prevention, and control.* Toronto: Hogrefe & Hans Huber.

Riley, D., & Mayhew, P. (1980). *Crime prevention publicity: An assessment*. Home Office Research Study No. 63. London: HMSO.

Rinn, R. C. (1976). Effects of nursing apparel upon psychiatric inpatients' behavior. *Perceptual and Motor Skills, 43*, 939–945.

Riordan, C. (1978). Equal status interracial contact: A review and revision of the concept. *International Journal of Intercultural Relations, 2*, 161–185.

Rivlin, L. G. (1987). The neighborhood, personal identity, and group affliations. In I. Altman & E. Zube (Eds.), *Neighborhood and community environments* (Vol. 9, pp. 1–34). New York: Plenum Press.

Robinson, T. D. (1990). *International dependence, basic needs provision, inequality and political violence: A cross-national analysis*. Unpublished master's thesis, Florida Atlantic University.

Robriquet, F. (1841). *Crime commis dans la corse*. Paris. Cited in R. D. Hunter. (1988). *The relationship of selected environmental characteristics to the incidence of convenience store robbery within the State of Florida*. Unpublished doctoral dissertation, Florida State University.

Rodin, J. (1976). Density, perceived choice and responses to controllable and uncontrollable outcomes. *Journal of Experimental Social Psychology, 12*, 546–578.

Rogers, E. M., & Shoemaker, F. F. (1971). *Communication of innovations*. New York: Free Press.

Rohe, W. M. & Burby, R. J. (1988). Fear of crime in public housing. *Environment and Behavior, 20*, 700–720.

Rohe, W. M., & Nuffer, E. L. (1977). *The effects of density and partitioning on children's behavior*. Presented at American Psychological Association, San Francisco.

Rohe, W. M., & Patterson, A. J. (1974). *The effects of varied levels of resources and density on behavior in a day care center*. Presented at Environmental Education Research Association, Milwaukee.

Romero, J. J. (1985). *A situational analysis of sexual assault among age-groups of female victims*. Unpublished doctoral dissertation, Temple University.

Rommel, R. C. S. (1959). Personality characteristics and attitudes of youthful accident-repeating drivers. *Traffic Safety Research Review, 3*, 13–14.

Roncek, D. W. (1981). Dangerous places: Crime and residential environment. *Social Forces, 60*, 74–96.

Roncek, D. W., & Bell, R. (1981). Bars, blocks, and crimes. *Journal of Environmental Systems, 11*, 35–47.

Roncek, D. W., & Faggiani, D. (1985). High schools and crime: A replication. *Sociological Quarterly, 26*, 491–505.

Roncek, D. W., & Lobosco, A. (1983). The effect of high schools on crime in their neighborhoods. *Social Science Quarterly, 64*, 598–913.

Roncek, D. W., & Maier, P. A. (1991). Bars, blocks and crimes revisited: Linking the theory of routine activities to the empiricism of "hot spots." *Criminology, 29*, 725–753.

Roncek, D. W., Bell, R., & Francik, J. A. (1981). Housing projects and crime: Testing a proximity hypothesis. *Social Problems, 29*, 151–166.

Rose, T. L. (1981). Cognitive and dyadic processes in intergroup contact. In D. L. Hamilton (Ed.), *Congitive processes in stereotyping and intergroup behavior*. Hillsdale, NJ: Erlbaum.

Rosenberg, M. (1975). The dissonant context and the adolescent self-concept. In S. E. Dragastin & G. H. Elder (Eds.), *Adolescence in the life cycle*. Washington, DC: Hemisphere Publishing.

Rosenfeld, R. (1986). Urban crime rates: The effects of inequality, welfare dependency, region and race. In J. Byrne & R. Sampson (Eds.), *The social ecology of crime*. New York: Springer-Verlag.

Roth, F. (1986). A practice regimen for diagnosis and treatment of child abuse. *Child Welfare, 54*, 268–273.

Rothbart, M. (1981). Memory processes and social beliefs. In D. L. Hamilton (Ed.), *Cognitive processes in stereotyping and intergroup behavior*. Hillsdale, NJ: Erlbaum.

Rotter, J. B. (1954). *Social learning and clinical psychology*. Englewood Cliffs, NY: Prentice-Hall.

Rotton, J., & Frey, J. (1985). Air pollution, weather, and violent crimes: Concomitant time-series analysis of archival data. *Journal of Personality and Social Psychology, 49*, 1207–1220.

Rubel, R. J. (1977). *Unruly school: Disorders, disruptions, and crimes*. Lexington, MA: D. C. Heath.

Rumsey, M. G., & Rumsey, J. M. (1977). A case of rape: Sentencing judgments of males and females. *Psychological Reports, 41*, 459–465.

Runciman, W. G. (1966). *Relative deprivation and social justice*. Berkeley: University of California Press.

Russell, G. (1991). Athletes as targets of aggression. In R. Baenninger (Ed.), *Targets of violence of aggression*. North Holland: Elsevier.

Russell, J. A., & Ward, L. M. (1982). Environmental psychology. In M. R. Rosenzwieg & L. W. Porter (Eds.), *Annual review of psychology* (Vol. 33). Palo Alto, CA.

Ryen, A. H., & Kahn, A. (1975). The effects of intergroup orientation on group attitudes and proxemic behaviour: A test of two models. *Journal of Personality and Social Psychology, 31*, 302–310.

Rynders, J., Johnson, R., Johnson, D. W., & Schmidt, B. (1980). Producing positive interation among Down's syndrome and nonhandicapped teenagers through cooperative goal structuring. *American Journal of Mental Deficiency, 85*, 268–273.

Saenger, G. (1953). *The social psychology of prejudice*. New York: Harper.

Saenger, G., & Gilbert, E. (1950). Customer reactions to the integration of Negro sales personnel. *International Journal of Opinion and Attitude Research, 4*, 57–76.

Saile, D. G. (1985). The ritual establishment of home. In I. Altman & C. M. Werner (Eds.), *Home environments*. New York: Plenum Press.

Sampson, R. J. (1983). *The neighborhood context of criminal victimization*. Dissertation, State University of New York at Albany.

Sampson, R. J. (1985). Neighborhood and crime: The structural determinants of personal victimization. *Journal of Research in Crime and Delinquency, 22*, 7–40.

Sampson, R. J. (1986). Neighborhood family structure and the risk of personal victimization. In J. M. Byrne, & R. J. Sampson (Eds.), *The social ecology of crime*. New York: Springer-Verlag.

Sandler, I. N., Miller, P., Short, J., & Wolchik, S. A. (1989). Social support as a protective factor for children in stress. In D. Belle (Ed.), *Children's social networks and social supports*. New York: Wiley.

Savitz, L. (1970). Delinquency and migration. In L. Savitz & N. Johnson (Eds.), *Crime in society*. New York: Wiley.

Scherdin, M. J. (1986). The halo effect: Psychological deterrence of electronic security systems. *Information Technology and Libraries* (September, 232–235).

Schlesinger, H., & Meadow, K. (1972). *Sound and sign: Child deafness and mental health*. Berkeley: University of California Press.

Schmid, C. (1960). Urban crime areas. *American Sociological Review, 25*, 527–542.

Schmidt, D. E., & Keating, J. P. (1966). Human crowding and personal control: An integration of the research. *Psychological Bulletin, 86*, 680–700.

Schoggen, P. (1989). *Behavior settings*. Stanford, CA: Stanford University Press.

Schopler, J., & Stockdale, J. E. (1977). An interference analysis of crowding. *Environmental Psychology, 1*, 81–88.

Schuerman, L., & Kobrin, S. (1986). Community careers in crime. In A. J. Ress & M. Tonry (Eds.), *Communities and crime*. Chicago: University of Chicago Press.

Schuessler, K. R., & Cressey, D. R. (1950). Personality characteristics of criminals. *American Journal of Sociology, 55*, 476–484.

Schuessler, K. R., & Slatin, G. (1964). Sources of variation in U.S. city crime, 1950 and 1960. *Journal of Research in Crime and Delinquency, 1*, 17–23.

Scott, R., & McPartland, J. (1982). Desegregation as national policy: Correlates of racial attitudes. *American Educational Research Journal, 19*, 397–414.

Seaman, D. (1979). *A geography of the lifeworld*. New York: St. Martin's Press.

Segall, M. H., Dasen, P. R., Berry, J. W., & Poortinga, V. H. (1990). *Human behavior in global perspective*. New York: Pergamon.

Seligman, C., Brickman, J., & Koulack, D. (1977). Rape and physical attractiveness: Assigning responsibility to victims. *Journal of Personality, 45*, 554–563.

Shannon, L. W. (1954). The spatial distribution of criminal offenses by state. *Journal of Criminal Law and Criminology, 45*, 264–273.

Sharfman, M. (1980). Drug overdose and the full moon. *Perceptual Motor Skill, 50*, 124–126.

Shaw, C. R. (1929). *Delinquency areas*. Chicago: University of Chicago Press.

Shaw, C. R., & McKay, H. (1931). *Social factors in juvenile delinquency*. Washington, DC: U.S. Government Printing Office.

Shaw, C. R., & McKay, H. (1969). *Juvenile delinquency and urban areas* (rev. ed.). Chicago: University of Chicago Press.

Sheldon, W. H. (1949). *Varieties of delinquent youths*. New York: Harper.

Sheridan, M., Henrion, R., Robinson, L., & Baxter, V. (1990). Precipitants of violence in a psychiatric inpatient setting. *Hospital and Community Psychiatry, 41*, 776–780.

Sherif, M., Harvey, O. J., White, B. J., Hood, W. R., & Sherif, C. W. (1961). *Intergroup cooperation and competition*. Norman: University of Oklahoma.

Sherman, L. W., Gartin, P. R., & Buerger, M. E. (1989). Hot spots of predatory crime: Routine activities and the criminology of place. *Criminology, 27*, 27–55.

Sherrod, K. B., O'Connor, S., Vietze, P. M., & Altemeier, W. A. (1984). Child health and maltreatment. *Child Development, 55*, 1174–1182.

Shinn, M., Lehmann, S., & Wong, N. W. (1984). Social interaction and social support. *Journal of Social Issues, 40*, 55–76.

Shorkey, C. T. (1980). Sense of personal worth, self-esteem, and anomia of child abusing mothers and controls. *Journal of Clinical Psychology, 36*, 817–820.

Shumaker, S. A., & Brownell, A. (1984). Toward a theory of social support: Closing conceptual gaps. *Journal of Social Issues, 40*, 11–36.

Siegel, L. M., & Senna, J. J. (1991). *Juvenile delinquency: Theory, practice and law*. St. Paul: West.

Silverman, T. A. (1974). Victim precipitation: An examination of the concept. In I. Drapkin & D. Vieno (Eds.), *Victimology: A new focus.* Lexington, MA: Lexington Books.

Silverstein, B., & Krate, R. (1975). *Children of the dark ghetto.* New York: Praeger.

Simmel, G. (1950). *The sociology of Georg Simmel.* New York: Free Press.

Simon, L. (1991). *Victim-offender relationships in crimes of violence.* Dissertation, University of Arizona.

Singer, J. E., Brush, C. A., & Lublin, S. C. (1965). Some aspects of deindividuation: Identification and conformity. *Journal of Experimental Social Psychology, 1,* 356–378.

Skogan, W. G. (1990). *Disorder and decline.* Berkeley: University of California Press.

Skogan, W. G., & Maxfield, M. G. (1981). *Coping with crime: Individual and neighborhood reactions.* Newbury Park, CA: Sage.

Skolnick, J. & Bailey, D. (1986). *The new blue line.* New York: Free Press.

Slaby, R. (1992). Media influences on violence. In American Psychological Association, *Report of the American Psychological Association Commission on Youth Violence.* Washington, DC: Author.

Slavin, R. E. (1977). How student learning teams can integrate the desegregated classroom. *Integrated Education, 15,* 56–58.

Slavin, R. E. (1983). *Cooperative learning.* New York: Longman.

Slavin, R. E. (1985). Cooperative learning: Applying contact theory in desegregated schools. *Journal of Social Issues, 41,* 45–62.

Slavin, R. E., & Madden, N. A. (1979). School practices that improve race relations. *American Educational Research Journal, 16,* 169–180.

Slavin, R. E. & Oickle, E. (1981). Effects of cooperative learning teams on student achievement and race relations. *Sociology of Education, 54,* 174–180.

Smelser, N. J. (1962). *Theory of collective behavior.* New York: Free Press.

Smith, M. D., & Parker, R. N. (1980). Type of homicide and variation in regional rates. *Social Forces, 59,* 136–147.

Smith, P. K., & Connolly, K. J. (1976). Social and aggressive behavior in pre-school children as a function of crowding. *Biological Social Life, 16,* 601–620.

Smith, S. M., & Hanson, R. (1975). Interpersonal relationships and child-rearing practices in 214 parents of battered children. *British Journal of Psychiatry, 127,* 513–525.

Snyder, J., & Patterson, G. (1987). Family interaction and delinquent behavior. In H. C. Quay (Ed.), *Handbook of juvenile delinquency.* New York: Wiley.

Snyder, M. (1981). On the self-perpetuating nature of social stereotypes. In D. L. Hamilton (Ed.), *Cognitive processes in stereotyping and intergroup behavior.* Hillsdale, NJ: Erlbaum.

Solnit, A. J., & Provence, S. (1979). Vulnerability and risk in early childhood. In J. D. Osofsky (Ed.), *Handbook of infant development.* New York: Wiley.

Sommer, R. (1966). *Personal space: The behavioral basis of design.* Englewood Cliffs, NJ: Prentice-Hall.

Sorrells, J. M. (1977). Kids who kill. *Crime and Delinquency, 23,* 312–320.

Sparks, R. F. (1982). *Research on victims of crime: Accomplishments, issues, and new directions.* Rockville, MD: Center for Studies of Crime and Delinquency.

Spearly, J. L., & Lauderdale, M. (1983). Community characteristics and ethnicity in the prediction of child maltreatment rates. *Child Abuse and Neglect, 7,* 91–105.

Stark, E., & Flitcraft, A. H. (1988). Women and children at risk: A feminist perspective on child abuse. *International Journal of Health Services, 18,* 97–118.

Staub, E. (1993). The mob. In American Psychological Association, *Report of the American Psychological Association Commission on Youth Violence,* Washington, DC: Author.

Steadman, H. J. (1982). A situational approach to violence. *International Journal of Law and Psychiatry, 5,* 171–186.

Stefanko, M. S. (1989). *Rates of secondary school vandalism and violence: Trends, demographic differences and the effects of the attitudes and behaviors of principals.* Unpublished doctoral dissertation, Claremont Graduate School.

Stephan, W. G., & Brigham, J. C. (1985). Intergroup contact. *Journal of Social Issues, 41,* 1–8.

Stephan, W. G., & Rosenfeld, D. (1979). Black self-rejection: Another look. *Journal of Educational Psychology, 71,* 708–716.

Stinchcombe, A. L., Adams, R., Heimer, C., Scheppele, K., Smith, T., & Taylor, D. G. (1980). *Crime and punishment in public opinion.* San Francisco: Jossey-Bass.

Stokols, D. (1978). On the distinction between density and crowding: Some implications for future research. *Psychological Review, 79,* 275–278.

Stokols, D., & Altman, I. (1987). *Handbook of environmental psychology.* New York: Wiley.

Stoks, F. G. (1982). *Assessing urban public space environments for danger of violent crime—Especially rape.* Unpublished doctoral dissertation, University of Washington.

Stouffer, S. A., Suchman, E. A., DeVinney, L. C., Star, S. A., & Williams, R. M., Jr. (1949). *The American soldier: Adjustment during army life* (Vol. 1). Hillsdale, NJ: Erlbaum.

Strauss, M. A. (1977). Wife-beating: How common and why? *Victimology, 2,* 443–458.

Streufert, S., & Streufert, S. C. (1979). The development of international conflict. In W. G. Austin & S. Worchel (Eds.), *The social psychology of intergroup confilict.* Monterey, CA: Brooks/Cole.

Suedfeld, P. (1987). Extreme and unusual environments. In D. Stokols & I. Altman (eds.), *Handbook of environmental psychology.* New York: Wiley.

Sullivan, M. L. (1989). *Getting paid: Youth crime and work in the inner city.* Ithaca, NY: Cornell University Press.

Sumner, W. G. (1906). *Folkways.* New York: Ginn.

Sutherland, E. H., & Cressey, D. R. (1974). *Criminology.* New York: Lippincott.

Suttles, G. D. (1958). *The social order of the slum.* Chicago: University of Chicago Press.

Suttles, G. D. (1972). *The social construction of communities.* Chicago: University of Chicago Press.

Tajfel, H. (1970). Experiments in intergroup discrimination. *Scientific American, 223,* 96–102.

Tajfel, H. (1978). The achievement of group differentiation. In H. Tajfel (Ed.), *Differentiation between social groups.* London: Academic Press.

Tajfel, H., Flament, C., Billig, M. G., & Bundy, R. F. (1971). Social categorization and intergroup behaviour. *European Journal of Social Psychology, 1,* 149–177.

Taylor, M. & Nee, C. (1988). The role of cues in simulated residential burglary. *British Journal of Criminology, 28,* 396–401.

Taylor, R. B., & Brower, S. (1985). Home and near-home territories. In I. Altman & C. M. Werner (Eds.), *Home environments.* New York: Plenum.

Taylor, R. B., & Gottfredson, S. (1986). Environmental design, crime, and prevention: An examination of community dynamics. In A. J. Reiss & M. Tonry (Eds.), *Communities and crime.* Chicago: University of Chicago Press.

Taylor, R. B., & Hall, M. M. (1986). Testing alternative models of fear of crime. *Journal of Criminology and Criminal Law, 77*, 87–101.

Taylor, S. E. (1981). The interface of cognitive and social psychology. In J. H. Harvey (Ed.), *Cognition, social behavior, and the environment*. Hillsdale, NJ: Erlbaum.

Taylor, S. E., & Fiske, S. T. (1981). Getting inside the head: Methodologies for process analysis in attribution and social cognition. In J. H. Harvey, W. Ickes, & R. F. Kidd (Eds.), *New directions in attribution research*. Hillsdale, NJ: Erlbaum.

Terr, L. (1970). A family study of child abuse. *American Journal of Psychiatry, 127*, 665–671.

Thoits, P. A. (1982). Conceptual, methodological and theoretical problems in studying social support as a buffer against life stress. *Journal of Health and Social Behavior, 23*, 145–159.

Tien, J. M., O'Donnell, V. F., Barnett, A., & Mirchandani, P. B. (1979). *Phase I report: Street lighting projects*. Washington, DC: U.S. Government Printing Office.

Tietjen, A. M. (1980). *Social networks and social services as family support systems in Sweden*. Presented at World Congress of Sociology, Uppsala, Sweden.

Tikalsky, F. D. (1982). Historical controversy, science, and John Wesley Powell. *Journal of Arizona History* (winter), 407–422.

Tillman, W. A., & Hobbs, G. E. (1949). The accident-prone automobile driver. *American Journal of Psychiatry, 106*, 321–331.

Toch, H. (1980). *Violent men*. Cambridge, MA: Schenkman.

Toch, H. (1985). The catalytic situation in the violence equation. *Applied Social Psychology, 15*, 105–123.

Toch, H. (1986). True to you, darling, in my fashion: The notion of contingent consistency. In A. Campbell & J. J. Gibbs (Eds.), *Violent transactions: The limits of personality*. Oxford: Basil Blackwell.

Townsend, P. (1974). Poverty as relative deprivation: Resources and style of living. In D. Wedderburn (Ed.), *Poverty, inequality and class structure*. Cambridge: Cambridge University Press.

Turner, C. W., & Thrasher, M. (1970). *School size does make a difference*. San Diego: Institute for Educational Management.

Turner, C. W., Layton, J. F., & Simons, L. S. (1975). Naturalistic studies of aggressive behavior: Aggressive stimuli, victim visibility, and horn honking. *Journal of Personality and Social Psychology, 31*, 1098–1107.

Turner, C. W., Simons, L. S., Berkowitz, L., & Frodi, A. (1977). The stimulating and inhibiting effects of weapons on aggressive behavior. *Aggressive Behavior, 3*, 355–376.

Turner, J. C. (1975). Social comparison and social identity: Some prospects for intergroup behaviour. *European Journal of Social Psychology, 5*, 5–34.

Turner, J. C. (1978). Social comparison, similarity and ingroup favouritism. In H. Tajfel (Ed.), *Differentiation between social groups*. London: Academic Press.

Turner, J. C. (1980). Fairness or discrimination in intergroup behaviour? A reply to Branthwaite, Doyle and Lightbown. *European Journal of Social Psychology, 10*, 131–147.

Turner, J. C. (1981). The experimental social psychology of intergroup behavior. In J. C. Turner & H. Giles (Eds.), *Intergroup behavior*. Chicago: University of Chicago Press.

Turner, J. C. (1983). Some comments on..."the measurement of social orientations in the minimal group paradigm." *European Journal of Social Psychology, 13*, 351–367.

Turner, R. C., & Killian, L. M. (Eds.). (1972). *Collective behavior* (2nd ed.). Englewood Cliffs, NJ: Prentice-Hall.

Turner, S. (1970). *The ecology of crime and delinquency*. Unpublished doctoral dissertation, Temple University.

Tygert, C. (1980). Student social structures and/or subcultures as factors in school crime. *Adolescence, 15,* 13–22.

U.S. Department of Justice. (1988). *Report to the nation on crime and justice*. Washington, DC: U.S. Government Printing Office.

U.S. Riot Commission Report. (1968). New York: Bantam.

Unger, D. G., & Wandersman, A. (1985). The importance of neighbors: The social, cognitive, and affective components of neighboring. *American Journal of Community Psychology, 13,* 139–169.

Unnithan, N. P. (1983). *Homicide and the social structure: A cross-national analysis of lethal violence rates, 1950–1970*. Dissertation, University of Nebraska.

Vaughan, G. (1978). Social categorization and intergroup behaviour in children. In H. Tajfel (Ed.), *Differentiation between social groups*. London: Academic Press.

Vaux, A. (1988). *Social support*. New York: Praeger.

Volkan, V. D. (1988). *The need to have enemies and allies*. Northvale, NJ: Jason Aronson.

von Hentig, H. (1947). *Crime: Causes and conditions*. New York: McGraw-Hill.

Voss, H. L., & Hepburn, J. R. (1968). Patterns in criminal homicide in Chicago. *Journal of Criminal Law, Criminology, and Police Science, 59,* 499–508.

Wagner, U., & Schonbach, P. (1984). Links between educational status and prejudice: Ethnic attitudes in West Germany. In N. Miller & M. B. Brewer (Eds.), *Groups in contact: The psychology of desegregation*. San Diego: Academic Press.

Walden, T. A., Nelson, P. A., & Smith, D. E. (1981). Crowding, privacy, and coping. *Environment and Behavior, 13,* 205–224.

Walker, N. (1980). *Punishment, danger and stigma: The morality of criminal justice*. Totowa, NJ: Barnes & Noble.

Wallis, A., & Ford, D. (1980). *Crime prevention through environmental design: An operational handbook*. Washington, DC: U.S. Department of Justice.

Walsh, D. (1978). *Shoplifting: Controlling a major crime*. London: Macmillan.

Warren, D. I. (1980). Support systems in different types of neighborhoods. In J. Garbarino & S. H. Stockings (Eds.), *Protecting children from abuse and neglect*. San Francisco: Jossey-Bass.

Warren, M. Q. (1983). Applications of interpersonal-maturity theory to offender populations. In W. S. Laufer & J. M. Day (Eds.), *Personality theory, moral development, and criminal behavior*. Lexington, MA: Lexington Books.

Webb, S. D. (1972). Crime and the division of labor: Testing a Durkheimian model. *American Journal of Sociology, 78,* 643–656.

Webster's Ninth New Collegiate Dictionary. (1984). Springfield, MA: Merriam-Webster.

Weeks, S. (1976). Security against vandalism. *American School and University, 48,* 37–46.

Weiner, N. A., & Wolfgang, M. E. (1985). The extent and character of violent crime in America, 1969–1982. In L. A. Curtis (Ed.), *American violence and public policy*. New Haven, CT: Yale University Press.

Weinstein, C. S. (1979). The physical environment of the school: A review of the research. *Review of Educational Research, 49,* 577–610.

Weisner, T. S. (1989). Cultural and universal aspects of social support for children. In D. Belle (Ed.), *Children's social networks and social supports*. New York: Wiley.

Weiss, R. S. (1974). The provisions of social relations. In Z. Rubin (Ed.), *Doing unto others.* Englewood Cliffs, NJ: Prentice-Hall.

Werner, C. M., Altman, I., & Oxley, D. (1985). Temporal aspects of homes: A transactional perspective. In I. Altman & C. M. Werner (Eds.), *Home environments.* New York: Plenum Press.

Westinghouse Electric Corporation (1978). *Crime prevention through environmental design: Technical guidelines—planning public outdoor areas.* Arlington, VA: Author.

Wetherell, M. (1982). Cross-cultural studies of minimal groups: Implications for the social identity theory of intergroup relations. In H. Tajfel (Ed.), *Social identity and intergroup relations.* Cambridge: Cambridge University Press.

Wetherell, M. S., & Vaughan, G. M. (1979). *Social class, sex, nationality and behaviour in minimal group situations.* Unpublished master's thesis, University of Auckland.

Wetzel, J. R. (1989). School crime: Annual statistical snapshot. *School Safety,* Winter, 8.

White, G. F. (1990). Neighborhood permeability and burglary rates. *Justice Quarterly, 7,* 57–67.

Whyte, W. F. (1943). *Street corner society.* Chicago: University of Chicago Press.

Wiatrowski, M., Gottfredson, G., & Roberts, M. (1983). Undertaking school behavior disruption: Classifying school environments. *Environment and Behavior, 15,* 53–76.

Wicker, A. W., & Kirmeyer, S. (1977). From church to laboratory to national park: A program of research on excess and insufficient populations in behavior settings. In D. Stokols (Ed.), *Psychological perspectives on environment and behavior: Conceptual and empirical trends.* New York: Plenum Press.

Wilbanks, W. L. (1985). Predicting failure on parole. In D. P. Farrington & R. Tarling (Eds.), *Prediction in criminology.* New York: State Univeristy of New York Press.

Wilder, D. A. (1981). Perceiving persons as a group: Categorization and intergroup relations. In D. L. Hamilton (Ed.), *Cognitive processes in stereotyping and intergroup behaviour.* Hillsdale, NJ: Erlbaum.

Wilder, D. A. (1984). Intergroup contact: The typical member and the exception to the rule. *Journal of Experimental Social Psychology, 20,* 177–194.

Wilder, D. A. (1986). Cognitive factors affecting the success of intergroup contact. In S. Worchel & W. G. Austin (Eds.), *Psychology of intergroup relations* (pp. 49–66). Chicago: Nelson-Hall.

Wilder, D. A., & Allen, V. L. (1978). Group membership and preference for information about other persons. *Personality and Social Psychology Bulletin, 4,* 106–116.

Wilder, D. A., & Thompson, J. E. (1980). Intergroup contact with independent manipulations of in-group and out-group interaction. *Journal of Personality and Social Psychology, 38,* 589–603.

Williams, C. L., Henderson, A. S., & Mills, J. M. (1974). An epidemiological study of serious traffic offenders. *Social Psychiatry, 9,* 99–109.

Williams, J., & Giles, H. (1978). The changing status of women in society: An intergroup perspective. In R. J. Brown (Ed.), *Differentiation between social groups.* London: Academic Press.

Wilson, J. Q. (1968). The urban unease: Community versus the city. *The Public Interest, 12,* 25–39.

Wilson, J. Q., & Kelling, G. L. (1982). Broken windows: The police and neighborhood safety. *Atlantic, 249,* 29–38.

Winsborough, H. H. (1965). The social consequences of high population density. *Law and Contemporary Problems, 30,* 120–126.

Wirth, L. (1939). Urbanism as a way of life. *American Journal of Sociology, 44,* 1–24.

Wolfe, D. A. (1987). *Child abuse: Implications for child development and psychopathology.* Newbury Park, CA: Sage.

Wolfgang, M. E. (1958). *Patterns in criminal homicide.* Philadelphia: University of Pennsylvania Press.

Wolfgang, M. E. (1967a). A sociological analysis of criminal homicide. In M. E. Wolfgang (Ed.), *Studies in homicide.* New York: Harper & Row.

Wolfgang, M. E. (1967b). Victim-precipitated criminal homicide. In M. E. Wolfgang (Ed.), *Studies in homicide* (pp. 72–87). New York: Harper & Row.

Wood, D. (1991). In defense of indefensible space. In P. J. Brantingham & P. L. Brantingham (Eds.), *Environmental criminology.* Prospect Heights, IL: Waveland Press.

Worchel, S. (1979). Co-operation and the reduction of intergroup conflict: Some determining factors. In W. G. Austin & S. Worchel (Eds.), *The social psychology of intergroup relations.* Monterey, CA: Brooks/Cole.

Worchel, S., Andreoli, V. A., & Folger, R. (1977). Intergroup co-operation and intergroup attraction: The effect of previous interaction and outcome of combined effort. *Journal of Experimental Social Psychology, 13,* 131–140.

Worden, M. A. (1980). Criminogenic correlates of intermetropolitan crime rates, 1960 and 1970. In D. E. Georges-Abeyie & K. D. Harries (Eds.), *Crime: A spatial perspective* (pp. 109–122). New York: Columbia University Press.

Yancy, W. L. (1976). Architecture, interaction and social control: The case of a large scale housing project. In H. M. Proshansky, W. H. Ittleson, & L. G. Rivlin (Eds.), *Environmental psychology: People and their physical setting.* New York: Holt, Rinehart & Winston.

Yochelson, S., & Samenow, S. E. (1976). *The criminal personality.* New York: Aronson.

Zajonc, R. B. (1976). Social facilitation. In C. Fisher (Ed.), *Psychology of sport: Issues and insight.* Pala Alto, CA: Mayfield.

Zalba, S. R. (1967). The abused child: 2. A typology for classification and treatment. *Social Work, 12,* 70–79.

Zillman, D. (1979). *Hostility and aggression.* Hillsdale, NJ: Erlbaum.

Zillmann, D. (1983). Arousal and aggression. In R. Geen & E. Donnerstein (Eds.), *Aggression: Theoretical and empirical reviews* (Vol. 1, pp. 75–102). New York: Academic Press.

Zillman, D., Bryant, J., Cantor, J. R., & Day, K. D. (1975). Irrelevance of mitigating circumstances in retaliatory behavior at high levels of excitation. *Journal of Research in Personality, 9,* 282–293.

Zimbardo, P. G. (1969). The human choice: Individuation, reason and order versus deindividuation, impulse and chaos. In W. J. Arnold & D. Levine (Eds.), *Nebraska Symposium on Motivation.* Nebraska: University of Nebraska Press.

Zimbardo, P. G. (1978). The psychology of evil: On the perversion of human potential. In L. Krames, P. Plinern, & T. Alloway (Eds.), *Aggression, dominance, and individual spacing* (pp. 155–169). New York: Plenum Press.

Zimmerman, D. (1983). Moral education. In Center for Research on Aggression (Ed.), *Prevention and control of aggression.* New York: Pergamon.

INDEX

187